BEHIND FROM THE START

Behind from the Start

HOW AMERICA'S WAR ON THE POOR IS HARMING OUR
MOST VULNERABLE CHILDREN

Lenette Azzi-Lessing

OXFORD
UNIVERSITY PRESS

OXFORD
UNIVERSITY PRESS

Oxford University Press is a department of the University of Oxford. It furthers
the University's objective of excellence in research, scholarship, and education
by publishing worldwide. Oxford is a registered trade mark of Oxford University
Press in the UK and certain other countries.

Published in the United States of America by Oxford University Press
198 Madison Avenue, New York, NY 10016, United States of America.

Library of Congress Cataloging-in-Publication Data
Names: Lessing, Lenette, author.
Title: Behind from the start : how America's war on the poor is harming our most vulnerable
children / Lenette Lessing.
Description: New York : Oxford University Press, 2017. |
Includes bibliographical references and index.
Identifiers: LCCN 2016013030 | ISBN 9780190459031 (hardback)
Subjects: LCSH: Poor children—United States—Social conditions—21st century. |
Children—United States—Social conditions—21st century. | Child welfare—United States. |
United States—Social policy—21st century. | BISAC: SOCIAL SCIENCE / General. |
SOCIAL SCIENCE / Social Work. | POLITICAL SCIENCE / Public Policy / Social Services & Welfare.
Classification: LCC HQ792.U5 L47 2016 | DDC 362.7/756900973—dc23
LC record available at https://lccn.loc.gov/2016013030

9 8 7 6 5 4 3 2 1

Printed by Sheridan Books, Inc., United States of America

For Ben.

Contents

Foreword
by Lisbeth B. Schorr

Senior Fellow at the Center for the Study of Social Policy

Lenette Azzi-Lessing's book stands alone among important social policy books in synthesizing the critical knowledge from all of the domains that must be connected if ambitious social change is to succeed. She draws on the most current findings from research and from experience. She documents the unmet needs of vulnerable young children, adolescents, and their families, and puts it all together to identify the unparalleled opportunities now at hand to address those needs.

Professor Azzi-Lessing's own wide-ranging experience runs from creating a school for disruptive adolescents, to organizing multiple service providers to work coherently with marginalized families, to advocating for the policies that could support high-quality, responsive services and supports. It extends from cuddling an affection-starved three-year-old in a children's shelter to her decision to join the academic world in search of the most powerful levers to bring about audacious change. She persuasively makes the case that our social policies need to move beyond scaling up isolated "evidence-based" programs to establishing the systems and providing the resources that could bring about bright futures for the children now destined for grim tomorrows.

In writing this book, Azzi-Lessing also aims to increase the American public's understanding of the plethora of interconnected circumstances that conspire to keep millions of children poor in the world's richest country. She explores the disconnect between what most Americans believe about plentiful government assistance to poor families and the diminished and fragmented resources that are actually available. She examines the ways in which the safety net continues to fray, with consequences that are often catastrophic for young children in families stuck at the bottom.

Drawing on the newest research that demonstrates that much of the physical structure of the human brain is developed in the first few years of life, she explains how the stress of being raised in poverty can harm young children's intertwined learning ability and emotional stability and how adversity in children's earliest years can interfere with the physical "wiring" of the brain affecting lifelong capacities for learning as well as physical and mental health. Azzi-Lessing argues that although the public and policymakers are attracted to simple, piecemeal, and inexpensive fixes, the current patchwork of dysfunctional and disjointed programs and policies is insufficient to make a lasting difference for the most vulnerable families. She documents how the widespread illusion that there are simple, cheap fixes for the complex array of interconnected problems poor families face and the fetishizing of medical-model, randomized trials as the only ways to determine which programs work have contributed to rising levels of public and political cynicism and the miserly allocation of funding for identifying and building real solutions.

Azzi-Lessing does not stop at describing the problems of the children and families left behind by America's prosperity, or the weaknesses of fragmented and underfunded attempts to help. She also lays out what she has termed the extra-strength strategies that could lift families out of poverty and improve their children's futures.

She calls for the development of innovative, comprehensive initiatives that address multiple needs simultaneously rather than piece by piece and that build on the strengths present in even the most vulnerable families. She describes how the shape and scope of efforts to help would benefit from including the voices, needs, and preferences of families targeted by antipoverty and child development initiatives. She points up the importance of supporting innovation and experimentation in trying and testing more powerful approaches aimed toward breaking the cycle.

She calls attention to the fact that the situation of many of the most fragile families is the culmination of generations of deprivation and living in the margins of society. If these families are to become financially self-sufficient and to meet the needs of their children, they need more long-lasting and more skilled, respectful help than they are now offered.

One of the great values of Azzi-Lessing's book is her emphasis on how much we know about "what works":

- Relationships hold the power to change lives.
- The quality of care a young child receives affects lifelong physical and emotional health.
- When caregivers—be they parents, foster parents, or child carestaff members—have the support and assistance they need, they are much better equipped to successfully nurture the children in their care.
- Chronic and complex problems require long-term and multifaceted interventions.
- The most promising strategies recognize and build upon the strengths found in even the most vulnerable families.

To act on the wealth of knowledge that we have now accumulated, Azzi-Lessing recommends the development and testing of (1) newer, long-lasting, comprehensive, and customizable extra-strength family support programs and (2) a cadre of extra-strength early care and education programs, including specialized preschool programs for highly vulnerable children. Of course, the prevailing pattern of restrictive and siloed funding makes it hard to act on these recommendations, which will require pooling and reallocating a large portion of the funds already being spent, and augmenting these with additional, carefully targeted resources to develop and test these and other promising approaches.

Azzi-Lessing points out that documenting the results of interventions is a critical component of the comprehensive strategies she proposes. Policymakers should not have to choose between relying on evidence produced by randomized trials and tolerating low levels of accountability. It is essential to find ways to document the impact of complex, interactive interventions, because—as Azzi-Lessing wisely points out—"We can't afford to waste public credibility any more that we can afford to waste public dollars."

She calls for an emphasis on systematic learning, encouraging program developers to identify the core components of their interventions that can be transported to other communities and organizations, allowing room for adaptation and adding components and other customization so that the program will work in the unique conditions of diverse settings. Systematic learning becomes ever more important as we learn that the most promising interventions have to respond to several generations at once, and take time to show results.

Among this book's many valuable contributions is Azzi-Lessing's exploration of the problem of targeting. She believes that it is now time to allocate significant resources to building, testing, and bringing to scale programs that are specifically targeted toward meeting the multiple and complex needs of the most vulnerable

children and their families. She points to the findings of Dr. Jack Shonkoff of the
Harvard Center on the Developing Child that

> large numbers of young children and families who are at greatest risk, par-
> ticularly those experiencing toxic stress associated with persistent poverty
> complicated by child maltreatment, maternal depression, parental sub-
> stance abuse, and/or interpersonal violence, do not appear to benefit sig-
> nificantly from existing programs.

Azzi-Lessing agrees with Shonkoff that these disappointing results arise because
the needs of children growing up in families and neighborhoods that cannot
support healthy development are far more extensive than those in the general
population. They outstrip the capacity of most existing early intervention programs. The needs of families facing exceedingly complex social and economic
disruptions—when they do participate—typically overwhelm conventional early
childhood program staff whose expertise is often restricted to child development
and parenting education.

Azzi-Lessing challenges the conventional wisdom that the voting public will
not support high-quality programs unless they are available to poor and nonpoor
alike. She suggests that a larger segment of the public would support investments
in programs aimed primarily toward impoverished children and their families if
these programs were to demonstrate their effectiveness—with both stories and
numbers—in making sustained, meaningful differences in outcomes, and if the
public could be encouraged to see the opportunities to help these families with
both their economic and child-nurturing prospects.

Virtually uniquely among the experts deeply involved in improving services
and programs for vulnerable families, Azzi-Lessing's vision extends beyond the
programmatic. She also explores the opportunities to change lives through major
policy changes, including strengthening systems that address child protection,
income supports, and work readiness and job training.

Dr. Donald Berwick, the preeminent health care reformer and change agent,
has written that "People committed to science ought to supply not just skepticism but also hope." In this important book, Lenette Azzi-Lessing couples the
findings from science and experience with her sharp analytic skills to provide us
with the hope we need if we are to counter, in her words, "the cumulative, harmful impacts of poverty, family and community violence, impaired parenting, and
other serious risk factors that threaten the optimal development of millions of
young children."

Acknowledgments

THIS BOOK IS the product of many influential experiences and conversations over many years, as well as an amalgamation of the work of numerous individuals and organizations. I must first express my appreciation to the staff and board and to the families served by Children's Friend, who taught me about the lives of vulnerable families and what is possible when dedicated individuals work together to improve those lives. A special thank you to Tina Laprade, and Lenore Olsen for many encouraging and insightful conversations. I also am grateful to the board and staff of the Economic Progress Institute for a transformative education regarding economic policy, and to my colleagues from the Advisory Board of the former National Center for In-Home Services and those at Children's Rights for a similar education regarding the child welfare system. A special thank you to Stephanie Pierce and Christine Buckner for sharing their stories on how that system does and doesn't work, and to Linda Orrante for her perspective on home-visiting programs.

I am indebted to my colleagues at Wheelock College who supported this work in many ways, especially by awarding me the Gordon Marshall Fellowship, and to David Fernie, Janine Bempechat, Stephen Dill, and Wendy Williams for their advice and encouragement. I must thank Jessica Black and my fellow participants in Boston College's "Social Work and Neuroscience Intersections" symposium for sharing their expertise regarding the connections between children's early experiences and their lifelong prospects. Having had the good fortune to learn from experts in other nations, I also appreciate the insights shared by Alison Garnham, director of Britain's Child Poverty Action Group, and by colleagues at the University of Fort Hare and its surrounding community in the Eastern Cape of South Africa. I am also grateful to staff members at the National Center for Children in Poverty, the Economic Policy Institute, and the National Coalition for Evidence-Based Policy for generously sharing their work.

I want to thank Dana Bliss, my editor at Oxford University Press, for recognizing from the beginning the potential of this project, and for his guidance in making this book accessible to the wide audience I intended to reach. I owe a great debt to Lisbeth "Lee" Schorr for her mentorship, suggestions, and reading of draft chapters and for so generously writing the book's foreword. Through her own highly influential and important writing, Lee provided an invaluable compass that has guided much of my work in academia as well as in the field. Many thanks to Charlie Milner, who helped me think through the messaging aspects of antipoverty initiatives. And I am forever indebted to Sandra Enos for many illuminating conversations, ideas, and advice, and to her and Deoshore Haig for their friendship and loving encouragement throughout the writing process.

Lastly, I must express my appreciation to my family for their love and support. During the writing of this book, our daughters, Rachel and Madeline Lessing, grew into lovely, courageous young women who cheered me on from beginning to end. And no one inspired and encouraged the work on these pages more than Ben Lessing, my husband of many years. For your endless reading of multiple chapters, late-night listening sessions, and most of all, your faith in this project and me, I dedicate this book to you with much love and gratitude.

BEHIND FROM THE START

1 Introduction

MY JOURNEY TOWARD writing this book began more than twenty years ago when I was an administrator in a community mental health center in Rhode Island, charged with developing a range of counseling and other services for troubled children and their families. During that time, one experience seared itself in my memory like no other. I was visiting a nearby children's shelter to discuss with its director ways in which we might collaborate in ensuring that the children living there could access the specialized mental health services they needed. The shelter was funded by the state child welfare agency, the Department for Children and Families (DCF), as a short-term setting for children who had been removed from their biological families due to maltreatment. I knew that the children living in the shelter would have significant needs for the services my agency provided, as I realized that most came from deprived circumstances in poor families, a situation that often results in delays in child development and learning abilities. I also realized that the trauma of having been abused or severely neglected, combined with the additional trauma of having been abruptly removed from their families, meant that the children in the shelter were likely to have behavioral and emotional problems requiring specialized and intensive therapy.

Being aware of all of these things did not prepare me for what I experienced during my visit. When I walked into the shelter, which was in a converted two-story house, I was stunned by how rundown and stark the children's living quarters were. The walls were pitted and dirty, as were the old wooden floors. There was a large television but few toys or games with which to engage the children and stimulate learning. There were even fewer books. Most of the furniture, including a few large sofas near the TV, was severely worn and dirty. Given that it was a weekday, all but the youngest children had gone to school.

The shelter's director greeted me and offered me a tour of the rest of the building. I had accepted the invitation when Joey, a pale, brown-haired three-year-old boy, appeared and without saying a word, took my hand and led me to a worn wooden rocking chair that was in the middle of the room. He pointed for me to sit down. Surprised, I did so and he immediately climbed into my lap, curled up in my arms, put his thumb in his mouth and relaxed. I did the only thing I knew to do, which was to keep my arms around Joey and gently rock the chair. The director sighed and told me that Joey frequently attempts to elicit cuddles from visitors and shelter staff members alike.

As I rocked Joey, the shelter director and I talked about the well-known syndrome of nurturance-starved children seeking adult attention and physical contact in order to make up for the care and affection they haven't received, even to the point of eliciting nurturance from complete strangers. She wistfully told me that state funding for the shelter was not sufficient to hire enough staff members to adequately respond to the many needs of the children there, including those like Joey, who wanted little more than to be cuddled like most three-year-olds routinely are. The director also shared some of the many challenges in meeting the needs of children at such wide ranges in age. She knew that what preschoolers need to cope and thrive varies dramatically from the needs of adolescents; however, the shelter routinely housed a mix of preschoolers, teens, and children at various ages in between.

As our meeting ended and I carefully placed a drowsy Joey on one of the threadbare sofas, I wondered what most taxpayers would think about the bereft conditions at the shelter and how the system they charged with nurturing and protecting children like Joey too often left them with these basic needs unmet. I hoped that those unsympathetic to the disruptive and frightening symptoms often demonstrated by maltreated adolescents in thousands of similar shelters across the country might be moved by children like Joey, whose life course was sharply pointed toward a rotten outcome, at the tender age of three. I wondered if everyone else would be as appalled as I was at what I have come to see, over and over again, as poor care for poor children.

Another experience while at that same job strongly influenced not only the writing of this book but the trajectory of my career. I was charged with creating a school for adolescents whose behaviors were too disruptive for them to remain even in the specialized classrooms provided by the local public school districts. This alternative school was to have low teacher–student ratios, specially trained and well-supported teachers, and therapeutic and family engagement services— resources that were in short supply in special education programs in the public schools. With funding from two urban school districts along with a few startup grants, we hired carefully selected teachers, therapists, and outreach workers and opened the school in a building that once housed a Catholic school.

The alternative school was a success in that a number of additional school districts began referring their more troubled students to the program. In fact, we were receiving so many referrals that the program quickly outgrew its initial home. It now operates in a number of locations throughout Rhode Island, serving hundreds of students with severe behavior and learning problems. In the school's earliest months of operation, I took on the task of reviewing the records of the youths who had been referred to the program. Nearly all of them were from very low-income families and most were either black or Hispanic. Most of these youths were referred to our program after having threatened and/or attacked classmates or teachers or frequently engaging in behavior so disruptive that even in classrooms with special education teachers, they prevented other students from learning. Not surprisingly, many of the students in our program already had encounters with the criminal justice system.

I noticed something else in the records accompanying students referred to our alternative school program. In nearly every case, these boys had begun exhibiting behavioral and/or emotional problems early in life, usually by the age of three or four. In most cases, their parent—usually a single mother—had attempted to get help but was unsuccessful. Reasons for this varied. Sometimes the mother had brought her child to counseling sessions, but the family's services were terminated because they missed a few appointments. In other cases, mothers sought help in caring for and disciplining their children but learned that no such help was available, or that it required private insurance or had unaffordable fees. For many families, a lack of reliable transportation to where services were located made getting help even more difficult.

What I saw in the records of the tough, indifferent, angry, and disruptive youths referred to our alternative school was how relatively small, early life problems had spiraled into much larger and often-intractable ones, with little intervention until they become too much for even special education programs to handle. I read story after story of young mothers trying to find and access services that either didn't exist, weren't available to families like theirs, or were too much hassle in the way of transportation and inconvenient appointment times. There were also stories of teachers and other school staff members encountering similar barriers when they tried to link these families with appropriate services. Such attempts typically took place once the child's behavior had become very disruptive and teachers and parents were overwhelmed. These records were not only stories of the early life experiences of each of the children referred to the program, they were also maps that showed—in stark terms—the pathways from early life challenges toward what Harvard professor Mary Jo Bane long ago termed "rotten outcomes": school failure, unemployment, significant mental health problems, too-early parenthood and, for many of the children, juvenile crime.[1]

A Call to Focus on Vulnerable Young Children

Following the course of those maps and witnessing situations like Joey's led me to quit my job at the mental health center and begin building an organization that would address the needs of impoverished families with young children in a comprehensive and responsive way. Those same experiences also sent me back to school to pursue a doctorate, as I sought to learn more about how extreme disadvantage is passed from one generation to another. During that time, I learned that much of the human brain is formed in the earliest years of life rather than before birth, and that the conditions under which babies and young children live play a major role in their lifelong ability to learn and succeed. I read studies showing how nature and nurture influence one another over time and over generations, essentially locking in advantage for some families and disadvantage for others. The more research I read, the more I realized just how important it is to intervene early in the lives of children at risk for rotten outcomes if we want to help these children avoid such outcomes and have a decent shot at a healthy and successful life.

Building and leading an organization dedicated to intervening early and effectively in the lives of poor families with young children provided an education of a different kind. I quickly realized that the reason good services weren't widely available to these families was that only a small portion of government funding for services to children and families was aimed toward young children. Most of the funding was—and still is—absorbed by programs and services grappling with the learning and behavior problems, the mental health problems, and the juvenile crime that result when the needs of vulnerable young children and their families go unmet. It took a great deal of persistence and creativity to find and access funding to respond to some of these early life needs. And once we did access funding, the programs we offered to poor families with young children were routinely placed on the chopping block whenever the state or federal government was looking to cut back on outlays for human services—even when these programs showed promise in reducing risk for school failure, child maltreatment, and other rotten outcomes. Sadly, despite increased national attention focused on the importance of what happens in early childhood, this is a scenario known only too well by today's leaders of organizations focused on improving the life chances of young children in poverty.

Despite these challenges, the agency I started grew, eventually merging, in the mid-1990s, with Children's Friend and Service, Rhode Island's longest standing child-service organization and one of the oldest in the nation. We christened the consolidated agency "Children's Friend" and began linking and combining programs in order to offer well-coordinated, comprehensive services to highly vulnerable families with young children in the Greater Providence area. Although deeply gratifying, this work was also very frustrating, in part because of the fragile nature of the grants and contracts we cobbled together to create those services. Even more frustrating was seeing that the needs of so many of the families we served typically went far beyond the counseling, home visits, child care, and other services Children's Friend offered. On a daily basis we saw families affected by homelessness, community violence, substance abuse, and other major mental health problems; parents with educational deficits; children poisoned by lead paint; and many other hardships. Unfortunately, resources to address these and other needs of poor families with young children were perpetually in short supply in the communities that most needed them.

I served as Children's Friend's director until leaving in 2007 to focus more attention on the policy arena, something my current position as a college professor enables me to do. Many years on the front lines of addressing the needs of highly vulnerable families has deepened my understanding of the problems faced by these families as structural problems, perpetuated by ineffective policies and programs that make breaking poverty's cycle nearly impossible. I have also come to see how little the public really knows and understands about the complex factors that cause and sustain our nation's stubbornly high rates of poverty, and child poverty in particular. Most Americans hear little about poverty, and what they do hear typically disparages poor parents, such as when one of these parents is caught trading food stamps for drugs or collecting benefits beyond those for which his or her family qualifies.

Missed Opportunities and Pathways to Rotten Outcomes

Few Americans realize the extent to which early life poverty plays a role in putting youths like those I just described on a pathway toward needing an alternative school program. When these now-difficult-to-help youths were babies and toddlers, most of their mothers lived in high-crime neighborhoods with few supports and sources of help. When these young moms did reach out for help, they encountered obstacles that prevented them from getting the guidance and resources they needed to successfully raise their children. Many of these mothers were unable to get and maintain jobs because of their own educational deficits and untreated mental health problems. They and their young children became overwhelmed by the stress that often accompanies poverty, stress from past traumas compounded by the ongoing stressors of community violence, inadequate housing and homelessness, and having their basic needs unmet. Given their backgrounds, it was not at all surprising that the children in these families grew up with serious behavioral, emotional, and/or learning problems. In fact, it would have been surprising if these youths had emerged from childhood without serious challenges that would dim their chances of a healthy and successful life.

And what about young children like Joey? I wish that I could say that Joey's surroundings and unmet needs for nurturance were an artifact of an earlier era and that we could be assured that all children, and young children in particular, in state custody today received the care and support necessary for them to have a decent shot at life. Sadly, since meeting Joey, I have seen far too many inadequate and even unsafe children's shelters and group homes. I have seen foster homes with too many children and not enough supervision, let alone individual nurturance and support for learning. Being involved, over many years, in efforts to improve and reform the child welfare system has given me an understanding of the ways in which this system often harms the very children it is charged with protecting. This occurs not because state child welfare agencies lack competent, dedicated, and caring professionals, but because states starve these agencies of the resources necessary to keep children safe, and pay little attention until tragedy strikes and local news media uncover the dysfunction that contributed to a child's death. Other than in the wake of such tragedies, the public hears little about the heroic efforts of child protective workers to help maltreated children—the largest group of whom are younger than age six—despite inadequate support, a dearth of decent foster homes, and antiquated systems for tracking highly vulnerable families. Average Americans hear even less about the ways in which the dysfunction of our child protective system helps perpetuate, rather than remedy, the cycle of intergenerational poverty for children like Joey.

I bring these and many other observations and experiences to my writing on these pages. As someone who has spent more years outside the halls of academia than within them, I see my role as an interpreter, gathering research findings and other knowledge across a wide array of fields and disciplines, and synthesizing them in a way that helps a broad range of readers understand one of most important public policy problems we face. In doing so, it is not my intention to place a disproportionate amount of blame for our nation's failure to substantially reduce poverty upon the shoulders of voters and elected officials from either major party or ideology. While conservatives are more likely to perpetuate negative stereotypes of impoverished families and advocate for reducing spending on these families, progressives often stand in the way of meaningful progress by protecting inadequate and ineffective programs and by perpetuating the myth that intergenerational poverty can be solved by simple and cheap solutions. All of these tendencies contribute to maintaining high rates of poverty for millions of children and their families.

The Purpose of This Book

The purpose of this book is to help readers deepen their understanding of five important aspects of this topic:

1. Why the U.S. poverty rate remains stubbornly high, and is the highest among similarly developed but less-wealthy nations
2. The devastating consequences of our poverty rates being highest among children under six years of age
3. The many ways in which our responses to family poverty harm children and help maintain poverty's cycle
4. How the programs and policies currently in place are too weak and ineffective to make a real and lasting difference
5. What it would really take—from both a policy and programmatic standpoint—to substantially improve the life chances of children born to poor parents.

My aim is to help readers connect the dots between our failed programmatic and policy approaches to poverty, our ineffective child-and-family-serving systems, and the harsh rhetoric and unfair reporting that drives much of the discourse on family poverty. I write not to present original research or to inform other academics about the many ways in which poverty harms the development and dims the life chances of young children; there are plenty such books already published, several of them collections of excellent chapters, each distilling the findings of researchers in the various silos that address this topic. Instead, my purpose is to help concerned individuals make sense of the onslaught of information bubbling up from research in fields as diverse as neuroscience, economics, developmental psychology, public policy, and environmental science, to name a few. I believe that this understanding is critical. As Jack Shonkoff and Susan Bales of Harvard's Center on the Developing Child have noted, research findings do not speak for themselves, and we can expect neither policymakers nor members of the voting public to wade through complex studies and academic journals in order to understand the profoundly harmful effects of child poverty and why it persists at such appallingly high rates.[2]

In sharing experiences from the front lines of this work and explaining key research findings from a wide range of fields and how they relate to our policies and programs regarding poor families with young children, I seek to engage and inform students and practitioners in these fields, those working in the trenches to help impoverished families, policymakers, and anyone else who is concerned about the stubborn rate of child poverty in the United States. Ultimately, my purpose is both to shine additional light on the complex causes of intergenerational poverty and to sharpen the focus of our search for meaningful solutions.

The child poverty rate in the United States remains high despite decades of antipoverty programs and policies. As I explain in the chapters ahead, our past and current approaches to intergenerational poverty haven't done enough of the right things for enough children and families in order to meaningfully lower that shameful number. In the last two chapters of this book, I propose improved programmatic strategies and call for dramatic changes in a wide range of policies that affect the well-being and life chances of disadvantaged young children. We need to do more, however, than identify or create better strategies. It has become painfully clear that new antipoverty strategies will not succeed without the support and commitment of the American people, something that is sorely lacking at this point in time. To muster that support we must all do a better job of educating ourselves, our neighbors, and our colleagues about the causes and consequences of millions of children growing up with their needs for safety and well-being unmet. Moreover, we must demand honesty and real accountability from those who promise dramatic impacts from the programmatic interventions they are advocating, and we must understand that meaningful and lasting change for families ensnared in poverty will take time as well as an influx of new resources spent in better ways than in the past.

We must push our political leaders and members of the media to provide insightful, accurate, and balanced analysis and reporting regarding this issue, so that the American public can develop an understanding of the plethora of interconnected circumstances that conspire to keep millions of children poor in the world's richest country. Only through widespread understanding and acknowledgment of the complex nature of the factors that perpetuate poverty can we begin to make real progress toward solving this problem. It is toward this end that I have written this book.

The Chapters Ahead

The next chapter sets the context for our discussion. It provides a brief perspective on poverty in the United States and summarizes efforts over the past fifty years to improve the life chances of poor children. It includes information on the scope of the problem and who is most affected, as well as how this country's poverty rates compare with those of other, similarly developed nations. I also discuss how economic factors and racism intersect in ways that perpetuate higher rates of impoverishment among blacks and certain other racial groups. I address three areas of widespread misunderstanding that underlie our current antipoverty policies: that we can punish poor parents into self-sufficiency; that government does too much to help poor families, and that our public schools can undo the harm inflicted upon young children born into poor families.

Chapter 3 traces the national discourse of shaming and blaming poor parents, from Ronald Reagan's "welfare queens" to the inflammatory rhetoric used by present-day politicians and commentators. I provide examples of how news reports often sensationalize relatively small instances of welfare cheating and how often-harsh public discourse has made low-income parents one of the last safe targets for ridicule in the public arena. This chapter also highlights the disconnect between what most Americans believe about government assistance to poor families and the diminished and fragmented resources that are actually available, especially since the passage of welfare reform legislation in 1996. I examine the impacts of government policies on poor families since then and illustrate the ways in which the safety net continues to fray, with often-catastrophic consequences for young children in families stuck at the bottom of our economy.

In Chapter 4, I examine those consequences. I explain how the stress and neglect of being raised in poverty can harm young children's learning ability and emotional stability. Drawing on research that demonstrates that much of the physical structure of the human brain is developed in the first few years of life, I show how adversity in children's earliest years can interfere with the physical "wiring" of the brain and can affect lifelong capacities for learning, as well as physical and mental health. This chapter exposes many of the other ways in which living in poverty harms children, and young children in particular. I examine findings from public health research showing that America's poorest children are far more likely than other children to be exposed to toxins that can impair lifelong learning ability. Moreover, I explain how increased segregation—by both race and class—in our poorest urban neighborhoods harms and restricts opportunities for the children and families living there.

In Chapter 5, I focus on the plight of children who rely on our underfunded and poorly monitored child protective system, one in which young children, impoverished families, and poor African American families in particular, are overrepresented. I examine implications of the little-known facts that family poverty is the most potent risk factor for child maltreatment, and that very young children represent the largest group of children in foster care. I point out that foster care harbors its own threats to their safety and well-being. I show how public and political apathy toward children and families in the protective system plays a role in allowing millions of children to experience multiple disrupted relationships, as they bounce from foster home to foster home. Lastly, I trace the life course of the thousands of children who languish in facilities until they "age out" of the system.

Chapter 6 shows how some of the interest groups focused on breaking poverty's cycle are, instead, contributing to its continuation by advocating for the expansion of programs that do little or nothing to improve the life chances of highly vulnerable young children. I help readers understand the often-misinterpreted "evidence" regarding the effectiveness of a number of popular programs aimed toward helping these children and their families. I separate the facts from the hype that is often used to oversell what can be expected from programs, particularly preschool and home visiting programs. In this chapter, I also argue that although the general public and policymakers are attracted to simple and inexpensive fixes, such piecemeal approaches are insufficient to make real and lasting differences in the lives of families caught in poverty's intransigent cycle.

Chapter 7 examines what the previous chapters tell us about what we must do from a programmatic standpoint in order to begin eradicating intergenerational poverty in the United States. In advocating for dramatic change from the current approach, I examine a number of strategies for building a system of programs that holds greater promise for improving the well-being and life chances of disadvantaged young children than the so-called system currently in place. These extra-strength strategies would utilize findings from brain development and other areas of research, along with experience from a range of more recently developed approaches, to deliver services that truly meet the complex needs of these children and their families in the current era. I also discuss funding strategies and examine the issue of accountability

In the eighth and final chapter, I call for a carefully crafted, comprehensive policy strategy for ensuring that far fewer American children experience the lousy outcomes that are caused by and that perpetuate intergenerational poverty. This strategy would address the economic factors that keep families stuck in poverty's clutches, while at the same time fostering the development of stronger, more effective programmatic approaches for helping poor families succeed. It would include ensuring that work pays and that supports are available to families headed by low-wage–earning parents, as well as restoring and improving the safety net for our most fragile families. I emphasize the importance of reforming systems, including the child welfare, immigration, and criminal justice systems, that play a significant role in perpetuating disadvantage. In closing, I call for a national movement to end child poverty and cite the successes and the challenges encountered as Great Britain mounted such a campaign and cut its child poverty by half over a ten-year period.

My most fervent hope is that once you have walked this journey with me, you will have a deeper understanding of the many factors that conspire to maintain intergenerational poverty in the United States, key reasons why we haven't made deeper inroads into solving this problem, and promising strategies for achieving much better results than have been realized by the programs and policies of the past.

2 Poor Policies for Poor Families
A LOOK AT OUR CURRENT SITUATION

FIFTY YEARS AGO, Americans and their leaders set out to right the gross injustice of widespread poverty in the world's richest country. As Attorney General Robert Kennedy, trailed by television cameras and newspaper reporters, toured parts of Appalachia and the South in the mid-1960s, much of the nation was horrified by the large numbers of impoverished individuals and families and the degree of deprivation Kennedy found. Thousands of families were living with little to no income, and going hungry was a fact of life. What most outraged Kennedy and average citizens, however, were the photographs and television footage of young children who were malnourished and living in substandard housing, many of them diseased, and facing a bleak future similar to that of their parents. These images played a significant role in rallying the nation to support the expansion of a wide variety of antipoverty programs, including the reauthorization of the Economic Opportunity Act of 1964, which had been signed into law by President Lyndon Johnson and became known as the War on Poverty.

The fact that many of the impoverished children and families shown in print and television images were African American in places like Mississippi, where agricultural jobs had dried up and meager aid programs such as food stamps were doled out at the discretion of white bureaucrats, demonstrated racial segregation and oppression's role in perpetuating poverty. This connection helped fuse the Civil Rights movement with antipoverty activism in what became a national campaign for both social and economic justice. The Civil Rights Act—also passed in 1964—was no less important than the Economic Opportunity Act in reducing poverty, as it opened the door to employment for African Americans who had been barred from many workplaces due to racial discrimination. Along with Kennedy and Johnson, the Rev. Martin Luther King Jr. and his civil rights agenda, including its Poor People's Campaign, advocated for ensuring that all Americans had access to the economic opportunity necessary to living a decent life.

While the 1960s and early 1970s were a time of great upheaval, with a bitterly protested war in Vietnam, civil rights marches and riots, the peak of the feminist movement, and the so-called sexual revolution, much of the American public were optimistic that our greatest problems could be solved. At least part of that optimism was well founded, as the nation cut its poverty rate in half between 1959 and 1973.[1] The multiple antipoverty initiatives launched during the Johnson administration, a booming postwar economy, and greater access to employment for African Americans due to civil rights legislation contributed to this achievement.

Of course, poverty didn't disappear during this period, and too many children were still being raised in deprived circumstances that set them behind their more privileged peers in school and in life. Significant racial disparities in income persisted. And using government resources to fight poverty was, as it always has been, a tough sell to the American public. As longtime antipoverty activist Peter Edelman puts it:

> It has always been hard to galvanize broad support for public policy directed at reducing poverty. Too many Americans are skeptical about public policy to help the poor, especially as they view the "poor" in their mind's eye. Beginning with the Bible and continuing through Elizabethan poor laws, throughout history there has been an instinctive belief among some that the poor have no one to blame but themselves. A special version of this exists in the United States, the Horatio Alger myth that one makes it (or doesn't) on one's own. The pioneer spirt and rugged individualism—values to be admired on the whole—contribute to the American version of the "blame the poor" story. (p. xvi)[2]

Our individualist culture notwithstanding, in the 1960s and early 1970s Americans supported, and their political leaders acted upon, a commitment to the goal of providing economic opportunity for everyone, and to creating policy solutions toward achieving this goal.

Unfortunately, the America of today is far more cynical, less optimistic, and much more at odds on the issue of poverty than it was in those earlier decades. The differences that divide our two major political parties and various ideologies are more stark, and the public has grown increasingly skeptical that much of anything will get done to address our most pressing problems on the domestic front, including failing schools, a broken immigration system, crumbling roads and bridges, and income inequality, to name a few. More than fifty years after the War on Poverty and the Civil Rights movement were launched, we find that poverty, racism, and the problems that spring from them are still with us, in a form that feels more insidious and less amenable to change than they were when Lyndon Johnson was president and Dr. King led marches.

A Rich Nation with Shamefully High Poverty Rates

As I show in the next chapter, public attitudes toward low-income individuals and families have deteriorated over time, as elected officials and various media outlets have become increasingly harsh in their "blame the poor" rhetoric, rhetoric that has also become increasingly racialized. When we follow the trajectory of the public discourse regarding poverty and poverty and race in the United States, we can easily see the correlation between deteriorating public attitudes toward the poor and the ramping up of public policies that punish individuals and families for being poor. Nearly 47 million Americans are poor and some 16 million of them live in deep poverty, with an income that is below half the Federal Poverty Threshold, commonly known as the poverty line.[3] An example of a family living at the poverty line is two parents and one child with an annual income of $18,751. For this same family to live in deep poverty means that they are subsisting on half that amount, or about $9,375 per year.[4]

Our high rates of poverty, and deep poverty in particular, are an anomaly in the developed world. Despite being the wealthiest, most innovative nation in the world, the United States has fallen far behind other similarly developed nations in ensuring economic opportunity for families and an adequate standard of living for its children.

A report by the nonpartisan Economic Policy Institute (EPI) compares countries in the Organization for Economic Cooperation and Development (OECD) with a ratio of gross domestic product (GDP) per hour worked similar to that of the United States. As Figure 2.1 illustrates, using the widely accepted international standard of poverty as at or below 50% of national median income, the United States had the highest poverty rate among the twenty-three countries that were compared, with 17.3% of its population living in poverty. The U.S. rate

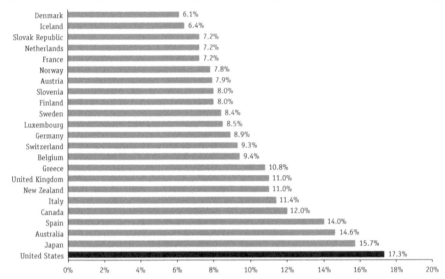

FIGURE 2.1 Relative poverty rate in the United States and selected OECD countries, late 2000s

Economic Policy Institute (2014). U.S. poverty rates higher, safety net weaker than in peer countries. Retrieved from http://www.epi.org/publication/ib339-us-poverty-higher-safety-net-weaker/.

was slightly less than double the unweighted 9.6% average of the OECD countries that were examined.[5]

The United States fares even worse when its child poverty rate is compared with that of other OECD countries. At 23.1% in 2009, the United States had the highest rate of child poverty, almost five times higher than Iceland, which had the lowest rate, and more than twice as high as the unweighted average of 9.8% among the twenty-three similarly developed countries (Fig. 2.2).

Things don't look much better when measuring child poverty by our own government-issued standards. Rather than measuring income alone, the 2012 U.S. census, using the Supplemental Poverty Measure (SPM), which takes into consideration noncash government benefits to poor families such as food stamps and subsidized child care and health care, found that more that 19%, nearly one in five, of America's children live in poverty. This more conservative measurement determined that more than 13 million children live in poor families.[6] Children are more likely to be poor in our nation than are adults and the elderly, and poverty rates are highest among children of color.[7] According to the National Center for Children in Poverty (NCCP), nearly 38% percent of black children live in poor families, as do 32% of Hispanic children and 35% of American Indian children, compared to 13% of white children.[8] Nearly 8.5% of American children, or 6.1 million, live in families with incomes less than half the federal poverty rate. The rate

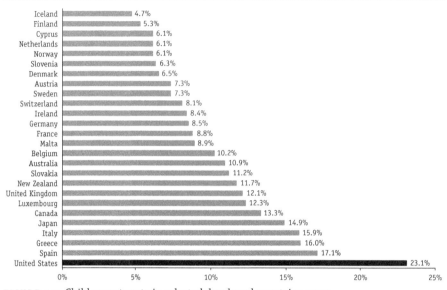

FIGURE 2.2 Child poverty rate in selected developed countries, 2009
Retrieved from the Economic Policy Institute website: http://www.epi.org/publication/ib339-us-poverty-higher-safety-net-weaker/.

of deep poverty is also higher for black, Hispanic, and American Indian children than it is for white children.

Equally disturbing is that poverty rates are highest of all among the approximately 24 million American children who are under the age of six. Nearly half of these children live in low-income or poor families. In 2014, 24%, or 5.5 million, of our nation's babies, toddlers, and preschoolers were growing up in families categorized as poor, meaning their income was at or below the poverty level—for example, about $16,300 for a single mother and her child. Many lived in households with less than half that amount of income.[9] Three million poor families with young children live in deep poverty, with annual incomes of half the poverty level—about $8,000 or less for a single mother and child.[10] The NCCP reports that the rate of deep poverty among families with young children has grown by 2% since 2008.[11] Figure 2.3 illustrates higher rates of low income and poverty among families with young children as opposed to those whose youngest child is age six or older.

Poverty in Young Children: A Perfect Storm of Risk for Rotten Outcomes

The fact that children under eighteen are more likely to be poor than adult or elderly Americans should be of grave concern to anyone who cares about our

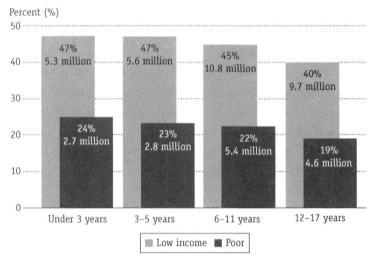

FIGURE 2.3 Percentage of children in low-income and poor families by age, 2014

nation's future, as poverty early in life typically does greater harm and longer-lasting harm than it does in adulthood.[12] Being poor in childhood is a strong risk factor for low educational achievement, school dropout, teen parenthood, and other undesirable outcomes. Growing up poor robs millions of children of the opportunities necessary to become a well-functioning adult and a contributor to, rather than a drain on, the nation's economy. We should be even more concerned that American children under the age of six are more likely to be poor and to live in extreme poverty than older children. These, our youngest and therefore most vulnerable children, are three times more likely to be poor than seniors age sixty-five and older.

As I explain in Chapter 4, there is a plethora of evidence to show that poverty, especially extreme poverty, early in life strongly affects a child's long-term life chances. Research suggests that this is due, in large part, to the relative malleability of babies' and young children's brains in early life, and the rapid brain development that occurs at this life stage. The bodies of babies, toddlers, and preschoolers are also more vulnerable to maltreatment, malnourishment, and other hazards that often go along with being poor.[13] Poverty, especially deep poverty, in early childhood decreases the odds that a child will be successful in school and in life, enjoy good health, and develop healthy and supportive relationships throughout his or her life.[14]

One of the many mechanisms that contribute to poor outcomes for poor children, for instance, is that being raised in poverty increases the odds that a child will be abused or neglected and/or placed into foster care.[15] Both child maltreatment and foster care placement are powerful risk factors for poor outcomes, especially if either or both occur in the first few years of life, when the human body is most fragile and the brain is undergoing its most rapid growth and development. These early years are when consistent nurturing and stable relationships are most crucial. As I report in Chapter 5, nearly half of the approximately700,000 children abused and/or neglected in the United States each year are under the age of six, and most of these children are poor.[16] This example illustrates a few of the many ways in which poverty occurring early in children's lives creates, in effect, a perfect storm of powerful risk factors combined with high levels of vulnerability—a combination that too often leads to bleak futures for millions of American children.

Poverty and Racism

As Figure 2.4 illustrates, poverty rates are significantly higher for black, Hispanic, and American Indian children ages five and under. A majority of young children in these racial groups are low income; more than 40% of black and American Indian families and about 35% of Hispanic families with young children are poor.

The topic of how race intersects with poverty is a complex one and fraught with myths, misinformation, and widely held stereotypes. What makes any discussion of this topic particularly daunting is the stubborn tendency of many Americans to mistake correlation (blacks as well as Native Americans and Latinos are more likely to be poor than whites) with causation (the widespread belief that there

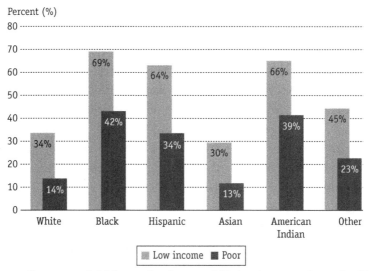

FIGURE 2.4 Percentage of children under six years old in low-income and poor families by race/ethnicity, 2014

is some innate tendency in individuals in these racial groups to eschew educa-tion and employment and remain dependent on government benefits). This belief has been nurtured in a number of ways, from how films and television pro-grams portray African Americans and other nonwhites to the use of terms such as "the culture of poverty" by certain politicians and commentators in referring to low-income black families. So-called scholarly publications such the 1994 best-seller *The Bell Curve: Intelligence and Class Structure in American Life* (co-authored by Charles Murray, whose writing I discuss in the next chapter) that purport to show a research basis for the innate inferiority of individuals of color have also buoyed mistaken beliefs about why we have such vast gaps in economic status across racial groups.[17]

Theories that blame the attitudes and behavior of people of color for the high rates of poverty within these groups appeal to many Americans because they offer a simple explanation to an extremely complex and stubborn phenomenon.[18] One of the many problems with these theories, however, is that they ignore the powerful role of past and present context and place the blame for economic dis-parities between whites and other racial groups squarely on the shoulders of poor individuals themselves. In doing so, they fail to examine how our unfair and heavily biased social and economic systems foster high levels of economic inequality between racial groups. Blame-the-poor theories typically ignore many decades of American history throughout which such disparities, often based on racism, have become deeply imbedded in our social and economic systems.

LACK OF OPPORTUNITY, SEGREGATION, AND POVERTY

The causes of disproportionately high rates of poverty among African Americans are rooted in slavery and segregation and persist today due to a cascade of mul-tiple factors. As renowned sociologist William Julius Wilson first charted, the manufacturing base in Northeastern and Midwestern cities began to erode after World War II, as corporations sought cheaper labor in the South and later, over-seas in countries like China and India with even cheaper labor costs and fewer costly worker protections. Driven by American consumers' demand for low prices on manufactured items and shareholders' demands for higher profits, this shift eliminated most of the stable, working-class jobs that once supported millions of black families. With little, in most urban centers, to replace those jobs, the number of marriageable (i.e., breadwinner) African American men dwindled, contributing to a rise in single mother–headed households within largely black communities. Decades of research show that being raised by a single parent in-creases the likelihood that children will grow up in poverty and will therefore encounter some of the harmful risk factors associated with both being poor and living in a single-parent family.[19]

Despite the civil rights breakthroughs in the 1960s, including the enactment of the Fair Housing Act of 1968, racial discrimination and segregation in housing, employment, education, and other areas have persisted, leaving many major cities "hyper-segregated," with high concentrations of black and Hispanic families living in the poorest, most isolated neighborhoods.[20] Extreme levels of racial segregation in many of America's larger cities remain in place today, as do shamefully high rates of child poverty. Detroit, for instance, has a child poverty rate of nearly 59%; Newark's child poverty rate is nearly 45%, and about 44% of Miami's children live in poverty.[21]

In his acclaimed book *Stuck in Place: Urban Neighborhoods and the End of Progress toward Racial Equality*, sociologist Patrick Sharkey documents how extremely difficult it is for families living in areas of high disadvantage to escape their circumstances. These families tend to remain, over generations, in the same impoverished communities—communities devoid of economic opportunity and plagued by failing schools, inadequate housing, and high crime rates. They do so not because they choose to live in poverty and all the ills that accompany it, but rather because they have such limited access to opportunities for meaningful social and economic mobility. Blacks and other minority groups continue to experience high rates of both housing and employment discrimination that thwart the upward mobility of their families and help drive the cycle of poverty. As Sharkey puts it, "The problem of urban poverty in the post-civil rights era is not only that concentrated poverty has intensified and segregation has persisted *but that the same families have experienced the consequences of life in the most disadvantaged environments over multiple generations*" (p. 26).[22] Sharkey's book documents how the wear and tear of extreme disadvantage over generations impact black individuals and families in multiple ways, affecting their physical and emotional health and chances for success in work and in life.

THE ROLE OF THE CRIMINAL JUSTICE SYSTEM

Another significant aspect of economic inequality across racial groups are extreme disparities in how our criminal justice system operates, including racial profiling of potential suspects, dramatically harsher prison sentences for offenses more frequently committed by African Americans, and racial disparities in granting parole.[23] The nation's deeply unjust and ineffective efforts to crack down on the selling and use of illegal drugs account for a large portion of these disparities. In the thirty years after President Ronald Reagan launched the "War on Drugs" (an unjust war sustained by every president who followed), the population of our prisons has exploded from around 300,000 inmates to over 2 million, largely due to drug-related arrests.[24] The United States now has the world's highest rates of incarceration and incarceration of its racial minorities—rates higher than even for countries with repressive governments, such as Iran and the Soviet Union.

As law professor Michelle Alexander writes in her devastating exposé *The New Jim Crow: Mass Incarceration in the Age of Colorblindness,*

> The United States imprisons a larger percentage of its black population than South Africa did at the height of apartheid. In Washington, D.C., our nation's capital, it is estimated that three out of four young black men (and nearly all those in the poorest neighborhoods) can expect to serve time in prison. Similar rates of incarceration can be found in black communities across America.[25]

Alexander reports that the use and selling of drugs in America occurs at similar rates for all races; however, in some states, the rate of incarceration for black men on drug charges is twenty to fifty times greater than for white men. Moreover, in low-income parts of our major cities, where the drug war is most intense, as many as 80% of young black men have criminal records that will limit their lifetime opportunities for education and employment—essential pillars for supporting a family. Alexander observes, "These young men are part of a growing under caste, permanently locked up and locked out of mainstream society."[26]

The problem of the disproportionate number of black men involved with the criminal justice system is rooted in our public schools, where students of color are suspended and subjected to other harsh disciplinary practices at rates far greater than for white students committing the same offenses.[27] These disparities, along with the underresourced, low-performing schools commonly found in poor neighborhoods that have a high concentration of families of color, place students of color, and black males in particular, at risk for school failure and dropout, factors that often lead to involvement in criminal activity. This school-to-prison pipeline plays a significant role in the mass incarceration of African American males. Moreover, it contributes to higher rates of single parenthood among black families, with children growing up without the presence or availability of their second parent. This helps keep black families trapped in poverty.

ADDITIONAL CHALLENGES FACING AMERICAN INDIANS AND HISPANICS

American Indians and Hispanics also face discrimination-based challenges regarding access to decent education, employment, and housing similar to blacks. Also like blacks, they are overrepresented in the criminal justice system. American Indians continue to experience the effects of government policies that stripped tribes of most of their land and relegated their members to reservations with inferior schools and few economic opportunities. The isolation and neglect of families living on reservations parallel, in many ways, conditions under which blacks and Hispanics live in our segregated inner cities. Over generations, American Indian families have had less access to health and mental health care than other Americans, and as a group they struggle with higher rates of chronic illnesses, obesity, substance abuse, and trauma-related mental health problems, in addition to high rates of unemployment and educational failure.[28] Moreover, the development of effective early childhood services aimed toward improving school success in American Indian communities has lagged far behind efforts in most other parts of the United States.[29]

In addition to racial discrimination in housing and employment, Hispanic families headed by parents who are recent immigrants encounter language barriers that limit their educational and employment opportunities. Public schools in many low-income communities lack adequate resources to meet the educational needs of students who are English-language learners, hampering these students' opportunities to fulfill their academic potential. Adding to these hardships, families headed by undocumented immigrants often remain in the shadows of the economy due to fear of arrest and deportation, a situation that hinders these parents' ability to earn a decent living.

Five and half million children in this country have at least one undocumented parent; most of these children are U.S. citizens. The 1.7 million undocumented children in this country live in constant fear that they and their families will be arrested, detained, and deported. Citizen children with undocumented parents grow up fearing a similar fate for one or both of their parents. They have reason to be frightened. In the first six months of 2011 alone, 46,000 parents of U.S. citizen children were deported by the Obama administration. Between 2005 and 2010, 87% of processed cases in New York City of adults living with U.S. citizen children resulted in deportation.[30]

Forty percent of children in recently immigrated families are poor, despite the fact that they are more likely than other poor children to have parents who are married and at least one parent who works. This is due to the low-wage jobs that the largest group of immigrants, Hispanics from South and Central America, typically hold. Immigrant parents who are undocumented face barriers in accessing work supports, such as job training programs and the subsidized health care and child care available to other low-income working families. Children of undocumented parents are less likely have health insurance, to be enrolled in early care and education programs, or to access the nutritional benefits of the food stamp (SNAP) program, even when, as citizens, they are entitled to these benefits.[31]

It is not uncommon for parents of even very young children to be arrested and detained by immigration authorities without having been able to arrange substitute care for their children.[32] Imagine the impact on children of having their parents fail to return from work at the end of the day. When a parent is deported, the children left behind often exhibit behavior and emotional problems and experience higher rates of homelessness and overcrowding than other poor children, and are more likely to experience chronic hunger.[33] Millions of children are being harmed by the economic and social hardships caused by our current immigration policies that fail to take into consideration their safety, needs, and aspirations.

Misperceptions and Misguided Policies

Given the complex set of factors that contribute to high poverty rates and the failure of various efforts and initiatives to reduce U.S. poverty rates to at least rates comparable to other developed nations, it is tempting to give up on trying to solve this problem. And that seems to be what a large portion of the American public and many of our elected officials have done. Even politicians and pundits on the left who frequently point out the shamefulness that the richest nation in the world has one of the highest rates of poverty, child poverty in particular, among its similarly developed peers seem to have little to offer in the way of a comprehensive vision for change. Although today we hear the topic of domestic poverty discussed more frequently in the public arena than in the past few decades, when it comes to proposing, developing, implementing, and evaluating promising, well-thought-out, viable strategies for change, there seems to be little progress on which to pin our hopes. And the populist movement, led by Senators Elizabeth Warren and Bernie Sanders, to address growing income inequality in the United States focuses largely on the growing gap between the wealthiest and middle and working class families, with less attention paid to the families who have been stuck at the bottom of our economy for decades.

Even those who lack compassion for the suffering endured by and the bleak life chances of the millions of young children growing up in impoverished families should understand that failing to significantly reduce poverty has harmful implications that extend far beyond the well-being of these children. Decades of research show that children who reach kindergarten ill prepared to learn and succeed in school cost taxpayers billions of dollars for special education and mental health services. Research also shows that poor children are at high risk to fail and/or drop out of school, a phenomenon that often leads to involvement in the juvenile justice system and the mental health system, and too-early parenthood, all of which cost taxpayers additional billions.[34] And that is before these troubled youths become adults, many of whom will become a chronic drain on rather than a contributor to the nation's economy.

And what about the life prospects of the children many of these disadvantaged youths will eventually have? Their prospects will be equally bleak, as long as we enable this vicious cycle to continue to siphon off untold quantities of both human and financial capital—human beings and national wealth—necessary for the United States to remain a competitive force in an increasingly globalized economy. The cost of child poverty to the U.S. economy has been estimated to be as high as $500 billion a year, or 4% of our GDP.[35] The magnitude and consequences of this siphoning of talent and treasure have led a number of leading economists, most notably Nobel laureate James Heckman, to advocate for wise investments aimed toward improving the life chances of America's disadvantaged young children.[36]

Viewed from any standpoint, the fact that the United States has a child poverty rate that is more than double the average of other developed nations, and that very young children, those most vulnerable to poverty's long-term effects, are more likely to be poor in America than any other age group is highly self-destructive. Yet these high rates persist. Why? Having spent my career working with poor families, developing programs to address their needs, advocating for them in the policy arena, and studying the research on antipoverty approaches across nations, I have identified three major misconceptions underlying U.S. policies that are largely to blame for our lack of progress. I will briefly discuss each of these widely held beliefs, the misinformation on which they are based, and how they contribute to America's failure to significantly reduce its high child poverty rates. In the chapters ahead, I show the many ways in which policies based on these and other misconceptions are not only hindering efforts to reduce poverty but are also harming our nation's most vulnerable children: the millions of babies, toddlers, and preschoolers who live in poverty.

MISCONCEPTION 1. PUNISHING POOR PARENTS WILL EVENTUALLY BREAK
THE CYCLE OF INTERGENERATIONAL POVERTY

The first misconception widely held by policymakers and the general public is that if we make life as miserable as possible for poor parents, they will become self-sufficient. As I recount in the next chapter, this appeared to have been the belief of most of those who championed welfare reform, the changes that became law in 1996 under the Personal Responsibility and Work Opportunity Reconciliation

Act (PRWORA), and of the majority of the American public who supported its passage. Many believed that harsher treatment of poor families, especially by dramatically reducing the government benefits they received, would force most of them to become economically self-sufficient.

Today, many Americans—including elected officials—still hold the view that the safety net for poor families helps maintain the cycle of intergenerational poverty by providing poor single mothers with increased funds for each additional child they have, and by allowing families to remain dependent on the system instead of fostering work. Given all the changes, including strict time limits, made to welfare and other safety net programs and the significant cuts they've endured at both the state and federal levels since 1996, these programs do anything but foster dependence. For instance, studies show that states withholding additional cash assistance from families for each new birth had no significant effect on the number of subsequent children born to mothers on welfare. Moreover, research on increased government spending on safety net programs during the Great Recession that began in 2008 found little evidence that it encouraged parents to eschew work in favor of accessing or remaining dependent on government benefits. Instead, as research by the Center on Budget and Policy Priorities (CBPP) concluded, "the U.S. safety net has become much more of a work-based safety net, providing consistently more assistance to low-income working families with children than in earlier decades and significantly less assistance to poor families without earnings."[37]

The shift toward a more work-based safety net has resulted in an increase in the number of extremely poor families who receive neither government cash assistance nor income from earnings.[38] We can see the effects of this policy shift in the fact that the number of families with children living in deep poverty has doubled in the period since welfare reform became law in 1996 to 2011.[39] These are typically families headed by a very young single mother, one who grew up poor and may have been sexually and/or physically abused and/or had "aged out" of our troubled foster care system.

Of course it would be much better if highly vulnerable young women like those I am describing did not have children, at least not until their own well-being and financial stability improved. Most Americans would likely be surprised to learn that in fact, the teen birth rate in the United States has been on the decline. It is now at a historic low, dropping 61% since 1991—10% during 2012 alone.[40] But the reality is, as I explain in the next chapter, that many of the teens and women in the current era who have children they can't support were themselves raised in poverty and came to single parenthood with very little hope of any other kind of future. Reducing or terminating assistance to these fragile families will not make the parents more employable, nor will failing to provide these families with adequate supports make it less likely that other vulnerable young women will avoid too-early parenthood. Instead, these harsh measures and the deprived conditions they create often place the children of these mothers on the path to continuing poverty's cycle.

Punishing parents who are working for low wages won't break the cycle, either. The strict measures of welfare reform in 1996 and, later, the economic hardships imposed by the Great Recession have moved the vast majority of employable, poor mothers into the workforce.[41] In many cases, the low wages that most of these mothers earn are subsidized by the remaining part of the safety net that assists low-wage–earner families with the costs of child care, health care, and food. Yet even with whatever government assistance is available, millions of these families are unable to provide their children with a stable, secure, and decent standard of living. Pushing the mothers of young children to work longer hours and/or take on additional jobs or cutting their already meager government benefits will not make these families more self-sufficient. Instead, it will increase already high levels of stress and hardship, especially for the children in these families. This will likely hit young children the hardest. For example, a number of studies have shown a decline in early learning abilities for poor children whose mothers were forced to work during their child's first year of life, and more hours worked per week were associated with stronger negative outcomes for these children.[42]

What about the fathers of children living in poverty? Many of these men lack the education and job skills necessary to support a family. The recent Great Recession, which created the longest postwar male jobless rate in U.S. history, made this situation even worse, and the manufacturing and construction sectors that employ large numbers of men with low levels of education have been particularly slow to recover. Young, less-educated men are far more likely to become nonresident fathers than those with college degrees.[43] Unfortunately, many of these men are chronically unemployed due to a multitude of barriers, including diminishing numbers of blue-collar jobs, a lack of job skills and access to job training, and criminal records.[44] Given the highly disproportionate rates at which men of color are incarcerated, it should surprise no one that many of the fathers unable to obtain steady employment due to criminal records are members of these same racial groups.

Nonresident fathers who are high school dropouts, and even those who have completed high school but lack a college degree, typically work at low-wage jobs that make it nearly impossible to pay child support in addition to supporting themselves. Punitive measures aimed toward increasing the amount of child support from underemployed nonresident fathers, including revoking driver's licenses, incarceration, and financial penalties, are often counterproductive, making conditions worse for poor children, as well as reducing the already limited contact they have with their fathers.[45]

Rather than helping to break the cycle of disadvantage, punitive policy measures that exacerbate stress and hardship in already struggling families help maintain intergenerational poverty by diminishing the prospects for young children to grow into healthy and productive adults. Studies show that as many as 60% of poor children live in households with one or more hardships, including difficulty affording adequate food, having utilities cut off, and/or overcrowding.[46] These stressors add to those caused by living in a violent neighborhood, experiencing child abuse or neglect, and other harmful experiences that go with being poor. As I explain in Chapter 4, high and chronic levels of family stress, especially when children are very young, often have detrimental effects on physical and mental health throughout life.

MISCONCEPTION 2. GOVERNMENT DOES TOO MUCH TO HELP POOR FAMILIES

A second misconception goes along with the notion that our policies should be more punitive, and that is that our government does too much to help poor families. Since the onset of welfare reform in 1996, the United States has been spending fewer and fewer dollars helping poor families with young children, with a modest uptick only during the most recent recession. As the economy continues to improve, the Congressional Budget Office projects that spending for programs that benefit low-income individuals and families—other than for health care—will fall below its forty-year average.[47] Also since the passage of welfare reform, the government has been spending an increasingly larger portion of its resources to help other groups of Americans, especially the elderly and disabled adults, rather than poor families with children. For instance, the nation's largest anti-poverty program, Social Security, lifts more Americans out of poverty than any other government program. In 2014, Social Security benefits raised the incomes of 27.4 million Americans, the majority of them elderly, above the poverty line.[48] The food stamp program, known as SNAP, lifted 4.7 million Americans out of poverty in 2014; more than half of its participants were adult or elderly citizens.[49]

This is not to say that income supports for struggling families with children don't also make a difference. In addition to SNAP, which kept more than 2 million children out of poverty in 2014, subsidized child care, targeted tax credits, health care through Medicaid, housing vouchers, and other safety net programs keep about 41 million people, including 9 million children, above the federal poverty line.[50] Without these programs, the U.S. poverty and child poverty rates would be nearly double what they are.[51] So we have plenty of evidence to show that the safety net works to help raise the standard of living above the poverty line for many families. The problem is that our safety net doesn't help enough families, given the 50 million Americans—13 million of them children—who remain in poverty, and that for those it does help, it doesn't help enough.[52]

To better understand what these numbers mean on a day-to-day basis, consider that an income near the poverty line is around $23,624 a year for a family of four with two children, an amount that even the most frugal family cannot stretch to make ends meet.[53] Although income above $23,624 would place that family above the official poverty line, it would take more than double that amount for such a family to adequately feed, clothe, and house its members and to afford transportation costs, basic educational items for their children, and other necessities, and far more than double for families living in major cities such as New York and Houston.[54] The U.S. safety net looks even less effective when compared to that of other developed Western countries, in which government benefits reduce poverty far more sharply. For instance, Germany's safety net reduces its overall poverty rate by 23 points, and the United Kingdom's reduces poverty by 18 percentage points. The United States is once again in last place, with a safety net that reduces its poverty rate by only 9 percentage points.[55]

Another way in which our government is doing too little to help impoverished families with young children is in failing to provide a well-coordinated system of carefully crafted programs and services that promote optimal development for children while helping their families overcome poverty and move toward self-sufficiency. Although adequate income in any form—whether it be a paycheck or a mix of employment income and safety net supports—would go a long way toward improving the life chances of young children in poor families, most experts agree that it isn't enough to help many of the most vulnerable families overcome the disadvantages of generations of poverty and deprivation.[56]

Given the multigenerational nature of much of the family poverty in the United Sates and the chronically inadequate resources available to these families, many of them face challenges that cannot be overcome by increased income alone. These challenges include low levels of parents' education and a lack of job skills; higher-than-average rates of depression, substance abuse, and other mental health problems; inadequate parenting skills; and higher levels of risk for child maltreatment. Moreover, children in poor families are far more likely to have experienced harmful levels of stress and to have developmental disabilities and/or to lag behind their nonpoor peers in regards to school readiness.[57]

Unfortunately, resources to address these and other needs common among impoverished families are typically most scarce in the communities in which most of these families live, whether it be in our segregated inner cities, in isolated rural areas, or on reservations. To substantially improve outcomes for their children, disadvantaged families need access to a range of services, including health and mental health care, parent training and parent support programs, early child development services, and remedial education programs and job training services for parents. They also often need help navigating the intake requirements, eligibility criteria, and other program rules and surmounting barriers, such as lack of transportation and language differences, that often stand in the way of families accessing the resources and services they need. Very few high-poverty communities contain an adequate supply and range of critical services and supports, nor do most offer families enough help in surmounting obstacles so that they can fully access the programs that are available.[58] The resources available in most such communities are, for the most part, poorly distributed and coordinated, and woefully inadequate to helping families overcome the often overwhelming problems related to intergenerational poverty.

MISCONCEPTION 3. EDUCATION REFORM IS ENOUGH TO CLOSE ACHIEVEMENT GAPS

A third misconception that underlies our failure to develop a comprehensive and effective strategy to substantially reduce poverty among families with young children is the notion that school reform alone is the answer. We can see the degree to which this belief is widely accepted in the plethora of recent books on early childhood poverty that focus on what schools should be doing for the disadvantaged young children who reach their doors. Of course, schools should do more to remedy early life disadvantage and to engage poor parents than they already do. And remedial education programs, teacher training and support, good afterschool programs, and strategies for engaging parents hold promise as useful tools in helping to close the achievement gap. However, pinning most of our hopes on schools to overcome the lagging development, deficits in early learning, and multiple traumas experienced by a large portion of children who have spent their first five years in poverty is folly. This narrow focus results in multiple lost opportunities to enhance children's development and engage parents in improving their children's life chances, well before impoverished children reach the kindergarten, or even preschool, door.

We must recognize that the achievement gap begins when children are born. Schools alone cannot undo the full measure of harm that has already been done to the prospects for success for hundreds of thousands of our nation's poorest children by the time they arrive at kindergarten. Moreover, the same conditions that created disadvantage for these children in their earliest years typically persist throughout their K–12 years of education. This includes living in families struggling to meet basic needs and with health, mental health, and substance abuse problems. It also includes educational disadvantages caused by multiple changes in schools due to homelessness and housing instability.[59] Moreover, given the degree to which so many of our communities are segregated by race and income levels, poor children are likely to attend inferior schools with lower-quality instruction and to be surrounded by low-achieving peers.

Other forces are at play as well. As poverty and education experts Greg Duncan and Richard Murname summarize,

> the rising economic and social inequality produced by technology and globalization has weakened neighborhoods and families in ways that make effective school reform that much more difficult. For a variety of historical reasons ... our nation has not learned how to provide the consistent supports that schools and teachers, especially those serving large numbers of low-income children, must have to succeed.[60]

In other words, school reform is moving too slowly, due in part to the very conditions that perpetuate family poverty. Duncan and Murname also point out that standalone "silver bullet" solutions, including charter schools, increased testing, and other widely touted strategies, have failed to achieve widespread improvements in the teaching and learning that take place in public schools in disadvantaged communities.

As I discuss in Chapter 6, much of the attention on schools as vehicles to address the achievement gap is now focused on the provision of universal preschool. However, given that universal preschool would result in adding preschool programs to the already struggling public schools in disadvantaged communities, disparities in quality are likely to be similar to those for K–12. And although making preschool available to all four-year-olds would likely benefit many disadvantaged children, more affluent children would benefit as well.[61] Therefore, making preschool available to all children is likely to extend downward—from age five to age four—unequal levels of school readiness and prospects for school success between poor children and their higher-income peers.

Looking Ahead

I address these three misconceptions in far more detail in the chapters ahead. But first, in the next chapter, I provide a brief overview of how America's War on Poverty has shifted over the past fifty years into a situation in which poor families are under siege by a wide range of forces, and how the safety net, established to ensure the safety and well-being of the children in such families, has become a shadow of its former self.

3 From the War on Poverty to the War on Poor Families
HISTORY AND IDEOLOGY

A NUMBER OF YEARS AGO, I found myself following, at close range, the governor of Rhode Island as he headed back to his office after speaking at an event in the state capital building. "Governor," I called, and then more loudly, "Governor," until he whirled around, startled to find me proffering my card and requesting a meeting with him. Governor Don Carcieri had just spoken at a press conference held by the Economic Progress Institute, a nonprofit that advocates on behalf of disadvantaged Rhode Islanders. The Institute arranged the press conference to report on the substantial decline in wages for the state's low-skilled jobs and to urge state leaders to do more to remedy these sorry statistics. As the Institute's new board president, my role was to welcome members of the media and other attendees and introduce the lineup of speakers.

Carcieri, who at that time had been in office only a year or two, had run as a maverick Republican; he was a wealthy, retired businessman who vowed to retool a state government controlled by special interests, and to restart the state's stalled economy. My colleagues and I knew that his conservative ideology ran counter to our view of government as having a responsibility to support vulnerable individuals and families as they moved toward self-sufficiency. However,

Carcieri had run as a leader who would work to create jobs and a thriving economy, something that the Institute recognized as critical to its agenda of lifting families out of poverty.

The governor's opening remarks repeated the mantra of trickle-down economics: give bigger tax breaks to businesses so that they will locate in Rhode Island and create more jobs, jobs that would help those who are willing to work to become self-sufficient. And then Carcieri paused, gazed out at his audience and announced that he felt compelled to talk about "the elephant in the room." Carcieri then stated his belief that what was really at the root of so many of the state's economic problems was that, "we have a situation today where we have too many single-parent households." He went on to say that welfare was "enabl[ing] a lot of bad decisions" by unmarried women "to have children they can't support." He urged those present to to help such women to "make more responsible choices.[1] He continued on with some standard personal responsibility rhetoric, pledged to work cooperatively with the Institute and other advocacy groups, and made a beeline for his office door, flanked by his state-trooper bodyguard and an aide. A collective gasp of disbelief echoed off the marble floors and gold-leafed ceiling of the room. I am not sure which was more startling: that the governor believed that the dwindling number of families on welfare in Rhode Island were to blame for the state's economic woes, or that he believed that becoming a poor, single mother was some sort of lifestyle choice. It was at that point that I found myself calling after Carcieri, intercepting him just as he was about to enter his office.

After I introduced myself, I told the governor that I had worked with single mothers and their families for nearly twenty-five years, and requested a meeting to discuss his remarks. His startled demeanor gradually gave way to his trademark affability; he replied that he would welcome a conversation about "the problem of single mothers." I agreed to contact his scheduler, and we shook hands and went our separate ways. Although I was as surprised as others that Carcieri engaged in this stock, blame-the-poor rhetoric before an audience of advocates for low-income families, I knew that he was far from alone in his views. The "welfare mother" has become an enduring icon of the class warfare and culture wars that have corroded political discourse on poverty in the United States over the past three and a half decades. Even as Americans are increasingly inclined to disapprove of negative, stereotyping remarks based on a person's race, gender, or sexual orientation, the welfare mother remains a safe target for scorn and ridicule. She is an effective trope, held up by conservatives as the symbol of a failed welfare state that drains taxpayers' dollars to foster dependence, laziness, and sexual promiscuity in poor women with children.

A Brief History of the War on the Poor

Fifty years after Lyndon Johnson launched the War on Poverty, Americans are deeply skeptical about government efforts to help poor families. This is not surprising, given how aggressively and consistently some politicians and commentators attack both antipoverty programs and the individuals and families who must rely on these programs. As a candidate for president in 1976, Ronald Reagan, remembered as "the great communicator," conjured images of welfare queens driving their expensive cars to pick up food stamps and other government handouts. He based these images on one actual case, a Chicago woman who was apparently a career criminal, accused of multiple crimes, including murder. She had cheated the government by fraudulently reaping benefits from a number of safety net programs.

Using this single story, Reagan framed a narrative in which reducing assistance to poor families went from being a heartless and shameful act to one that assumed the moral high ground. It portrayed women who depended on welfare benefits while raising their children as inclined to bilk the system that was designed to help them. Given that the woman he chose as his poster child for "welfare queens" was black, Reagan's narrative also reinforced the mistaken perception that most welfare recipients were racial minorities. Other comments reveal that Reagan was not, as his defenders have argued, innocently and inadvertently stoking racial resentment. For instance, speaking in the nearly all-white state of New Hampshire that same year, Reagan conjured the image of a "strapping young buck" buying T-bone steaks with food stamps. In doing so, he reinforced not only the worst stereotypes of welfare recipients as inclined to cheat, but also the perception of recipients as largely black, as the term "young buck" was then, and unfortunately still is, used by whites in the South as a pejorative description of large black men.

Reagan's narrative of the shiftless, undeserving welfare cheat endured in the political discourse throughout both of his terms. His successor, George H. W. Bush, attempted to soften the rhetoric regarding both race and poverty, calling for "a kinder, gentler" nation, while continuing his predecessor's trickle-down economic policies. Such policies are based on speculation that when the rich get richer they help the poor by creating jobs, as well as by increasing their charitable giving. We now know that trickle-down economic policies not only fail to help poor families but also contribute to vast inequality between the richest Americans and the rest of us. Rather than ridiculing poor single mothers as Reagan did, Bush promoted the notion that many of the needs of vulnerable citizens could be addressed without substantial government spending on programs to help them. Instead of programs paid for with tax dollars, Bush envisioned legions of volunteers from all walks of life rising up to help needy individuals and families, a notion he wrapped in the romanticized image of "a thousand points of light."

MURRAY, GINGRICH, AND THE CONTRACT WITH AMERICA

By the early 1990s the increasingly negative public image of families on welfare provided the ideal backdrop for some conservative commentators and politicians to attack government programs that assist impoverished families. The most prominent critic was Charles Murray of the American Enterprise Institute, who argued that instead of alleviating poverty, welfare benefits maintained poverty's cycle by encouraging dependence and discouraging parents from working. Murray is best known for co-authoring, in 1994, the highly controversial book *The Bell Curve*, which presents "evidence" (ultimately discredited) that individuals living in poverty and members of other marginalized groups, including blacks, are congenitally inferior to white, higher-achieving individuals. Prior to publication of *The Bell Curve*, Murray had gained fame from his 1984 book *Losing Ground*, in which he called for the complete termination of welfare assistance to impoverished families. He argued that the harsh consequences of attempting to raise children with no income at all would deter poor, single women from having children and would discourage additional births among such women who already had at least one child. As Murray put it, "restoring economic penalties translates into the first and central policy prescription: to end all economic support for single mothers."[2] When questioned about the millions of American children who would go hungry and homeless in families with no income, Murray proposed bringing back orphanages—not the dreary facilities depicted in Oliver Twist, mind you, but rather "modern facilities" with top-notch care.

Murray's and others' antiwelfare views resonated with an American public that was becoming increasingly hostile to the "something for nothing" image of welfare and other government benefits for poor families. By the time Bill Clinton ran for his first term in 1992, the backlash against these programs was so acute that "ending welfare as we know it" became a promise of Clinton's presidential campaign, helping to portray him as a new, centrist Democrat. Murray's anti–single-mother rhetoric was featured prominently in Newt Gingrich's 1994 Contract with America, which called for, among other things, legislation that would "[d]iscourage illegitimacy and teen pregnancy by prohibiting welfare to minor mothers and denying increased AFDC [welfare cash assistance, which was titled at that time Aid to Families with Dependent Children] for additional children while on welfare, cut spending for welfare programs, and enact a tough two-years-and-out provision with work requirements to promote individual re-sponsibility."[3] Gingrich shrewdly used phrases such as "discourage illegitimacy" and "promote individual responsibility" to portray cutting benefits to poor fami-lies as morally righteous. Echoing Murray, Gingrich also called for the revival of orphanages to care for the children of mothers who would be made destitute and homeless by massive cuts in welfare benefits. Even though many of the provi-sions of the Contract with America never made it into law, they resonated with a large portion of the American public. The Contract was instrumental in helping Republicans gain control of the House of Representatives for the first time in forty years and elevating Gingrich to House Speaker. Most importantly, it paved the way for Congress to pass and Clinton to sign the Personal Responsibility and Work Opportunities Reconciliation Act of 1996 (PRWORA), commonly known as welfare reform, that dramatically scaled back cash assistance to poor families with children.

In the years since Reagan's election, blaming chronic poverty on the poor choices made by irresponsible adults has become a tidy and convenient way for Americans to absolve themselves and their government of responsibility for solving this recalcitrant problem. Like Governor Carcieri and many other socially conservative politicians, large numbers of Americans are attracted to the simplistic "personal responsibility" response to a problem that is madden-ingly complex and has failed to succumb to a wide range of policy and pro-grammatic interventions over the past several decades. Moreover, viewing poverty through a personal responsibility lens helps those who are not poor to feel virtuous regarding their own choices and ability to defer gratification to lead more "responsible" and "self-sufficient" lives. This sense of righteousness is conveyed in comments posted on the websites of politics and news organiza-tions, in response to reports on family poverty, and profiles of families who rely on some form of government assistance. Although these comments vary, the common themes include, "I would never have children I couldn't support" and "I've had to make sacrifices and work hard to get to where I am today—why can't they?" Like much of what is posted online about poor Americans, however, the wording of such sentiments is often obscene, venomous, and denigrating toward those receiving what the writers consider to be undeserved government handouts.

THE INTERTWINING OF RACISM AND SEXISM

One of the many destructive consequences of the national discourse on pov-erty has been the racialization of the perceived negative characteristics of poor families. For decades, politicians and commentators have—subtly as well as blatantly—conflated disproportionate rates of out-of-wedlock births and family poverty to some innate weakness or moral defect in African Americans. They have done so despite the fact that for as long as the races of Americans in poverty has been tracked, whites have constituted the largest racial group. This type of racialized rhetoric is not unique to social conservatives and began long before Ronald Reagan moved into the Oval Office. One of the most famous— and infamous—examples of this is the 1965 report *The Negro Family: The Case for National Action*, written by New York senator and former Harvard sociologist Daniel Patrick Moynihan, a Democrat. In his report, Moynihan declared that the "weakening" structure of African American families "will be found to be the principal source of most of the aberrant, inadequate or antisocial behavior that did not establish, but now serves to perpetuate, the cycle of poverty."

Race, Single Motherhood, and Poverty

Moynihan's report was and continues to be harshly criticized for singling out black families and citing the single-parent structure of a higher proportion of these families as the main cause of chronic poverty and the disadvantages that accompany it. Legions of critics have faulted Moynihan for victim blaming, as he also located the key drivers of poverty primarily in individual behavior (i.e., "poor choices") and less in the historical, economic, and social factors that did and still do contribute heavily to the cycle of disadvantage, especially among blacks. However, more than fifty years after the release of Moynihan's report, its focus on individual behavior still underlies and stokes much of the debate regarding factors that maintain higher rates of intergenerational poverty among blacks. The question it raises is this: Are out-of-wedlock births, which are disproportionately higher for black women, the primary cause of family poverty or a result of it?

Given that intergenerational poverty is, by definition, a cycle, with girls of all races who grow up poor being far more likely to become teenage single mothers than girls in higher-income families, the answer must be: Both. Motherhood is one of the few paths to adulthood available to adolescent girls growing up in poverty, given their compromised start in life, as I describe in the next chapter, one that often leads to poor performance in school as well as to significant social and/ or emotional problems. When these girls fail in school and/or drop out, they typically lack basic job skills, and college is out of the question. Moreover, girls from poor families are more likely than their nonpoor peers to be victims of physical and/or sexual abuse and to suffer from untreated mental health problems related to abuse and other traumas. For so many of these girls, having a child is the only way to obtain a role in society and to eke out a living, however meager, traumatic, and humiliating.

Despite a large body of research that documents this trajectory,[4] many Americans, especially far-right politicians and commentators and their followers, cling to the "personal choice" explanation for single parenthood, ignoring the reality that growing up poor in America leaves millions of young women— a disproportionate number of them African American—with very few choices other than motherhood for constructing an adult life. As I put it to Governor Carcieri: Picture a girl who is born to parents in a stable relationship and whose needs for safety, good health, and early learning are consistently met, a girl who attends decent schools where she is encouraged to succeed and envision a future for herself. Do you really believe that such a young woman, at the age of 17 or 18, looks into the mirror and says, "Should I apply to college and have a successful career, or should I get pregnant so that my child and I can live in poverty for the rest of our lives?" Only if you believe that a large number of well-nurtured, young women ask themselves this question and that many of them choose the latter option does viewing single parenthood through the lens of "choice" and "personal responsibility" make sense.

It's hard to believe that most Americans envision such a scenario. Most of us understand that children who are well cared for and have access to a decent education have a good shot at growing into successful, or at least self-sufficient, adults. Most of us are also aware that the vast majority of young, single women who bear children they cannot support have themselves grown up in poverty and have little reason to see any other future. The facts confirm this: Young women from poor families are twice as likely to bear children while in their teens as those who are not poor.[5] No one should be surprised, then, to find higher rates of single motherhood among black teens when the poverty rate among black children (39%) is more than double that of white children (14%).[6]

There are other seemingly inevitable pathways to single motherhood, including what happens in our troubled foster care system. As I report in Chapter 5, adolescent girls who become stuck in foster care are far more likely to become pregnant by the time they are nineteen than their non–foster care peers. Moreover, girls who grow up in foster care also become teen parents at double the rate of those in the general population. The fact that children born to teen parents are twice as likely to be placed into foster care as are those born to older parents provides yet another demonstration of how the cycle of intergenerational poverty is anything but a choice for the young lives ensnared in it.[7] The latter fact helps explains higher rates of single parenthood and poverty among black mothers because, as I also discuss in Chapter 5, African American children are placed into foster care at rates higher than for white or Latino children, and they tend to languish there for longer periods of time. The longer children remain in the system, the more likely they are to experience multiple placements and their damaging effects, and the less likely they are to exit the system before they reach adulthood.

During my years of working with poor, single mothers of various racial backgrounds, I saw what the research shows: that economic deprivation in early life often leads to school failure, and that school failure, frequently compounded by maltreatment and/or other trauma, sets the stage for too-early parenting.[8] Before they became pregnant, these young women were largely invisible to society, with little hope for earning a decent living, let alone having a successful career and/or a stable marriage. Becoming a parent provided them with at least a role in society, as well as access to meager government assistance and support from community-based organizations, access and support they would otherwise have been denied. It is worth noting that among the array of nonprofit agencies in a typical low-income community, there are usually several whose mission is to help children and/or support families with children, and very few, if any, whose mission is to help disadvantaged, childless young women find a satisfying and self-sufficient future. Seen from this vantage point, single motherhood at an early age looks less like a "lifestyle choice" and more like one of the only choices for girls growing up in poverty.

For most of these mothers, the fathers of their babies also grew up poor and came to school ill prepared for school success.[9] These young men's academic failures left them with few prospects for employment and at risk for criminal activity, factors that dim their prospects for becoming reliable husbands and fathers.

Raising Ratings and Scoring Political Points

Ignoring the complex nature of intergenerational poverty, including the dynamics I've just described, blaming poor parents for their situation, and racializing poverty and welfare dependence continue to deliver strong returns for many talk show hosts and politicians. Fox News' Bill O'Reilly pounded the irresponsibility and race buttons in 2014 in observing the fiftieth anniversary of the Johnson administration's War on Poverty: "maybe we should have a war against chaotic, irresponsible parents. But America will never launch that kind of war because it's too judgmental and deeply affects the minority precincts. Therefore, cowardly politicians and race hustlers continue to bear false witness that our economic system is at fault rather than bad personal decision-making."[10] Here again, intergenerational poverty is blamed on "bad personal decision-making" rather than the bad luck of millions of children who happen to be born into poor families, often with inadequately educated and/or troubled parents, and into a society that shuns them. It is tempting for those on the left to dismiss O'Reilly's bombastic salvos as the kind of sensationalized noise that attracts like-minded viewers and incites controversy and debate, all of which the owners of Fox recognize as good for ratings. However, it is well worth noting that 62% of Americans get their news from O'Reilly and his colleagues on 24-hour cable news stations, with Fox as a ratings leader.[11] No doubt statements made on Fox News programs influence the attitudes and voting preferences of a significant portion of voters. Moreover, O'Reilly is wrong that "America will never launch that kind of war," given the pervasiveness of this type of rhetoric—much of it cleaned up and more subtle than O'Reilly's—coming from many of today's politicians and commentators, and the multiple ways in which this harsh discourse is reflected in our public policies.

From Reagan's welfare queens to presidential candidate Mitt Romney's "47 percenters" who are dependent on government benefits and cannot be convinced to "take personal responsibility and care for their lives," the war on poor families slogs on with its often misogynistic, racialized innuendo. Also in 2014, former governor of Arkansas and perennial Republican presidential candidate Mike Huckabee criticized proponents of government-subsidized health care for making low-income women "believe that they are helpless without Uncle Sugar coming in and providing them a prescription each month for birth control because they cannot control their libido or their reproductive system without the help of the government."[12] In addition to portraying low-income women who use birth control as promiscuous, Huckabee's comments demonstrate his apparent ignorance of the fact that preventing subsequent births among young, single mothers is important to their ability to move themselves and their children out of poverty. Having a second and third child makes finishing school and/or completing job training much more difficult and less likely to happen. Therefore, providing low-income mothers, especially teen mothers, with access to contraception is a smart, cost-effective component of any strategy aimed toward breaking the poverty cycle.

As Reagan's image of welfare-abusing "young bucks" demonstrates, it is not just poor women who are disparaged by politicians and pundits. In March 2014, Republican Congressman (now House Speaker) Paul Ryan blamed the "culture" of poor men for high unemployment and poverty rates in many urban communities. "We have got this tailspin of culture," Ryan stated, "in our inner cities in particular, of men not working and just generations of men not even thinking about working or learning the value and the culture of work, and so there is a real culture problem here that has to be dealt with."[13] Scores of commentators attacked Ryan for what they saw as his thinly veiled conflation of shiftlessness and black men, whose images are commonly conjured by the term "inner cities." They also criticized Ryan's implication that unemployment and poverty reside in "black culture."

Whether deliberately or otherwise, Ryan's statement evoked the most controversial and derided aspect of Moynihan's 1965 report, the use of the phrase "the culture of poverty" to describe and explain the recalcitrant problem of intergenerational poverty, poverty among blacks in particular. Moynihan, like Ryan, was accused of asserting that there is an innate tendency in blacks to eschew work and responsibility in order to live on the dole. Also similar to Moynihan, Ryan's observation seems to mistake correlation (higher rates of poverty among African Americans) for causation (being black causes one to turn away from work and gravitate toward government handouts).[14]

Denigrating Rhetoric Influences Public Policy

The regular flow of disparaging comments by pundits and politicians like O'Reilly and Huckabee and the barrage of other attacks on poor families in the media continue to demonstrate that the concerns voiced by Martin Luther King, Jr. in his response to Moynihan's report were warranted. In speaking about African American families living in poverty, King foresaw that

> As public awareness of the predicament of the Negro family increases, there will be danger and opportunity. The opportunity will be to deal fully rather than haphazardly with the problem as a whole—to see it as a social catastrophe . . . brought on by long years of brutality and oppression—and to meet it as other disasters are met, with an adequacy of resources. The danger will be that the problem will be attributed to innate Negro weaknesses and used to justify further neglect and to rationalize continued oppression.[15]

Fifty years later, it is clear that the dangers King feared, rather than the opportunities for comprehensive approaches he hoped for, have been realized, as ugly and often racist rhetoric continues to drive much of our social policy regarding families in poverty. King was, of course, speaking about black families and referring to the reverberating consequences of slavery, segregation, and racial discrimination, all of which contribute to disproportionate rates of poverty among black families. However, the attribution of poverty to some innate moral weaknesses of poor parents aptly describes much of the current discourse regarding poor families of all racial backgrounds. For example, a 2014 column by the *New York Times'*

Nicholas Kristof that profiled a young white child and his single mother living in extreme poverty in West Virginia elicited a slew of denigrating comments such as this: "You show a photograph of a fat woman with tons of tattoos all over that she paid for, and then we—boohoo—have to worry about the fact that her children aren't cared for properly?"[16] Virtually any web posting that profiles or discusses poor, single-mother families attracts streams of readers' remarks full of vitriol and contempt.

As a career social worker and social work educator, I am accustomed to hearing negative, stereotypical comments about poor families from casual acquaintances and occasionally even from some of my students. Although these remarks are not as mean-spirited and contemptuous as what is posted on the web, they make it clear that in an era of increasing social sanctions against those who make sexist, racist, or antigay comments, America's poor are the last group for which ugly stereotyping and denigrating comments are socially acceptable among large sectors of the general public. It has gotten so that even individuals who try to help the poor are criticized for doing so and are sometimes called degrading names such as "welfare pimp" or "poverty pimp." A particularly sad example of this was in the *Wall Street Journal* in 2014, when a mega-rich hedge fund manager criticized his teenage son for the boy's volunteer work providing food and personal hygiene supplies to homeless New Yorkers. Instead of demonstrating pride in his son's compassion, this father posited that such help only encouraged people to remain homeless.[17]

It would be easier to ignore such rhetoric, chalking it up to ignorance regarding what causes and perpetuates poverty, if not for the fact that public discourse strongly affects public policy. Blaming poverty on the poor means that neither the American public nor our elected officials feel responsible for improving the plight of families caught in poverty's snare. As another *New York Times* columnist, Charles Blow, pointed out in response to Speaker Ryan's comments on high rates of unemployment among black men:

> By suggesting that laziness is more concentrated among the poor, inner city or not, we shift our moral obligation to deal forthrightly with poverty. When we insinuate that poverty is the outgrowth of stunted culture, that it is almost always invited and never inflicted, we avert the gaze from the structural features that help maintain and perpetuate poverty—discrimination, mass incarceration, low wages, educational inequities—while simultaneously degrading and dehumanizing those who find themselves trapped by it.[18]

I wish that I could end my vignette about the governor of Rhode Island by describing how my colleagues and I convinced him that it is morally wrong and economically short-sighted to turn our backs on disadvantaged young children and their mothers. I would like to tell you that the governor began to understand how cutting the bare-bones assistance that the state provides to these families only further dooms their chances of ever becoming self-sufficient, that he acknowledged that each of the children in impoverished families is a potential member of the well-prepared workforce Rhode Island so desperately needs, and that it is vital—from an economic development perspective—to invest early in their well-being and school success.

I did get my meeting with the governor; in fact, I got two. I brought along colleagues with additional expertise on the needs of vulnerable families and the costs of neglecting poor children, along with research findings to back up our arguments. Carcieri, a friendly and intelligent man, appeared to be engaged and persuaded by what he heard. We were optimistic when the discussion turned toward developing strategies to help families break the poverty cycle, and how our tiny state could lead the country in demonstrating that such strategies, when carefully crafted, can succeed. But personal ideology is a powerful force, even in the face of research evidence and compelling arguments. The negative public discourse regarding poor families, especially those headed by single mothers, appears to have seeped into the very pores of so many elected officials. It too often drives much of the poverty-related policy in the United States and the disconnect between these policies and what research findings indicate we should do for vulnerable young children and their families. As Shonkoff and Bales conclude:

> although the negotiation of public policy provides a distinctive forum for shaping perspectives, there is little to indicate that patterns of thinking about complex social issues are different among policymakers compared to the general public. Moreover . . . investigators have found legislators to be highly reliant on verbal discourse, images in the public media, folk wisdom, common sense, and the views of their colleagues who have little expertise in science.[19]

Shortly after our second meeting, Governor Carcieri's aides stopped returning my phone calls. A year later, the governor's budget called for even deeper cuts in programs serving poor families with children.

THE WELFARE CHEAT CANARD

It is not just rhetoric from far-right commentators and politicians that stokes public resentment of poor families. In more subtle but no less damaging ways, other members of the media help maintain the image of parents receiving government benefits as dishonest and lazy. The constant barrage of news stories about parents selling their food stamps in order to buy drugs or alcohol, using welfare checks to support their gambling habits, or receiving benefits to which they weren't entitled gives the false impression that a high percentage of parents in families that receive these benefits are dishonest, if not criminal. To be clear, all fraudulent use of public funds is wrong, and there is no evidence that these news reports are based on inaccurate information. But the prominence of welfare-cheat stories and the sensationalized reporting on them are disproportionate to both the incidence and the cost of this type of fraud.

Comparisons with Other Government Programs

News reports often focus on fraudulent use of the federal food stamp program, whose official title is the Supplemental Nutrition Assistance Program (SNAP), so it seems fitting to make a few comparisons between SNAP and other government programs. In studying the period 2002–2005, the nonpartisan Government Accounting Office (GAO) found that across the country, improper payments in the food stamp program amounted to approximately 1% of the program's cost.[20] Government spending was approximately $28 billion for food stamp benefits in 2006, so improper payments of food stamp benefits cost taxpayers roughly $280 million dollars in 2006. That's a lot of money, and taxpayers should be concerned; however, it's mere pocket change compared to what's lost to mismanagement and fraud in other government programs.

For instance, an internal Pentagon report concluded that between 2001 and 2011, defense companies swindled the U.S. military out of $1.1 trillion; that's more than $100 billion (yes, billion) dollars a year, for ten years. It gets worse. The Defense Department paid more than $250 million to fifty-four defense contractors who were eventually convicted of criminal fraud; of that amount, $33 million was paid to companies *after* they had been convicted of defrauding the government.[21] Moreover, a report by the U.S. Congress' Commission on Wartime Contracting estimated that by 2011, waste and fraud in the war in Afghanistan ranged from 15% to 29% of the total funds spent. These figures include $360 million that the Commission estimated "ended up in the hands of people the American-led coalition has spent nearly a decade battling: the Taliban, criminals and power brokers with ties to both."[22]

This is shocking enough. However, it is not just the Defense Department that is losing several billion dollars a year in fraud and mismanagement; the Internal Revenue Service (IRS) has a dirty little secret known as the tax gap. Defined as the difference between the amount of taxes rightfully owed to the federal government and the amount actually paid by individuals and corporations, the tax gap for 2006—the year in which mismanagement in the food stamp program cost $280 million—was $385 billion (again, that's billion with a "b").[23] The latter amount reflects what remained unpaid after the IRS audited, investigated, and attempted to collect what was owed from those it identified as scofflaws. Of course, the $385 billion does not include fraud that the IRS hadn't uncovered; that is, whatever tax cheats got away with by underreporting their income, using foreign banks to hide assets, and so forth, just as there is no way to calculate the cost of undiscovered cheating in SNAP. However, when we compare the percentage of funds known to have been lost to errors and fraud by the IRS in what appears to be a typical year, an estimated 14.5% of payments due, the percentage of income tax revenue the IRS failed to collect was approximately 14.5 times higher than the 1% of total funds lost in the food stamp program.

Administrators of SNAP have continued efforts to reduce food stamp errors and misuse, with rates hovering between 1% and 3% in recent years. Despite what the facts are, however, some conservative pundits and lawmakers routinely cite excessive rates of food stamp fraud as partial justification for making big cuts in a program that prevents millions of low-income children and their families, as well as elderly and disabled adults, from going hungry.[24] Meanwhile, most Americans hear far less about the hundreds of billions lost to various forms of fraud in defense contracts and nonpayment of income tax.

Let's face it: Some form of cheating occurs in virtually every large-scale human enterprise. It takes various forms, from shoplifting in stores and credit card fraud, to defaulting on student loans, to making exaggerated claims for workplace injuries. It should come as no surprise, then, that cheating also takes place among the most desperate members of society, those relying on government benefits in order to keep themselves and their children housed and fed. It is also important to note that the lion's share of the fraud that occurs in government antipoverty programs is committed by unscrupulous third-party providers, like clinics and medical supply companies that falsify claims in order to obtain higher Medicaid and Medicare payments. Moreover, middle- and upper-income individuals commit a significant amount of fraud by accessing government benefits, such as disability payments, to which they are not entitled.[25]

Legal Ways to Pay Less and Get More

Another aspect of this topic on which the media seldom report is how, unlike low income families, wealthier individuals and families can afford tools to ensure that they pay as little in taxes and get the most out of government programs as possible. Even though many of the strategies employed to do so are perfectly legal, a number of them are unfair to those of us who can't afford expensive financial advisors. For example, a Boston radio station whose news reports frequently sensationalize stories about food stamp fraud and welfare abuse runs a commercial for a financial advising firm that helps older people, including those who are wealthy, avoid having to pay for nursing home care. How do they do that? By using legal strategies such as putting all of the patient's financial assets into a trust that is "owned" by his or her children or other trustees. Signing over the house to the children is another frequently employed tactic to make the person in need of expensive nursing home care appear destitute. In most of these scenarios, the elderly or disabled individual can retain unfettered access to his or her financial assets and home, even though on paper he or she no longer owns them. So who pays the costs of nursing home care for a patient who appears penniless after successfully shielding his or her assets? Taxpayers do through Medicaid, the program funded by federal and state governments to provide health care coverage for poor families and disabled adults and children. Most Americans would be surprised to learn that nearly one third of the $400 billion spent by Medicaid each year goes to nursing home care. (Medicare, the government health insurance program for elderly individuals of all income groups, does not cover the costs of ongoing nursing home care.) In fact, Medicaid spends more than five times as much on each elderly person in nursing homes and other forms of long-term care than it does on each poor child it covers, and even more per person on disabled adults in nursing homes and other facilities.[26]

To be sure, those using trusts and other mechanisms to effectively hide their assets in order to have taxpayers pay their bills probably make up a modest percentage of nursing home patients, and the government has taken steps to thwart such practices. Moreover, a greater number of nursing home patients on Medicaid are individuals who were unable to pay the high cost of care from the beginning, or whose assets were depleted early on in paying for their care, due to yet another hole in the safety net. Nevertheless, the ads for assistance in "protecting your assets from the high cost of nursing home care" continue to run, and such loopholes are rarely criticized by the media.[27]

The Effects of Biased Reporting

Given the disproportionate amount of reporting on welfare fraud, and the innuendo in many politicians' remarks, the general public could be forgiven for getting the impression that cheating is endemic among low-income individuals and families, and that the costs to taxpayers are enormous. The continuous sensationalizing of reports on even minor incidents serves to harden the hearts and attitudes of Americans against young families that must rely on government assistance to survive. Poor single parents, the vast majority of them mothers, have become our social pariahs. In casting these parents out as worthless, we also cast out their children, children who did not choose to be born poor. As I describe in Chapter 4, the effects of growing up amid extreme deprivation are often catastrophic. Young children bear the brunt of punishing policies as politicians and pundits use overhyped benefit-fraud reports to justify cutting or eliminating already meager safety net programs rather than calling for improved oversight of these programs. This is patently unfair, as Eric Schnurer of *The Atlantic* points out:

> Combatting fraud requires efforts and investments that target the real perpetrators, not cheap shots at beneficiaries and reflexive cuts in their programs. There are, after all, equal levels of fraud and theft in other fields, most notably finance—but we don't try to reduce it by shutting down the entire industry and blaming the customers.[28]

Public discourse on poor families shapes policy both at the state and federal levels as politicians pass legislation that is in line with the perceived attitudes and beliefs of their constituents—at least, if they want to be reelected. There is little doubt, for instance, that polls showing that 60% of Americans believed that poverty is caused by people not doing enough to help themselves played a major role in Bill Clinton's signing welfare reform into law in 1996, without strong provisions to protect the well-being of millions of children living in families that would be affected by the law's harsh restrictions on benefits. Interestingly, that number had decreased by 2014, with an NBC/*Wall Street Journal* poll showing that only 44% of Americans blamed poverty largely on the poor. Political scientists speculate that the recent decline probably reflects attitudes softened by the Great Recession that began in 2008, as large numbers of previously nonpoor Americans struggled to find and keep employment.[29]

It is worth keeping in mind, however, that even though the poll shows more empathy toward the poor, just under half of those responding still view poverty as the fault of those affected by it, rather than on circumstances beyond their control. Equally concerning are the results of a similar poll taken in 2013, in which a majority of respondents chose "too much government welfare that prevents initiative" as the leading cause of poverty over any other factor.[30] These findings demonstrate how deep-seated Americans' erroneous beliefs are in regards to antipoverty policies, as most seem oblivious to the fact that much of what they call "government welfare" has withered away since the 1996 passage of welfare reform legislation.

It is ironic that while the most recent recession may have reduced the number of Americans who blame poverty on the poor, the number who believe that government should help take care of those who are disadvantaged has also declined. A Pew Research Center poll found that the majority of Americans who support having a social safety net fell from 69% in 2007 to 59% in 2012. During that same period, the percentage who feel that government has a responsibility to take care of very poor people who cannot take care of themselves fell from 28% to 22%.[31]

The extent to which Americans' ambivalence regarding the role of government in helping the disadvantaged has become "baked in" to our culture can be seen in the results of a multinational poll conducted by Pew in 2011. Fifty-eight percent of Americans rated being free to pursue their life goals "without interference from the state" as more important than for government to play an active role in guaranteeing that "nobody was in need." To compare, between 30% and 38% of respondents in Britain, Germany, France, and Spain ranked providing unencumbered freedom to pursue one's life goals as a more important function of their government than working to eliminate need.[32] This helps explain why the poverty rate, the child poverty rate in particular, is much lower in these countries than in the United States, as is the case for almost every other similarly developed nation.

The Incredible Shrinking Safety Net

The shaming and blaming rhetoric, as well as overhyped news accounts of benefit fraud and misuse, makes assistance to poor families an appealing target for budget cuts. At the federal level and in most states, elected officials in both major parties routinely whittle away funding for these programs, in flush times as well as during economic downturns. However, many if not most Americans still seem to have the impression that the welfare system bestows generous benefits that enable single mothers to lead comfortable, even leisurely lives, with their largesse expanding with each additional child they bear—the old welfare queen canard. As those who work with poor families know, nothing could be further from the reality of these women's lives.

Although it can be argued that to some extent the old welfare program, AFDC, discouraged both marriage and employment and provided unintended (albeit very small) financial incentives for single mothers to have additional children, the cash assistance program that replaced AFDC, under the auspices of welfare reform, was designed to have the opposite effect. Moreover, cuts in food stamps, subsidized housing, and other antipoverty programs have made life increasingly harsh for children and families who rely on some form of government assistance. The following is a concise examination of the way in which antipoor family rhetoric has influenced and continues to influence U.S. policies regarding these families.

THE PASSAGE AND EFFECTS OF WELFARE REFORM

By the mid-1990s and in an atmosphere of frequent assaults on the welfare system by Murray, Gingrich, and others, ending "welfare as we know it" became one of the most pressing hot-button issues in the country, with polls showing a majority of Americans had soured on maintaining the safety net. In 1996, Congress passed and President Clinton signed PRWORA, commonly known as welfare reform. PRWORA created a five-year, lifetime limit on cash assistance to poor families and instituted work requirements for parents, while slashing funds in a number of federal programs that benefit those families. Cash assistance to poor families through AFDC was replaced with a program entitled Temporary Assistance for Needy Families (TANF). Unlike AFDC, TANF provides cash assistance through fixed block grants to states and requires states to supplement federal funds with their own revenue. States must enforce time limits on benefits and achieve specific rates of participation in work activities by TANF-recipient families in order to receive full funding from the federal government.

Welfare reform achieved mixed results. By extending government-subsidized child care and health care to families in which parents were able to get (mostly low-wage) jobs, PRWORA helped support the transition of these families from welfare to income earned from employment. A booming economy and unprecedented economic growth in the mid-1990s played an enormous role in the early success of welfare reform as they boosted the job prospects for even low-skilled parents. With overall unemployment during this time near 4%, its lowest rate in decades, the employment rate for poor mothers rose from 46.5% in 1994 to 65.4% in 1999, a 48% increase. During that time, the number of families receiving welfare cash assistance dropped significantly, by nearly 60%.[33] The number of single-parent families in poverty, however, dropped by only 22% for that same period, revealing that parents' employment at a low-wage job was insufficient to lift most poor families out of poverty. Instead of ending "poverty as we know it," one result of welfare reform was that the working poor constituted a greater share of all poor parents.[34] Moreover, PRWORA's efforts to limit family size by not increasing TANF payments for additional children has had little effect on subsequent births among poor, single mothers. The twenty-one states that chose not to increase the size of payments for additional children born to mothers on TANF found little to no impact on the number of subsequent births to these mothers.[35]

Despite its early success in dramatically reducing welfare rolls, and its less dramatic but nonetheless significant effects on the total number of families in poverty, welfare reform has done little to improve the lot of families stuck at the very bottom of the economy. As I discussed in Chapter 2, there has been a major shift in the focus of antipoverty spending away from families headed by poor single parents and toward less-poor or near-poor working families, seniors, and people with disabilities. While the percentage of low-income families has declined slightly since the implementation of welfare reform, the percentage of those living below 50% of the poverty line has actually increased.[36] As I noted earlier, such families include those headed by teen mothers, parents with limited literacy skills or English-speaking ability, those struggling with addiction and other mental health problems or domestic violence, and parents and/or children with physical or cognitive disabilities. These are the most fragile families whose children are at greatest risk for rotten outcomes. They are the families most often fated to perpetuate the cycle of poverty, a cycle that has kept the child poverty rate in the United States at shamefully high levels, especially when compared with other similarly developed nations. The dire circumstances of the children in these families is missing from much of the political debate on poverty, a debate that continues to recycle the well-worn themes of "choice" and "personal responsibility" and implies that poor parents could overcome the multiple challenges they face if they were just more motivated and worked harder.

From Cash Assistance to Marriage Promotion

By the early 2000s, the U.S. economy was slowing and unemployment rates were ticking upward as corporations continued to transfer many of their low-skilled jobs to foreign countries with lower wages and fewer labor protections and other regulations. Some of the progress made by welfare reform toward increasing family self-sufficiency began to roll backwards, as low-income parents experienced increased difficulty obtaining and holding on to employment. At the same time, government funding was shifting away from TANF and toward the earned income tax credit, which benefits only lower-income families in which at least one parent is employed. Moreover, food stamp (now known as SNAP) receipt among the poorest families declined as welfare reform had made accessing this benefit more difficult; however, food stamp expenditures on higher-income single-parent families increased.

Analysis by the National Bureau of Economic Research (NBER) found that by 2004, families in what they called "deep poverty" received less in government benefits than did low-income families that were not as poor, due largely to these shifts. Across the board, government resources spent to meet the basic needs of the poorest families with children declined, while spending on other groups, through programs such as Social Security, disability insurance, workers compensation, and unemployment insurance increased. As the NBER report put it,

> In fact, the very largest increases occurred for the highest income groups. This shows clearly that there has been a double redistribution of expenditure in the U.S. over time: within groups, expenditure has been redistributed from the very poor to the less poor and near poor, and, across groups, expenditure has been redistributed from the nonelderly, nondisabled to the elderly and disabled.[37]

Another factor that contributed to the decline in benefits for the poorest families with children was that unlike its predecessor AFDC, TANF was provided to states in the form of a block grant that could be used for a wide variety of other purposes. This provided states with an incentive to restrict cash assistance to as few destitute families as possible in order to utilize these funds for other priorities. The "compassionate conservative" agenda of George W. Bush's administration altered TANF in ways that were rarely reported on by the media but had significant impacts on what is left of the safety net. During Bush's eight years in office, federal funds in these block grants to states shrank considerably, as his administration shifted TANF away from supporting the basic needs of families and toward funding social service programs. Some of these programs, such as job training and job placement services, focused on promoting employment for low-income parents, something critical for families to obtain self-sufficiency. However, other programs supported by TANF funds were part of Bush's agenda to distribute a greater portion of federal antipoverty funding to the faith-based organizations he saw as critical to breaking the cycle of poverty.[38]

Perhaps the best known of Bush's faith-based programs was the Healthy Marriage Initiative, which amped up the Clinton administration's attempts to encourage poor, single parents to get married, and those already married to remain together. This initiative funded projects ranging from research studies of poor adults' perceptions of marriage to media campaigns that touted the benefits of being married. Although a few of the projects funded under the Healthy Marriage Initiative appeared to have achieved some modest results, hundreds of millions of federal dollars—funds that could have been allocated toward improving the literacy skills, mental health, and work readiness of impoverished parents—were wasted without measurably increasing marriage rates or decreasing child poverty rates.[39]

The War on Poor Families Continues

Barack Obama campaigned for doing much more than his predecessors to eliminate child and family poverty in the United States. In his bestseller *The Audacity of Hope*, Obama called for America to renew its commitment to ending poverty and ensuring that all children have the opportunity to thrive. In 2007, candidate Obama gave a speech on poverty in Anacostia, an impoverished neighborhood in southeast Washington, D.C. He described finding new solutions for reducing urban poverty as "the cause that led me to a life of public service almost 25 years ago." Obama stated that accomplishing this goal would "require the sustained commitment of the President of the United States."[40]

However, as President Obama was sworn in in 2009, the United States was deeply involved in fighting two wars, and the country, along with much of the world, was on the precipice of economic collapse. After the administration and Congress spent billions of dollars to bail out corporations whose irresponsible and greedy leadership led them—indeed, the entire economy—to the brink of ruin, record numbers of families lost their homes to foreclosure, and a long recession with high unemployment took its toll, Americans were not in the mood for efforts to raise up the country's most vulnerable families. Families headed by one or two parents earning a decent wage before the Great Recession did receive help from the Recovery Act passed at that time. The law included provisions to extend food stamp eligibility to a greater number of families and to provide health care coverage to millions of uninsured children by expanding Medicaid and the Children's Health Insurance Program (CHIP). Unemployment benefits were extended to more individuals for longer periods of time, and expanded tax credits helped millions of parents whose earning power had declined to weather the recession.

CONDITIONS WORSEN FOR FAMILIES AT THE BOTTOM

Although the Recovery Act helped families who were pushed into poverty by the Great Recession, it did little to improve conditions for millions of children who were already living in poverty. And although expanded access to health care under the Affordable Care Act helps moderately disadvantaged families and their children, the harsh conditions and intergenerational poverty in places like Anacostia in Washington, and the south side of the former president's adopted hometown, Chicago, remain largely unchanged from when he took office.

As the economy makes a slow but steady recovery, and with the stock market having hit record highs, Washington's war on poor families continues to take its toll, striking children the hardest. Caps on federal spending, known as sequestration, which Congress insisted upon in return for enabling President Obama to raise the debt ceiling, have had a devastating effect on children in the nation's poorest families. Sequestration caps on spending for subsidized housing, for example, caused the number of impoverished families receiving housing vouchers to fall by 100,000 in 2013 alone.[41] Over 1.3 million children and youth were homeless during the 2013–2014 school year, according to the U.S. Department of Education, an increase of 15% over the previous three years. Four fifths of these children were living in homes that were not their own, often in crowded and unstable conditions; the rest were living in shelters or on the street, in cars, or in abandoned buildings.[42] In 2013, not satisfied with sequester cuts in housing and other safety net programs, Congress cut funding for SNAP, a measure that resulted in an average loss of $29 in food stamps each month for a family of three, the equivalent of taking away sixteen meals a month.[43] The families affected by these cuts are among the poorest. Four in five food stamp recipients have gross incomes below the poverty line (about $23,500 for a family of four) and include many families with one or more low-wage earners.

Outside of Washington, the war on poor families rages on in the states. Because welfare reform converted cash assistance for poor families from a federal entitlement that rose and fell according to need to a fixed block grant for each state, state governments largely control the purse strings. This means that governors and legislatures can shift TANF funds to cover a wide range of expenses and programs that don't necessarily benefit families in poverty. That is exactly what has taken place. In the initial year of welfare reform, nearly 70% of the TANF block grant went to pay for basic cash assistance for poor families with children. By 2012, that portion had dropped to only 29%, despite the increased number of families who had fallen into poverty due to the recession.[44]

Some of the ways in which states are spending TANF funds reveal the incoherence of public policies pertaining to vulnerable families. For instance, when Georgia was court ordered to overhaul its dangerous and dysfunctional foster care system, the state tapped more than half its TANF block grant to pay for the improvements. *Mother Jones* writer Stephanie Mencimer noted the twisted logic in diverting funds from addressing the basic survival needs of poor families to shoring up the foster care system, highlighting the fact that "one of the goals of

TANF, of course, is to keep children out of foster care in the first place by reliev-
ing some financial strain from their parents."[45]

DIMINISHED HELP FOR STRUGGLING FAMILIES

By 2012, states were spending just 8% of TANF block grant funds on providing
transportation, job training, and other services intended to help parents transition from welfare into the workforce.[46] At the same time, most states require
parents to demonstrate that they have made an exhaustive attempt to find work
before their families can be enrolled in TANF; this was the case even during
the recession, when jobs, especially entry-level jobs, were nearly impossible to
find.[47] Research by the Center on Budget and Policy Priorities (CBPP) reveals that
maintaining a strong safety net for the poorest families is not a priority for most
states, nor is helping the parents in these families to become employed:

> In every state, TANF plays a markedly smaller role in providing cash assis-
> tance to very poor families to help them meet basic needs than AFDC did.
> Moreover, states have used only a modest share of their TANF resources to
> help individuals find employment, and few states have invested the neces-
> sary resources to help poor parents with the most serious employment bar-
> riers find and maintain work.[48]

The Great Recession that began in 2008 was the first major economic down-
turn since the passage of welfare reform and the block granting of TANF in 1996.
What happened at that time confirmed the greatest fears of antipoverty economists, as state governments tapped larger portions of safety net funds to plug
recession-induced shortfalls in revenue, while the needs of impoverished families rapidly grew. The CBPP summarized the harmful effects this perfect storm
of circumstances triggered:

> Under a block grant that provides a fixed level of funding that does not rise
> and fall with need, states bear all the financial burden of increased need
> when the economy slows or the state's low-income population grows for
> other reasons. And because states must balance their budgets even during
> recessions, they generally have been unable or unwilling to provide much
> added help when need increases—often choosing instead to reduce the as-
> sistance to needy families at the very time that poverty and hardship are
> swelling.[49]

States continue to cut back on cash assistance to their poorest families, even with the recovery from the Great Recession picking up steam. In 2014, the national TANF caseload was 14% lower than it was in 2006, while the number of families with children in poverty was 17% higher.[50]

Children Bear the Brunt

Lawmakers in a number of states have found additional ways to increase the misery of impoverished families. For instance, thirteen states have passed laws requiring parents in families receiving welfare benefits to undergo periodic drug tests. These laws cut off benefits to families headed by a parent who tests positive for using illegal drugs. Similar laws are being considered in additional states, despite the fact that federal courts have ruled against them and evidence that drug testing welfare recipients would cost states far more than they would save by eliminating benefits for the small percentage of families in which a parent did test positive (a meager 2.6% of benefit recipient parents tested in Florida).[51]

Stripping welfare benefits from poor families headed by a drug-using parent stands in stark contrast to the much more empathic response from politicians to the rising number of individuals addicted to opioids or heroin. Politicians of all stripes are calling for compassion and increased access to drug treatment programs for the largely white, suburban and rural individuals addicted to these more expensive drugs, although many of these same political leaders support ripping the fragile safety net from poor families affected by addiction to cheap street drugs.[52] The hypocrisy in the "drug testing welfare mothers" laws isn't the worst part. By stripping families of what may be their sole source of income, these laws also have the perverted effect of causing children who are already coping with the stress of having a substance abuse–affected parent to go hungry, become homeless, and/or suffer other hardships.

All of this leads me to wonder if the public understands that every budget cut and punitive measure aimed toward poor, single parents contributes to deprivation and suffering for the children in these families. Rather than eliminating families' need for government assistance, these harsh policies help ensure perpetuation of the poverty cycle by depriving young children of the basics, such as adequate nutrition and stable housing. In the mid-1990s, welfare reform pushed those parents who were able to get jobs to leave public assistance rolls. Right before PRWORA's passage, more than two thirds of children in poor families received cash assistance. Over the past two decades, that number has dwindled to an average of 23%; worse, in twelve states, only 10% of the poorest children receive cash assistance through TANF.[53] States made these drastic cuts even though the percentage of children, young children in particular, living in poverty has increased by 23% since 2006, with nearly 6 million children under the age of six years now living in poverty.[54]

The families who continue to receive now-meager welfare benefits are those plagued by mental illness, substance abuse, domestic violence, inadequate education, and other problems not easily solved. The babies and young children in these highly vulnerable families are at the greatest levels of risk for poor outcomes. And what about the millions of young children who were plunged into poverty during the recession, those whose families are unable to access assistance from a shriveled TANF program, or whose families have exceeded the lifetime limits on assistance? Our nation's war on the poor cannot punish the parents in these families into becoming self-sufficient. Instead, it helps guarantee that large numbers of our most vulnerable young children will grow up, as did many of their parents, with unaddressed mental health, physical health, and/or learning problems, poorly educated, and with few options other than too-early parenthood and involvement with the criminal justice system—the very problems that perpetuate the cycle.

In the next chapter, I discuss the various pathways through which poverty, especially during early childhood, harms the life chances of millions of American children.

4 Poverty Is Poison
MULTIPLE ASSAULTS ON YOUNG LIVES

AS I NOTED in the first chapter, poverty is more harmful to children's development when it occurs in the earliest years of life, a time in which the developing brain is more malleable and vulnerable to what is happening in the child's environment. Most Americans understand that inadequate nutrition, inferior early learning opportunities, and hazards such as exposure to lead paint can put poor children at a disadvantage for success in school. However, far fewer are aware that early life poverty and the stressful living conditions poverty brings can cause lasting harm to individuals' physical and mental health and their prospects for economic self-sufficiency and satisfying social relationships. As I explain in this chapter, some of this harm is the result of inadequate nurturance at a time in which it is most important, and some is due to young children's especially high vulnerability to the effects of severe and chronic stress. Moreover, a wide array of additional factors, described in this chapter, contribute further in stacking the odds against a healthy and successful future for young children growing up in poverty.

Lessons from Neuroscience

Relatively recent findings from brain science provide compelling evidence that extreme and/or chronic stress and neglect, the kind that frequently occurs in poor families, can have profound effects on a child's ability to learn and love and to succeed in work throughout his or her life. This is due in large part to the fact that the physical construction of the human brain is not nearly complete at birth; instead, our brains continue developing from infancy well into adulthood. And given that the most rapid brain formation occurs in the first few years of a child's life, what happens in those early years, how he or she is cared for and raised, creates the foundation for future development, learning, and behavior. That is why it is critically important that all babies and young children, not just those in middle- and upper-income families, have the supports necessary to build the strongest foundation possible. Sadly, the United States continues to fail at fulfilling its responsibility to provide these supports for millions of its children.

Although discoveries in brain science have recently found their way into newspapers and magazines, those who study human development have known for much longer that the earliest years of life are critical to lifelong learning and success. With the publication in 2000 of *From Neurons to Neighborhoods: The Science of Early Development*, the neuroscientists, pediatricians, and developmental psychologists of the National Scientific Council on the Developing Child informed a wider audience—including many policymakers—regarding recent research findings on the timing of and the mechanisms by which the human brain develops.[1] This highly influential book explained what scientists were learning at the time about the intricate and rapid process of brain development that occurs during the prenatal stage and throughout the earliest years of life. *From Neurons to Neighborhoods* showed how critically important children's earliest experiences and environments are to their future well-being and success. Its publication a decade and a half ago led to calls for bold action on the part of policymakers to ensure that all children have the best possible start in life.

The fact that this call remains largely unheeded has tragic consequences for millions of our youngest and most vulnerable children. The years since *From Neurons to Neighborhoods* was published have seen a rapid expansion in research in early brain development, as well as in research-based recommendations for how to support optimal development of children in families and in early care and education programs. Today, we have much more knowledge than ever that tells how important the earliest years of life are. Despite this knowledge, we also have persistently high numbers of young children in poverty and a steadily shrinking safety net that places today's poor, young children at even greater risk for rotten outcomes than their year-2000 counterparts. This chapter shows how findings from groundbreaking research in neuroscience, early childhood development, and other fields converge to inform our understanding of the insidious and lasting effects of extreme poverty in early life. It examines the challenges that poverty poses to building resilience against adversity in highly vulnerable infants, toddlers, and preschoolers.

EARLY BRAIN DEVELOPMENT 101

To understand how poverty can cause permanent harm to the brains of young children, it is first necessary to have an understanding of how the human brain develops. Experts in neuroscience commonly use the terms "wiring," "circuitry," and "architecture" to explain how human brains are formed over time and how they operate. "Wiring" refers to neurons, the nerve cells in the brain that are rapidly forming connections with one another before birth and in the early years of life. These connections continue to develop, although at a slower pace, throughout adulthood. As neurons connect, they form circuits, and as children grow and develop, increasingly complex circuits are built onto those that developed earlier. This brain circuitry controls thinking, as well as emotional and social capabilities. As infants and young children explore their world, play, and, most importantly, interact with their parents and other caregivers, they are building the physical structure, or architecture, of their brains. This "wiring" process sets the course for how children will learn and behave as they grow up and throughout their lives.[2]

Until recently, the development of cognitive capacities (those that enable thinking and learning) was thought of as somewhat separate from the development of social and emotional capacities (those that affect relationships and behavior). In the past, the mistaken perception that each of these capacities develops in its own space or silo, separate from the others, was at the center of debates about whether early childhood programs should focus on early learning skills such as phonics and counting, or on social and emotional skills, like getting along with others and learning to manage one's emotions. New discoveries in neuroscience, however, have made such debates obsolete; they show that the development of each of these capacities is tightly intertwined with the development of the other two, and this remains so over the course of life. This means that what happens in the development of one of these capacities affects and is affected by what happens in the other two.[3]

To illustrate this intertwining, I encourage my students to imagine a strong braided cable consisting of three strands of wire: one strand represents the capacity for cognitive tasks (thinking and learning), the second strand represents emotional capacity (feeling and managing emotions), and the third strand represents social capacity (interacting and developing relationships with others). If one of the wires in such a cable began to rust, so would the other two, and if one wire is much thinner than the others, the entire cable would be less strong.[4] Similarly, when infants and young children develop close, loving relationships with their parents, other caregivers, family members, and friends, they are developing not only their social and emotional capacities but are also expanding their abilities for thinking and learning.

Recognition of the interconnectedness of learning capabilities is at the center of various efforts now under way to encourage parents, especially those who are poor and uneducated, to interact with their babies and preschoolers in nurturing and stimulating ways. A number of early childhood programs encourage parents to make frequent eye contact with their babies and toddlers, to sing and coo to them, and to play games such as peek-a-boo. Programs now promote these types of interactions not only because they help build strong relationships between babies and their parents, but also because they stimulate the development of lifelong feeling, thinking, and learning capacities. Similarly, scientific confirmation of the intertwined nature of cognitive, emotional, and social learning is strongly influencing practices in early care and education. The discovery that good social and emotional development are crucial to building academic skills has led to greater focus in early childhood programs on encouraging young children to play and to develop satisfying relationships with adults and other children. It has also caused many early care and education experts to rethink the way that early academic skills, such as math skills and literacy, are fostered in programs for young children.

The Role of Genes

What role does a child's genetic makeup play in how his or her brain develops? Findings from genetic research in recent years show that genes influence far more than physical traits, such as eye and hair color, height, and body shape. Scientists have found that the foundation of personality, referred to in child development studies as "temperament," is influenced by the genes that an individual inherits from his or her parents. This helps explain why some infants are described by their parents as easy and happy, while others are more fussy and difficult to soothe. As a child grows towards adulthood, his or her genetic makeup influences whether others will describe him or her as shy or outgoing, how he or she will manage stress, and how he or she will deal with anger and other emotions. Genes also play a role in an individual's vulnerability to addiction and other forms of mental illness. However, scientists do not yet fully understand the various mechanisms involved in contributing to these and other vulnerabilities.

Powerful as they are, however, genetic tendencies are only one part of the equation in determining one's life chances. Over the course of life and especially in the earliest years, a person's genes interact with his or her experiences to shape personality, behavior, and learning style. For example, if a young girl with a genetic tendency (temperament) to be introverted has many opportunities to develop rewarding relationships with other children and with adults, she is likely to be less socially withdrawn as she grows up than another introverted child who has far fewer such opportunities. This example shows how experiences, over time, interact with temperament to shape an individual's level of comfort and competence in social situations. Similarly, a boy born with a genetic tendency to be exceptionally active is less likely to be identified as having a behavior problem in school if his parents consistently set reasonable and firm limits regarding acceptable behavior. Parents can also help channel a child's tendencies to be very active into socially acceptable activities such as sports and help their child learn to control the appearances of these tendencies in less acceptable settings, such as in a classroom.

An individual's environment and experiences and his or her genetic makeup continue to interact and influence one another from before birth and throughout life.[5] Research documenting this process of ongoing mutual influence makes the phrase "nature versus nurture," which implies that either genetic makeup or experiences dominate human development, obsolete. Instead, the interaction of nature (genes and other inherited characteristics) and nurture (the experiences a child has and how he or she is raised) more closely resembles a dance in which partners respond to each other's movements rather than a tug of war, in which they pull in opposite directions. In emphasizing the reciprocal influence of genes and experiences, scholars now describe human development—in near poetic terms—as a process of "nature dancing with nurture over time."[6]

The dance between genes and experience affects the development of the human brain in profound ways. Not only does an individual's genetic makeup influence how he or she reacts to experiences in life, but scientists have found evidence that the reverse is true: experiences can affect one's genetic makeup. That is, an individual's experiences over time contribute to the muting or "turning off" of certain genes and the amplifying or "turning on" of other genes. At no point do experiences affect genes more acutely than in the prenatal, infancy, and early childhood stages of life, when the brain is still rapidly being formed.[7] This is one of the key reasons why the quantity and quality of experiences between infants and young children and their parents and other caregivers are so important. In fact, experts refer to frequent and responsive interaction between infants and young children and their caregivers as the "active ingredient" that interacts with genes to shape the architecture—the hardwiring—of the developing brain.[8]

The Power of "Serve and Return"

As babies develop strong attachments to their parents, they create and expand their capacities for trust and mutual caring and for appropriate and satisfying interactions with other human beings. These first relationships lay the groundwork for the relationships individuals will form throughout their lives. Child development experts have long understood that a healthy attachment to a parent or other consistent caregiver is fundamental to good mental health. In the past, we viewed attachment as somewhat static, and focused on the behaviors of parents (primarily mothers) as the key determinants of whether an infant or toddler became securely attached and developed a capacity to form satisfying relationships with others. We now know that the creation of secure attachments between infants and their parents and other caregivers involves a highly interactive process in which both participate. In this process, infants and young children invite their parents to interact with them, and the parents' response to that invitation determines what happens next. Early childhood development researchers often refer to this process as "serve and return."

When a parent responds to the child's invitation to interact, the child typically responds in kind, prompting an additional response from the parent. This back-and-forth interaction continues, much like the serve and return of a tennis or Ping-Pong match.[9] Anyone who has raised a child knows how automatic and instinctive serve and return seems to be, for babies as well as for their parents. The back-and-forth cooing, endless games of "peek a boo," and a parent picking up and cuddling an infant when he or she begins to fuss demonstrate how deeply serve and return is integrated into typical parent–child interactions. It is how a child learns that he or she matters and has an impact on the behavior of other humans, as well as that he or she can count on adults to be responsive in meeting his or her expressed needs. When interaction of this type occurs frequently over time, it "turns on" or stimulates the expression of genes that promote not only a child's emotional and social development but healthy physical development and learning capacity as well. The mutual action of serve and return is a primary way in which what happens in a child's environment affects aspects of the genetic makeup he or she will carry throughout life.[10]

One of my favorite home videos is of my daughter, Rachel, at about nine or ten months old. In the video, I am talking to her in that nonsensical way that seems automatic for most parents with infants. My voice rises and falls as does the degree of its urgency as I lean forward and engage her; my tone changes from questioning, to repetition of a phrase, to excitement. Rachel's eyes are wide and locked onto mine as she kicks her legs and pumps her arms. Her entire tiny body is animated as she giggles and coos in response to the sound and gestures I am making. I respond to her giggles and coos by making similar sounds; she repeats these sounds and we continue back and forth. I wasn't aware, all those years ago, that Rachel and I were engaged in a session of "serve and return" that was building the circuitry of her brain and expanding her lifelong capacity to love and to learn, but I did know instinctively, as most parents seem to, that what was going on was good for our relationship and good for Rachel's development.

What science now tells us is that interactions like this are essential to the development of healthy brain circuitry; they build the child's learning and social capacities while simultaneously strengthening the bonds between the child and his or her parents. It also tells us that when parents or other caregivers consistently fail to respond to a child's invitation for interaction, and diminish the amount of serve and return the child experiences, it impedes the wiring process that forms critical brain circuitry. This unresponsive caregiving, if it occurs over time, can turn off certain genes and harm a child's capacity to manage his or her emotions and to develop and maintain healthy relationships. Moreover, because social development and emotional development are so tightly braided together with cognitive development, limited and inconsistent serve-and-return interactions with parents and other caregivers can reduce a child's capacities for thinking and learning.

An understanding of early brain development is critical for informing how we care for infants and young children, and the environments in which early care takes place. This is not only because formation of the architecture of the human brain occurs most rapidly in the earliest years of life, but also because the ability of experiences to influence the way in which the brain is developing—something researchers refer to as "plasticity"—decreases over time. Like a melted piece of plastic or molten glass that hardens once it cools, the human brain's malleability and capacity for change diminish as children become older. As children grow older it becomes increasingly challenging to repair or enhance aspects of the brain's architecture that are compromised due to missed opportunities in infancy and early childhood.[11] That is why the slogan "catch them while they're young" underlies much of the growing interest in how best to intervene with vulnerable children during the earliest years of their lives.

HOW STRESS AFFECTS YOUNG BRAINS

Research in brain science has also begun to reveal how young children's biological responses to highly stressful situations can directly harm their developing brains, jeopardize their physical and mental health, and limit their capacity to learn. Most of us are familiar with the "flight or fight" or "stress" hormones released by the brain that cause our pulse rates to quicken and our hearts to pound in stressful situations. The stress hormone cortisol appears to play the most significant role, but the human body releases other hormones as well in such situations. The purpose of these hormones is to physically arouse us in order to meet stressful challenges or to quickly remove ourselves from hazardous situations.[12] Anyone who has taken a stress-management class is familiar with the terms used to categorize stress in adults: positive stress and harmful stress. We typically use the term "positive stress" to describe the rush of adrenaline and other hormones a person experiences when preparing to speak in public or compete in a sporting event. In positive stress circumstances these hormones help increase our alertness and ability to focus.

Most of us understand "harmful stress," on the other hand, as the type that arises in more dire and long-term situations, such as when a person is in a very troubled emotional relationship, reports to a boss who bullies him or her, or witnesses extreme violence, such as being in combat. We know that although the hormones released when we encounter positive stress are benign and can be even beneficial, the types and amounts of stress hormones released when an individual encounters harmful stress, especially over a prolonged period of time, can take a large toll on one's emotional and physical well-being. Consistent presence of large amounts of cortisol and other stress-related hormones in the body contributes to anxiety disorders, obesity, heart disease, and other serious illnesses.[13] Fortunately, some of the impacts of harmful stress can be buffered by the support of family members and friends and by participating in psychotherapy, exercising regularly, and using other stress-management strategies.

A Concentrated Effect on Babies and Young Children

As one might expect, stress has a much more potent effect on the developing fetus during pregnancy and on babies and young children because the architecture of their brains is undergoing rapid development and their brains are more malleable than at any other time. The scientists and physicians on the National Scientific Council on the Developing Child have become increasingly concerned about the high levels of stress experienced by pregnant women and young children in poverty and its potential impact on both physical and mental development throughout these children's lives. By studying the types of stressors that babies and young children encounter and how they react to stress, research-ers have identified three distinct ways in which children's bodies respond to vary-ing levels of stress: positive stress response, tolerable stress response, and toxic stress response. Each of these types of response has a different impact on the developing brain.[14]

Studies show that children usually produce a positive stress response when the stressor is mild and/or short-lived and is buffered by the support of a caring adult. A three-year-old child starting the first day at a new child care center or who has an accident during toilet training is likely to experience mild stress. When there are supportive adults available to comfort and reassure the child, this type of stress provides opportunities for him or her to learn and practice healthy responses to challenging experiences. For this reason, positive stress responses are thought to be helpful to a child's development. A tolerable stress response, on the other hand, results from experiences that pose a greater set of challenges and or threats.[15] Being in a car accident or experiencing the death of a loved one is a type of occurrence that is likely to trigger tolerable levels of stress in young children. This kind of stress is not likely to cause lasting harm as long as a child receives enough emotional support and reassurance.

Research findings make clear that the responsiveness of caring adults is the critical ingredient in a child's ability to tolerate such disturbing events. Such adults can help the child process and manage stress, as well as develop coping skills and a sense of control in the wake of troubling events.[16] For instance, when a young boy has been in a minor car accident, his parent will typically buffer the stress by holding him and reassuring him that he is OK, that accidents are rela-tively rare, and that riding in a car is generally safe. Even when this type of buff-ering takes place, some young children may show short-term symptoms, such as bedwetting or nightmares, following a stressful event or loss. In such cases, specialized play therapy may be necessary to help the child process the event and return to his optimal level of well-being.

When Stress Becomes Toxic

Although stress hormones are usually not harmful to young children at the relatively short-term and low levels triggered by positive and tolerable stress responses, they can become hazardous when activated at high levels and for prolonged periods of time.[17] The third type of stress response, toxic stress re-sponse, occurs when a child encounters severe, chronic, and/or unrelenting stress at a time in which support and nurturance from an adult is inadequate or missing. A toxic stress response triggers changes in the child's heart rate and blood pressure and causes the release of an overdose of cortisol and other stress hormones that can damage the developing brain and other organ systems.[18] Many of the risk factors related to growing up in poverty, such as domestic violence, parental substance abuse, and living in high-crime areas, can trigger this type of response and the release of high levels of stress hormones in babies and young children. The rapid pace of brain development in young children, along with the malleability of their brains, make them highly susceptible to the toxic effects of having their brains bathed in these hormones on a frequent or chronic basis.

Scientists now know that toxic stress responses to the harmful conditions that often accompany poverty can alter the architecture—the actual physical structure—of different regions of the developing brain. When a pregnant woman experiences high levels of anxiety over extended periods of time, her body releases and exposes her unborn child to large amounts of potentially hazardous stress hormones, which can harm the rapidly forming brain of her fetus.[19] After the child is born, being raised in conditions that cause the frequent and/or chronic release of large doses of these same hormones can permanently change his or her brain in a way that causes him or her to experience high levels of stress, even in nonstressful situations, and to become excessively fearful and anxious. As the child grows, and especially as he or she enters elementary school, these changes appear to contribute to the development of mental illnesses, such as attention-deficit disorder, hyperactivity, and anxiety disorders, and/or severe behavior problems.[20]

The connection between growing up in a highly stressful environment and having a heightened stress response helps explain why diagnoses of mental illness and behavior problems are more common among children growing up in poverty.[21] Poor children are often confronted by overwhelming stressors that frequently recur and/or become chronic, causing their small bodies to release higher-than-normal amounts of stress hormones. Permanent changes in the brain's level of cortisol and other hormones can have harmful, long-term effects on children's well-being and functioning. Scientists now refer to stress-induced biological changes in systems within young children's bodies as the "biological embedding" of stress:

> Biological embedding primarily occurs early in development and leads to physiological individual differences that have a substantial, although not inevitable, influence on health and behavior. Further, early experiences with chronic stress, such as those engendered by living in poverty, tend to

have a cumulative effect on human physiology, gradually calibrating biological systems to be increasingly inflexible and maladaptive.[22]

This helps explain the many ways in which being raised in poverty can impair children's capacities for self-control, learning, memory, and problem solving, and therefore affect their ability to learn and succeed in school. Moreover, children's increased vulnerability to depression and other mental illnesses brought about by chronically high levels of stress hormones in their bodies can interfere with learning and school success.[23]

The Multiple and Lasting Effects of Early Life Adversity

In addition to grave implications for children's ability to learn and succeed in school, harsh, stressful experiences in early life place individuals at high risk for serious and chronic health and mental health problems throughout their lifetimes. This is the key finding from the Adverse Childhood Experiences (ACE) study conducted by the U.S. Centers for Disease Control and Prevention and the HMO Kaiser Permanente. In the 1990s, 9,508 adults who received their health care through Kaiser completed a survey in which they reported whether, as a child, they had experiences known to create high levels of stress.[24] The categories of adverse childhood experiences used in the study included psychological, physical, or sexual abuse; domestic violence; and living with household members who abused drugs and/or alcohol, were mentally ill and/or suicidal, or had been imprisoned.[25] The number of adverse experiences reported by each participant in the study was compared to measures of high-risk behaviors, such as heavy alcohol or drug use, health status, and diseases he or she experienced as an adult.

Researchers found that individuals who reported experiencing four or more types of stressful experiences in childhood were four to twelve times more likely than individuals with fewer or no adverse childhood experiences to be struggling with substance abuse, depression, and suicidal tendencies, as well as other severe mental and physical health problems, as adults. The connection between having a rough start in life and being more likely to have mental health and behavior problems had been recognized long before the ACE study was conducted; however, the degree to which early adversity raised the odds of such a large number of harmful outcomes surprised even those who study such connections. Even more stunning and equally concerning, the study found that the more instances of highly stressful childhood experiences study participants reported, the more likely they were to develop a serious physical illness, including heart disease, cancer, and lung and liver diseases, later in life.[26]

The ACE study provides the most compelling evidence to date of the pervasive role severe adversity in early childhood plays in contributing to physical and mental health problems throughout life. Viewing findings from the ACE study in the context of what we now know about the impact of toxic stress on the rapidly developing brains and bodies of young children demonstrates how the wear and tear of growing up amid the problems and dangers that frequently plague poor families helps perpetuate the cycle of disadvantage. These findings bring to light how severe and chronic stress not only has harmful effects on the learning and behavioral capacities of young children but also contributes to the development of chronic physical and mental illnesses later in life, illnesses that can interfere with employment and create other hardships for struggling families.[27]

The ACE study also sheds light on some of the pathways through which severe disadvantage in early childhood contributes to poor outcomes in adulthood. It found that children who grew up in highly stressful situations were more likely to use alcohol and drugs, smoke, become obese, and engage in reckless sexual behavior once they became adolescents.[28] Decades of additional research show that youths who engage in such high-risk behaviors are more likely to fail and drop out of school, join gangs, be chronically unemployed and/or homeless, commit violent crimes, and become single parents.[29] All of these findings confirm that the babies of poor, young, and troubled parents are at risk to experience similar levels of adversity and dysfunction as did their parents, and to grow up to perpetuate the cycle of chronic poverty and disadvantage.

ESPECIALLY HARMFUL SOURCES OF STRESS FOR YOUNG CHILDREN

Poverty alone can be extremely stressful to families who are unable to meet their most basic needs for food, housing, and safety. Adding to that strain are many of the conditions that commonly occur in poor neighborhoods, such as frequent episodes of violence and other crimes, rundown housing, and limited opportunities for recreation and socializing. These conditions also heighten the isolation experienced by the families forced to live there.[30] Young children are affected by the stress and worry of their parents, as both factors can cause poor parents to be less than attentive to the emotional needs of their children and to provide far less serve and return and other types of social stimulation than young children need.[31]

There is even more to the story. Research has identified three family risk factors that, when accompanied by poverty, are particularly dangerous to the development of young children: maternal depression, maternal substance abuse, and family violence.[32] Although none of these conditions is unique to families living in poverty, the stress of being poor, combined with having few social supports to buffer that stress, often conspires with one or more of these conditions to harm the development and threaten the future well-being of young children, precisely at the time when their bodies and brains are most vulnerable.[33]

Depression is far more common among single mothers in poverty than for women in general. Studies of low-income mothers indicate that as many as one third to one half of these women suffer from depression.[34] This would come as no surprise to anyone who has observed the many challenges that poor mothers encounter and the lack of hope that accompanies growing up poor and remaining so as an adult. The isolation, shame, and sense of having few prospects for a better life that I observed while working with low-income mothers help account for high rates of depression. Being cared for by a depressed mother can very harmful to young children, especially in homes without fathers or other nurturing adults to assist with childrearing.[35] This is because, as we have seen, the emotional attachments that babies and toddlers form with their parents are the foundation for emotional and social development, as well as for thinking and learning capacity. A number of studies show that depressed mothers tend to be less responsive to their children's needs and interact with their children far less than mothers who are not depressed.[36]

This lack of nurturing and attention can damage the critical relationship between babies and toddlers and their mothers, because these relationships require frequent and consistent positive interaction, especially the "serve and return" kind. When an infant or toddler is being cared for by a depressed mother who is unable to provide a warm and loving response to his or her cues, the child's budding capacities to engage in rewarding relationships, manage his or her emotions, and learn are thwarted. No wonder numerous studies show that maternal depression, especially when it is chronic and severe, is not only harmful to the development of young children but also places these children at greater risk for developing depression themselves, as well as behavioral problems, as they grow up.[37] Moreover, being depressed hampers parents' ability to protect young children from harm and meet their needs for nutritious food, health care, and other basics.[38]

Struggling with depression makes low-income mothers even more vulnerable to other dangerous risk factors, including drug and/or alcohol abuse and domestic violence.[39] Counselors who work with poor, depressed mothers commonly observe a process of self-medicating: using alcohol, prescription drugs, and/or illegal drugs in order to feel less depressed. While working in a program that provided home-based services to poor, substance abuse–affected mothers and their children, I was struck by how many of the mothers had been sexually and/or physically abused. Many of these mothers had been beaten or raped as children, by their own fathers or other family members, or abused as adults, by their husbands or boyfriends. Sadly, many had endured abuse both as children and as adults. Most of these women had never received proper therapy for their traumas, and not surprisingly many of them met the criteria for a diagnosis of depression, which, in most cases, had gone untreated. It wasn't hard to see why these mothers would reach for alcohol and/or other drugs as a means to cope with the haunting aftereffects of such traumatic experiences, combined with the many hardships of being poor.

The prevalence of alcohol and other drug abuse among low-income mothers of young children is harder to measure than that of depression. Substance abuse has greater stigma attached to it, and parents who disclose it risk involvement with child protective services and law enforcement authorities. Estimates of substance abuse among poor mothers are as high as 37%.[40] As one might expect, when mothers are frequently intoxicated it affects serve-and-return patterns and other aspects of the crucial mother–child relationship in ways similar to maternal depression and has similar, harmful effects on their children.[41]

Like depression, maternal substance abuse also places young children at greater risk for child abuse and neglect, as parents who are drunk or high are less able to protect their children from harm and to control violent impulses.[42] Substance abuse and depression are often intertwined with domestic violence, especially in impoverished families.[43] A study by the Government Accounting Office (GAO) found that 65% of women on welfare had been victims of domestic violence at some point in their lives.[44] This type of violence included being beaten, kicked, stabbed, strangled, dragged by the hair, and shot with a gun. In addition to impairing mother–child relationships and mothers' ability to care for their children, violent acts often severely traumatize the children who witness them. Young children who witness acts of domestic violence are likely to experience extreme levels of stress that, without proper treatment, can lead to severe emotional disturbance and learning and behavior problems.[45]

STRESSFUL CONDITIONS HELP PERPETUATE DISADVANTAGE

It is clear that, by themselves, poverty, maternal depression and/or substance abuse, and domestic violence can have lasting harmful effects on the development of young children. As the ACE study confirms, when two or more of these are present in a single family, as is often the case in poor families, the level of risk to the well-being and development of young children escalates.[46] Too often, the interactions between these risk factors create a cycle of extreme stress in these families that is very difficult to interrupt. For example, being poor makes women more vulnerable to depression, and being poor and depressed increases the likelihood that a woman will begin abusing drugs and/or alcohol and use poor judgment in forming relationships with men. When a mother is depressed and/or struggling with addiction, taking the steps necessary to protect herself and her children from an abusive boyfriend or husband is far more difficult than it already would be. Under such conditions, leaving an abusive relationship is likely to feel impossible. Conversely, these risk factors also make it more difficult for a mother to escape poverty, as they are likely to impair her ability to become and remain employed.

Combining findings in early brain development with those from studies that examine the impact of various types of stress on how the brains of young children develop helps us understand how extreme adversity in early life can have dire consequences for the well-being and future prospects of young children. These studies confirm that when parents experience high levels of chronic stress, their ability to nurture and protect their children is impaired.[47] This can compromise children's lifelong capacities for learning and successful relationships. Examining these findings in the context of those from the ACE study adds to our understanding of the potential toll taken on a person's lifelong physical and mental health by the early life adversity that poverty typically brings. This research helps explain why the cycle of intergenerational poverty is so difficult to break, as it shows the many ways in which children raised in extreme disadvantage are at much greater risk than their peers to spend their lives in poverty and to create families that are also plagued by disadvantage. Genes may play a role in perpetuating the cycle as well. Emerging research in the field of epigenetics suggests that stress- and trauma-related changes to an individual's genes can be transmitted from parent to child, passing on higher levels of vulnerability from one generation to the next.[48]

Multiple Risk Factors Accumulate to Cause Rotten Outcomes

Unfortunately, the story doesn't end there. Young children growing up in poor families are exposed to many other sources of harm and have access to far fewer resources that promote healthy development and resilience against adversity than do their nonpoor peers. For too many young children, multiple risk factors pile up and interact with one another to darken their life chances. Here are some of the other ways, besides experiencing inadequate nurturance and high levels of stress, in which being poor harms children.

POOR CHILDREN ARE MORE LIKELY TO BE BORN WITH HEALTH
PROBLEMS OR DISABILITIES

As I noted earlier, the disadvantages that poverty brings to children often take hold well before birth. Expectant mothers who were themselves raised in poverty are likely to experience far higher levels of stress throughout their pregnancies than are nonpoor pregnant women. This can trigger the release of correspondingly high amounts of stress hormones that saturate the brains and bodies of their unborn children.[49] Poor expectant mothers are also more likely be adolescents who haven't yet reached physical and emotional maturity. Moreover, these mothers are less likely to receive prenatal care, follow a nutritious diet, and abstain from smoking or from using drugs and alcohol than are nonpoor expectant mothers. These risk factors contribute to higher rates of premature births, low birth weight, and babies born with health problems and/or developmental disabilities.[50]

Infants born prematurely are often underweight and less healthy at birth than full-term infants.[51] Despite breathtaking advances in neonatal care for such infants, low birth weight and premature birth still increase babies' risk for dying during the first few weeks or months of life. When they survive, these babies are typically more challenging to care for, something that can overwhelm the capacities of poor young mothers, especially those who have few sources of social and emotional support. Moreover, premature and/or low-birth-weight children are more likely to have serious physical disabilities, mental health disorders, and behavior and learning problems that can hamper their ability to succeed at school and in life.[52]

POOR CHILDREN RECEIVE LESS STIMULATION THAT PROMOTES EARLY LEARNING

Just as disparities exist between poor and nonpoor infants in the quality and frequency of opportunities they have for "serve and return" interactions with caregivers, there are additional disparities that affect learning ability that continue well beyond infancy. For instance, a number of studies show that low-income parents tend to spend less time talking to their young children than do parents with higher incomes. The well-known research of Betty Hart and Tod Risley found that the quantity, quality, and responsiveness of parents' speech to their children varied strongly by income and education levels. Parents categorized as "professional class" spoke to their infants and toddlers nearly four times more frequently than parents receiving welfare and used two and a half times as many words. Higher-income parents were also far more likely to engage their children in conversation than poor parents. Hart and Risley found that when poor parents spoke to their children, it was usually for the purpose of directing their behavior rather than initiating back-and-forth conversation that would engage and appeal to the children.[53]

These differences matter because children gain most of their earliest learning capacities and skills from interacting with their parents and other caregivers. Parents who have the skills and the time to engage their children in conversation and familiarize them with a plethora of words and phrases in the critical, early years of development provide their children with a powerful head start toward lifelong learning and success. Such children enter school with the advantage of not only having a much larger vocabulary than their low-income peers, but also being more advanced in developing a range of social, emotional, and cognitive skills that underlie and support formal learning. Other powerful ways in which higher-income parents support the developing architecture of their children's brains and prepare them for success in school are by frequently reading to them and exposing them to lots of books by taking them to the library, two activities far less common among poor families. The fact that young children in higher-income families typically watch far fewer hours of television than do their low-income peers, and have greater access to educational toys and games, further tips the scales in favor of nonpoor children.[54]

These and other disparities practically guarantee that children from poor families will lag behind their nonpoor peers in school readiness and many of the basic skills necessary for school success. Research suggesting that gaps between poor and nonpoor students in learning and school achievement remain stable from age four through high school tells us that early life disadvantage has pro-foundly negative effects on poor children's odds for school success.[55] And as we know, school performance strongly affects a child's life chances in a number of ways, one of the most important of which is whether he or she will be able to earn enough money to avoid poverty and its harmful consequences.

Disparities in early learning opportunities continue, even when low-income parents are employed and able to enroll their children, often with the help of public subsidies, in early care and education centers. The ratio of children to teachers tends to be higher at centers in low-income communities, which means each child gets less adult attention than he or she would receive at an early care center in a higher-income community. Moreover, a number of studies show that teachers and caregivers in centers in low-income communities are less likely to engage young children in ways that stimulate learning and cognitive development.[56] For instance, a study that compared the behavior of teachers in child care centers with children from different income groups found those serving low-income children to be less sensitive, less likely to respond to children's needs, and more harsh toward the children than teachers and caregivers serving children from middle- and high-income households.[57] What this and other studies tell us is that many of the children who are in greatest need of warmth, stimulation, and attention from adults are less likely than their higher-income peers to receive nurturing and stimulating care. Although the federal government and a number of states are investing considerable resources in improving the quality of the early care and education that low-income children receive, far too many situations of "poor care for poor children" still exist.

POOR CHILDREN ARE MUCH MORE LIKELY TO BE HOMELESS OR TO LIVE IN HOUSING THAT IS INADEQUATE, DANGEROUS, AND/OR OVERCROWDED

More than 1.5 million American children live in homeless families and more than 40%, or 600,000, of these children are under the age of six.[58] Being homeless contributes to a number of physical and mental illnesses, behavior and learning problems, and other hardships for children, and for young children in particular. The harm begins in pregnancy. Infant mortality rates for pregnant women living in shelters are much higher than for other pregnant women. Children born to women living in shelters are more likely to have low birth weight and to suffer physical ailments, including upper respiratory infections and stomach disorders, as well as emotional and behavioral problems.[59] Public health experts report that these problems are caused or worsened by the dilapidated conditions of so many homeless shelters in the United States. Many shelters expose pregnant women and young children to high levels of allergens such as mold and dust, poor ventilation, and crowded living conditions that help spread contagious diseases.[60] Not having access to nutritious food also harms families, especially those living in barebones shelter and motel rooms that lack refrigerators and appliances for cooking. Not surprisingly, the stress and uncertainty of homelessness also take their toll on both parents and children, increasing the likelihood that children will develop mental health problems.[61]

Millions of other poor children are living in inadequate and overcrowded apartments or houses. This problem intensified during the most recent housing bubble, when home prices and rents skyrocketed, resulting in higher numbers of families unable to find an affordable place to live. When that bubble abruptly burst and banks foreclosed on record numbers of properties, many low-income families were evicted from their houses and apartments. Seeing no other choices, many poor families began doubling and tripling up, with two or three families living in apartments designed for only a single family. A report on 22,000 low-income families with children under the age of three found that 41% of these families had been doubling up with another family or living in otherwise over-crowded conditions during the previous twelve-month period.[62]

Overcrowded housing impacts young children in a variety of ways, including ex-posing them to highly stressed adults and increasing risk levels for child maltreat-ment. Consequently, it also affects their sense of safety. A few years ago, one of my students described a poignant example of how overcrowding had affected the behavior of a young boy in a family that she had helped find a small apartment in Boston. For months after his family had moved into their own three-room apart-ment, this preschooler continued to close the door to whichever room he entered or was leaving. He had learned this behavior while he, his mother, and his sister were living, for several months, in one room of a four-room apartment that was also occupied by two other families. Closing the door had been essential during that time, because one single room was the only space this family of three was en-titled to use. It is difficult to imagine how any parent could come close to meeting the nutritional, hygiene, learning, and emotional needs of her two young children in a situation like this.

The Most Vulnerable Children in the Most Dangerous Housing

The lack of affordable, adequate housing for poor families often causes desperate parents to accept housing that is blatantly unsafe, sometimes with tragic con-sequences. For example, in 2010, a three-day-old baby and six other people died when fire broke out in an overcrowded apartment in an illegally converted attic in Chicago. A few years earlier in that same city, a toddler and a ten-month-old baby died in a fire inside an illegally converted basement in which ten people were living.[63] Even many of the so-called legal apartments available to poor fam-ilies are in violation of basic safety codes and present myriad dangers. Faulty wiring, unsecured windows and stairways, problems with heating and cooking appliances, and other hazards contribute to a higher rate of accidental injuries and deaths for low-income children.

"Making do" under such conditions is often the byproduct of desperation. In my days of making home visits, I observed parents trying to heat their apart-ments with flames from the burners of a gas cooking stove, trying to keep active young children away from dangling electrical wires, and discouraging their tod-dlers from getting near unprotected windows, the bottoms of which reached nearly floor level in second- and third-floor apartments. Many of these parents were extremely reluctant to report such housing code violations because they feared being evicted as retribution by their often-absentee landlords and had no-where else to go.

As one would expect, younger children are most vulnerable to household dangers. Studies show that 80% to 90% of fatal, unintentional injuries to young children occur in their homes. Here, too, we see disparities related to poverty and race. Low-income children under the age of five have the highest rate, among American children, of emergency room visits for accidental injuries in the home. Moreover, despite an overall decline over the past twenty-five years in the death rate for injuries in the home, the odds of dying from an accident at home remain substantially higher for African American children, children who are more likely to be poor than those in any other racial group.[64]

The Lead Poisoning Epidemic

Long before thousands of young children were poisoned by lead-infused water in Flint, Michigan, we knew that exposure to water from the lead pipes and lead paint often found in the old, rundown houses and apartments in which poor families are forced to live can damage young brains and cause serious, permanent behavior and learning problems. Living in housing that contains lead paint is especially hazardous for young children not only because their bodies are small and still developing, but also because children between the ages of one and six are naturally inclined to explore their world by putting things into their mouths. This hand-to-mouth behavior is primarily how flaking paint and lead dust gets into children's bodies. Tragically, this behavior coincides with the years in which brain development is occurring most rapidly and the brain is most vulnerable to toxins. There is no such thing as a "safe" level of lead ingestion—one proven to be not harmful to the development and well-being of children.[65] Despite much progress over the past thirty years in reducing lead exposure, more than 300,000 children in the United States have hazardous amounts of lead in their bloodstreams.[66]

As in Flint, elevated levels of lead are most commonly found among poor children, particularly those living in decaying urban neighborhoods. A number of studies show that the rate of unsafe lead levels in the blood of poor children is four times higher than for children living in higher-income neighborhoods.[67] In New York City, lead poisoning is found almost exclusively among African American and Latino children, with the rate for African American children being nearly four times higher than for white children.[68] This is similar to the situation in Flint. These statistics show yet another way in which disparities in income contribute to racial disparities in the exposure of children to harmful conditions. A team of community health experts sums up how lead exposure contributes to the cycle of intergenerational disadvantage: "The consequences of this continuing, disproportionately high prevalence of elevated lead levels in low-income communities include cognitive deficits and delays, leading to poor learning, diminished lifetime accomplishment, and perpetuation of poverty."[69]

Mold and other potentially toxic substances, as well as vermin (such as cockroaches, mice, and rats), are far more common in poor homes and frequently cause and exacerbate health problems, including severe headaches, allergies, and asthma. Moreover, poor ventilation, malfunctioning heating systems, and structural defects can expose children to harmful levels of radon, carbon monoxide, and toxic chemicals present in floor covering and other building materials.[70] Overcrowding and thin, damaged walls between cheap apartments increase children's exposure to second-hand cigarette smoke. These toxins take their toll. For instance, the highest rates of asthma in the United States are found among minority children living in poor neighborhoods, where as many as 23% of the children have asthma; this percentage is almost four times the national average.[71] Asthma and other chronic respiratory diseases increase children's vulnerability to other illnesses and cause children to miss school and limit their ability to participate in sports and other physical activity. Although childhood asthma will eventually resolve for about half the children who suffer from this ailment, abnormalities in the way their lungs function are likely to continue and can contribute to serious health problems throughout their lives.[72]

POOR CHILDREN EAT LESS-NUTRITIOUS FOOD

Families with very limited financial resources find it nearly impossible to feed their children a nutritious and balanced diet. This is due to a variety of factors, including the higher costs of fish, lean meats, and fresh fruits and vegetables in comparison to less-healthy foods; lack of access to supermarkets; and parents' lack of skill in preparing healthy foods as well as a poor understanding of the importance of doing so. One study found that wealthy neighborhoods in the United States had three times more supermarkets than did poor ones, and that white neighborhoods had four times as many supermarkets as did those populated mainly by African Americans.[73] Today, children growing up in poor neighborhoods across the United States suffer the effects of poor nutrition, while farmers' markets and organic food stores are proliferating in wealthier areas.

Not having a supermarket nearby means that families must choose between the inflated prices and limited selection—with an emphasis on highly processed and junk foods—in local convenience stores, or spend additional time and money for transportation to access the healthier foods and better prices at a distant supermarket. Nutrition experts refer to neighborhoods with few options for buying healthy foods as "food deserts." In a recent review of several studies on food deserts, researchers concluded that disparities in the availability of nutritious food across communities are worse in the United States than in the United Kingdom and Canada, and far worse than in Australia and New Zealand.[74] Somehow, the latter four nations are better able to ensure that the quality and variety of food available in their low-income communities more closely resemble what's available in wealthier areas.

Adequate nutrition is especially critical in the first years of life when children are developing most rapidly. Poverty contributes to a number of nutrition-related health challenges, including stunted growth and anemia.[75] Health problems caused or exacerbated by poor nutrition contribute to learning and behavior problems, and children with frequent and/or chronic illness miss more school and activities than do healthy children.[76] All of these factors threaten children's chances of succeeding in school. Moreover, poor nutrition sharply increases children's risk for becoming obese. More than one in eight preschoolers in the United States is obese, and children in poverty are 50% more likely to be obese than non-poor children. Obesity in early childhood dramatically increases the odds that a child will be overweight or obese as an adult and suffer physical problems, including chronic illnesses such as diabetes and heart disease.[77]

POOR CHILDREN ARE EXPOSED TO HIGHER LEVELS OF POLLUTION IN AIR AND WATER

Gary Evans, a Cornell professor of human ecology, writes about the "stark evidence of physical, environmental injustice among the poor in America."[78] Evans cites studies showing that impoverished families, when compared to middle- and upper-income families, live closer to toxic waste sites and have higher rates of exposure to pesticides and that the water and air poor families consume tend to be more polluted. He observes that because a high proportion of families at the lowest end of the income spectrum live mainly in densely populated, urban communities with heavy amounts of traffic and frequent traffic congestion, children in these families are typically exposed to higher concentrations of toxic chemicals emitted by cars and other vehicles. Bus garages and terminals and marine transfer stations, most often located in in low-income areas, are major sources of pollution from diesel fuel. Diesel engines emit far more toxic pollution than modern gasoline engines, making this proximity especially harmful. Moreover, waste incinerators and factories that release harmful chemicals into the air can also be found in or near the communities in which poor families live.[79]

Because their lungs and immune systems are still developing, children are more susceptible to the harms of air pollution than are adults,. Numerous public health studies point to a connection between high levels of air pollution and higher rates of miscarriage and infant death, as well as increased rates of childhood asthma and pneumonia, among families who live in highly polluted areas.[80] Airborne poisons affect a much higher portion of African American and Latino families, families who are more likely to live in poor and crowded urban neighborhoods. More than 50% of the families in these two racial groups live in areas that fail to meet two or more national clean air standards; only 33% of white families live in these highly polluted areas.[81]

POOR CHILDREN ARE MORE LIKELY TO LIVE IN SEGREGATED, DANGEROUS, RESOURCE-POOR NEIGHBORHOODS

Exposure to higher levels of pollution is just one of the ways in which living in poor neighborhoods harms individuals and young children in particular. As I noted in Chapter 2, Patrick Sharkey has documented the ways in which neighborhood segregation by race and income contributes to maintaining the cycle of poverty, especially for blacks and Latinos.[82] He found that 60% of black children in highly segregated areas live in high-poverty neighborhoods compared with less than 6% of white children.[83] Young black and Latino children typically attend kindergarten programs in which most of the children are poor, and studies have found that children fare worse in classrooms that contain mainly poor children compared to those in classrooms containing high percentages of nonpoor children.[84]

Significantly higher rates of violence, such as shootings and sexual assaults, as well as other crimes, such as drug dealing and robberies, create a great deal of stress for the families who are forced to reside in poor neighborhoods. As I discussed earlier in this chapter, high levels of stress threaten the capacity for parents to nurture their children. High crime rates also isolate families who are fearful about venturing outside with their children. These fears are not unfounded; the United States has the highest rate of child homicides among developed nations, and these deaths are concentrated in poor, urban areas. Although young children are more likely to be killed by an abusive parent or other caretaker, the homicides of older children and adolescents in particular typically result from the gun violence that is prevalent in our most impoverished neighborhoods.[85]

Living in such a neighborhood affects families in a variety of ways. Fear of being harmed by gunfire, sexual assault, and other forms of violence is an overlooked but pervasive problem for families in poor neighborhoods. Many Americans seem to assume that such families "get used to" living in a perpetually threatening environment. However, studies confirm that poor women with children are much more likely to be afraid of going out into their own neighborhoods than were nonpoor mothers.[86] For instance, a 2004 study involving African American mothers of young children in Baltimore's high-crime neighborhoods found that these mothers experienced high levels of chronic stress due to constant concern about their own and their children's safety.[87] Public health experts have linked the stress that comes from living in an unsafe neighborhood to a wide range of health and mental health problems, including worsening symptoms of asthma in children.[88]

A number of years ago, a few colleagues and I conducted interviews with parents of young children in a poor, high-crime community in Rhode Island as part of a needs assessment. Most of the young, single mothers we interviewed described living in fear that they or their children would be harmed if they ventured outside their small, shabby apartments. They also reported that men regularly pulled their cars up to where these mothers would be walking and—even if they were pushing their children in strollers—solicited them for sex in exchange for money. Several of these mothers described how the discarded needles and condoms, animal waste, and broken glass strewn about the few playgrounds in their neighborhood made it impossible for their young children to safely enjoy outdoor play. Because of such conditions, in addition to high crime rates, families in low-income neighborhoods often spend much of their time indoors. There is typically a shortage of opportunities for socializing and recreation in such neighborhoods. YMCAs, Little League teams, and craft classes are rare, and poor families are often unable to afford the fees for whatever programs are available. These factors help to explain how families become isolated even while living in crowded neighborhoods in densely populated communities.

Children growing up in unsafe and underresourced neighborhoods with few opportunities for recreation get less exercise than their nonpoor peers, increasing their risk for obesity and other health problems. Moreover, these factors limit opportunities for families to develop mutually supportive relationships, friendships that could help buffer the effects of stress for children and their parents.[89] Social isolation, like stress, contributes to adult and child vulnerability to depression, increases a family's risk for child abuse and neglect, and often deprives young children of opportunities to play with other children, something that is also important for healthy cognitive and social development and school readiness. To make matters worse, in many poor neighborhoods there are shortages of the mental health services and other supports that are often necessary to help overstressed, traumatized children and adults return to healthy functioning.[90] Without effective treatment, high levels of stress and trauma may lead to behavior and learning problems, anxiety disorders, and/or depression.

POOR CHILDREN ARE MORE LIKELY TO BE ABUSED AND/OR NEGLECTED

Every year, more than 1.2 million children in the United States are abused or neglected. The stress and isolation that come with being poor contribute to higher levels of risk for child maltreatment among impoverished families. Children in low-income households are three times more likely to be abused and seven times more likely to be neglected than nonpoor children. Of greatest concern is the fact that infants and toddlers suffer the highest rates of all types of child maltreatment.[91] Child abuse and neglect are harmful to the development of young children and, when severe, can have a catastrophic effect on the developing brain and other aspects of a child's health and well-being.[92] Every year, the physical abuse of children in the United States results in thousands of head injuries, broken bones, and deaths. Even less extreme incidents of physical abuse and chronic emotional abuse, in which parents harshly criticize or threaten their children, can cause injuries and trigger the release of toxic levels of stress hormones that damage the developing brain. A 2014 report, based on the conclusions of an expert panel convened by the federal government to examine the biological effects of child maltreatment, summarizes the pervasive and often lasting effects, especially for very young children:

> Data on the neurobiology of maltreatment show that child abuse and neglect alters brain development and is associated with alterations in neuroendocrine and immune function that are implicated in adult chronic diseases. Treatment of these diseases costs American taxpayers billions of dollars annually. Children are at the greatest risk of being victimized by abuse and neglect before the age of 3 years, which is *exactly* the point when the brain is undergoing rapid neuronal proliferation and pruning, synaptogenesis, and white matter development.[93]

Physical neglect often takes the form of parents failing to meet children's basic needs for adequate food and clothing and protection from a variety of dangers, such as accidental injuries and physical and sexual abuse by other adults. As I explain in the next chapter, the number of cases of child neglect identified each year far outnumbers cases of child abuse, and a large portion of physical neglect cases are, at least in part, a consequence of family poverty. Emotional neglect can be even more harmful. Given the critical role that "serve and return" plays in the development of children's brains and their lifelong capacity for learning and loving, it is easy to understand how severe emotional neglect in early life can have damaging effects. When a mother or other caregiver consistently fails to respond to a young child's attempts to engage him or her in interaction, or to the child's crying and other indicators of distress, opportunities for forming critical circuits in the brain are lost. Because of its potential impact on brain development and lifelong functioning, emotional neglect is considered by some experts to be the most destructive form of maltreatment. It is especially difficult to identify, however, because unlike a bruise or broken bone, gaps in the brain's circuitry and the "turning off" of genes that influence a child's capacity for empathy, affection, and learning are not readily observable, even by trained social service and health care providers.[94]

Risk Factors Interact to Put Children on Paths Toward Rotten Outcomes

The more that researchers in various fields study the effects of poverty on young children, the more new ways they find in which various poverty-related risk factors conspire to harm these children. It is important to understand that most risk factors, by themselves, do not account for the poisonous effects of childhood poverty. Instead, a combination of risk factors present in poor families and communities and the interactions between these factors damage children's prospects over time. For instance, interactions among early life risk factors put far too many children on a path toward failing in school. School failure, along with learning and behavior problems, dramatically increases the likelihood that children will experience rotten outcomes, such as drug and alcohol abuse, teen pregnancy, and juvenile crime. Such outcomes pave the way for a lifetime of poverty and hardship.[95]

What About Factors that Promote Resiliency?

However, not all children raised in poverty are fated to lousy outcomes. Adults who have managed to overcome severely deprived childhoods and growing up in violent communities are regularly profiled by the media; their inspiring stories remind us that succeeding in the face of substantial adversity is indeed possible. Paul Tough's 2012 bestseller *How Children Succeed: Grit, Curiosity and the Hidden Power of Character*, for instance, includes stories of young adults who are building rewarding lives despite having childhoods riddled with the stress of extreme poverty and inadequate parenting. Such stories are indeed inspiring. However, it is important to keep in mind that these stories receive a great deal of attention primarily because they portray the rare exceptions, rather than the typical outcomes, for children growing up in adverse situations. Unfortunately, statistics on rates of teen parenthood, school failure and dropout, criminal behavior, and other rotten outcomes for children raised in poor communities tell another story, one in which these unfortunate outcomes occur for large numbers of impoverished children.

Balancing Risk Factors with Those Known to Promote Resiliency

Over the past two decades, fostering resiliency has become increasingly recognized as an important aspect of improving the lives of individuals and families. Experts think of resiliency as stemming from a set of protective factors that counterbalance or offset the harmful effects of disadvantage and adversity. A number of personal characteristics and elements of one's environment appear to help promote resiliency. Decades of research on resilient individuals—disadvantaged children who have beaten the odds and found pathways to success in life—consistently point to three factors as particularly powerful in helping disadvantaged children overcome adversity: being born with a flexible, "easy" temperament; experiencing a consistent and long-lasting relationship with one or more nurturing adult; and having the opportunity to develop a special skill or unique talent.[96]

Temperament and talent are considered to be largely innate qualities, dependent upon the luck of genetics, rather than something that can be chosen or created through experience or intervention. However, the right type of support and training can help parents identify the positive traits in even the more challenging temperaments of their babies and young children, and encourage them to respond to their children in ways that foster a better fit between the child's innate tendencies and the parent's expectations and parenting style. High-quality early care and education programs include well-trained, skillful teachers who know how to create similar conditions in order to meet the unique needs of all of the young children in their classrooms. And certainly any level of talent a young child demonstrates can be nurtured, and skills can be built, through the support of caring adults and by programs in communities and schools, such as music and art classes and sports teams.

Unfortunately, being raised in poverty doesn't only create risk for young children, it also, in many cases, deprives children of opportunities to build personal resilience. Many poor communities lack appropriate parent support and training programs, as well as high-quality early care and education centers that offer individualized nurturance to support the success of children with challenging temperaments. Moreover, these communities typically offer little in the way of opportunities for children to develop their talents and skills beyond the academic skills fostered in their schools. Perhaps of greatest concern is the scarcity of supportive adults in the lives of many of our poorest young children, given that large numbers of these children are being raised by single mothers, many of whom struggle in the face of the social isolation and chronic stress that come with disadvantage. The degree to which poor parents are typically besieged, isolated, and ignored helps to push out of reach for many children the resilience that having a consistent, nurturing relationship with even one adult might foster.

This is not to say that some measure of resilience does not exist within individuals and families in poverty, or that resilience cannot be cultivated in children growing up in poor communities. As I explain in Chapter 7, identifying and recognizing strengths in individuals, families, and communities and building upon these strengths are at the very heart of what it will take to improve the life chances of disadvantaged children. Equally important, however, is recognizing the extreme and persistent nature of the multiple risk factors that plague many of today's impoverished families, and that many of these factors are beyond their control. As Larry Davis, Dean of the School of Social Work at the University of Pittsburgh, sums it up:

> We certainly should continue to look for strengths and protective factors, but we must be more willing to acknowledge the problems that the poor and minority populations are experiencing as a result of structural forces that are completely overpowering their personal strengths, their cultural strengths, or both.[97]

In the next chapter, I explore how the child welfare system, a system charged with protecting our most vulnerable children, often fails to do so and how, as a result, it overpowers the resilience of and harms too many of the children it has been charged to safeguard.

5 It Takes a Firestorm
HOW THE CHILD WELFARE SYSTEM PERPETUATES THE CYCLE

Twenty children, ages six and seven, along with six adults, were shot to death at the Sandy Hook Elementary School, in Newtown, CT, on December 15, 2012.

Four hundred seventy-seven children, the overwhelming majority of them ages five and under, died in Florida between the end of 2007 and March 2014. Seventy percent of the Florida children were ages two and under. Many of these children died brutal, horrible deaths in which they were trampled, beaten, and/or tortured.

If you are like most Americans, chances are you are very familiar with the information in the first statement, while completely unaware of the information in the second. Like me, you probably recall being stunned and horrified by the news of the mass shooting at the Sandy Hook Elementary School. For many Americans, being reminded of that tragedy still brings deep sadness, and we can be certain that every December in the foreseeable future will harbor additional reminders of the lives that were taken in that shooting and of the very young lives in particular. Given the degree to which the killing of innocents in Connecticut was closely covered by virtually every media outlet and haunts us still, why hasn't news of 477 child deaths in Florida in just over six years—an average of nearly eighty deaths per year—garnered at least as much national attention and outrage? Why didn't the fact that these children were known to the taxpayer-funded system charged with keeping endangered children safe attract intense media attention and public outrage before the body count became so high? I believe that a large part of the answer is that nearly all of the children killed in Florida were poor and many of them were of color.

A Scandal Breaks in Florida

Five-year-old Ashton-Lynette was born to a troubled seventeen-year-old who ran away from home when Ashton-Lynette was just a few months old. The child's mother was investigated at least three times by Florida's Department for Children and Families (DCF), which, due to her rampant drug use, referred her to a drug treatment program. The agency failed, however, to ensure that the mother was participating in that program and that her young daughter was safe. On October 21, 2012, Ashton-Lynette died from ingesting pills, including morphine and amphetamines. Florida's Child Protection Team, a unit that evaluates DCF's response to abuse and neglect cases, found that Ashton-Lynette's death was preventable. "The mother readily allowed her child to stay in her friend's home several times a week, knowing the home was filthy and that pills were everywhere and readily accessible to the child," the team reported.[1]

Emmanuel Murray was also born to a troubled seventeen-year-old in Florida. DCF was aware that Emmanuel's mother grew up in a violent home and that mother and baby were living with the mother's boyfriend. However, the agency failed to conduct a background check on the boyfriend and were, therefore, unaware of his violent history. When the baby was less than three months old, the boyfriend beat Emmanuel's mother so badly that she required hospital treatment. Concerned for Emmanuel's safety, DCF had his mother sign an agreement to end all contact with her abuser. Two weeks later, DCF terminated its involvement with this family. On March 5, 2009, just one week after DCF closed the family's case, the baby and his mother were in the boyfriend's car when he began beating her and threatening to kill Emmanuel. As the mother fled to get help, her boyfriend sped away, tossing Emmanuel onto the pavement, killing him.[2]

Beginning in 2013, prompted by a series of high-profile deaths to children in the care of Florida's DCF, a *Miami Herald* investigative team combed through six years of records to document the deaths of children who, like Ashton-Lynette and Emmanuel, had been in families that had had at least one encounter with DCF over the previous five years. The *Herald* discovered that DCF had been grossly underreporting the number of deaths of children with which it had contact, sometimes by as many as thirty-nine deaths per year. Most of the 477 children who died were ages five or younger; 70% were ages two and younger.

Additional numbers help tell the story of an underresourced, dysfunctional system. More than eighty of the 477 children died after their parents signed so-called safety plans, something Florida DCF often used instead of the more time-consuming and expensive process of obtaining court orders to mandate parents' participation in substance abuse or mental health programs, and other services aimed toward increasing safety for their children. Unlike court orders, the safety plans were not enforceable by law; therefore, these cost-cutting promises were useless in protecting children from harm. In several incidents, DCF staff members failed to heed multiple warnings indicating that children were in grave danger: thirty-four children were killed after the agency had received ten or more reports indicating that they were being maltreated.

Even more gut-wrenching than the numbers in the *Herald*'s "Innocents Lost" series are its chronicles of the short, traumatic lives and brutal deaths of Ashton-Lynette, Emmanuel, and many other Florida children whom DCF had been charged to protect. Anyone who reads these stories will be saddened by them, and—I would hope—outraged by the fact that many of these children would likely have been saved had the system worked as it should. Indeed, a number of Florida's elected officials, as well as members of the public, expressed outrage at the young lives lost within their dysfunctional child welfare system, something familiar to those of us in other states where media exposés uncovered similar tragedies. We have seen DCF directors resign under fire and the abrupt terminations of direct-service workers assigned to monitor the families in which a death occurred. And we have read and listened to the plethora of heated rhetoric pointing blame at state child welfare agencies and the governors under which they operate.

A portion of that blame is well placed. There is no denying that incompetent leadership, poor decision making, and shoddy casework played a role in many of the deaths in Florida, as they have in other states. The *Herald* pointed to a shift in Florida's child welfare system in recent years in which it moved away from placing at-risk children in foster care and toward allowing more of these children to remain with their own families. In hindsight, it's painfully clear that many of the children killed by their parents, or by someone in whose care their parents left them, should have been removed from the custody of their dangerous and/or highly neglectful parents. It's important to point out, however, that foster care is not panacea; it harbors its own risks, especially for babies and young children.

Firestorms in Other States

In a recent twelve-month period, ten children placed in foster care by the Texas Department of Family and Welfare Services (DFPS) died under suspicious circumstances. Among them was eleven-month-old Orien Hamilton, whose head was crushed under the knee of a violent caretaker. Several months later, two-year-old Alexandria Hill died after her foster mother slammed her head against the floor. Investigators found that in both Orien's and Alexandria's cases, the private agencies with which Texas contracts to find and supervise foster homes failed to conduct sufficient background checks before allowing the families to provide foster care to vulnerable, young children. After a review prompted by Alexandria's violent death, Texas suspended the licenses of several foster homes, citing serious safety concerns, including foster parents using physical punishment and withholding food from the children placed in their care. Children's Rights, a national organization that advocates for improvements in state foster care systems, recently sued Texas in federal court, claiming that the state violates the constitutional rights to safety and well-being of the children in its system.[3]

It is tempting to attribute the gaping holes and poor oversight of the Florida and Texas child welfare systems at least in part to the fact that they are both Southern states whose right-leaning politics sometime result in severe hardship and occasionally outright harm to the vulnerable children living in those states. Such stereotyping is understandable, given the high percentage of Texas children without health insurance, and the miserly per-child rate Florida allocates for its preschool programs. But a recent scandal in kid-friendly Massachusetts, that most progressive of states with its near-universal health care coverage and the nation's highest test scores, shows that even states with liberal governors and legislatures can be grossly negligent in funding and overseeing their child welfare systems.

In December 2013, the Massachusetts Department for Children and Families (DCF) received court approval to remove three children from their mentally ill, drug-addicted mother and her boyfriend, who had a history of violence along with a drug problem of his own. However, when DCF arrived at the home, one of the children, four-year-old Jerimiah Oliver, was missing. Months later, Jerimiah's body would be found along a highway. The death sparked public outrage when it became known that the family had a long history with DCF and that the system had failed to act in response to a series of reports indicating that the children were in danger. Equally appalling is that, over the eight-month period before DCF realized that Jerimiah was missing, his worker had failed to visit the family even once. Six months before Jeremiah's disappearance was discovered, his mother informed DCF that she no longer wanted the agency involved with her family, something that should have resulted in a court order to keep the family under DCF supervision. DCF failed to petition the court and lost track of the family. By the time new reports of abuse and neglect triggered a petition to remove the children, the four-year-old had disappeared.[4]

The circumstances surrounding Jeremiah's death sparked an investigation into DCF by the *Boston Globe* and the New England Center for Investigative Reporting. Massachusetts residents were stunned to learn that each year an average of nine or ten children under DCF's supervision were dying of maltreatment or suspected maltreatment, a rate six times higher than for children not involved with DCF. Those deaths included thirteen-month-old Kadyn Hancock, who was killed by his mother in 2010. Kadyn's aunt alleges that DCF ignored her concerns regarding the baby's safety and that it returned Kadyn to his mother's care a week after he had been treated for a broken arm. In 2013, three-month-old Chase Gideaka, a boy who had been under DCF supervision since being born with drugs in his system, was beaten to death by his mother's boyfriend. In the aftermath of Jerimiah Oliver's death, the social worker assigned to his family and two DCF supervisors involved in the case were fired. After published reports on additional child deaths, including that of Kadyn and Chase, revealed that DCF's problems went well beyond that single case, its director was forced to resign.[5]

A National Disgrace

After having spent more than twenty-five years working to improve services for families ensnared in child welfare systems, what happened in Florida, Texas, and Massachusetts is sickeningly familiar to me. I know the cycle triggered by shocking child fatalities all too well. In the aftermath of similar tragedies, I have comforted distraught social workers, participated in inquiries to determine what went wrong, and advocated for strengthening the systems charged with protecting endangered children. I have watched the focus of child welfare systems, caught in the glare of public scrutiny that often follows publicized child deaths, shift rapidly from supporting vulnerable families in safely caring for their children at home toward removing large numbers of children from even low-risk homes. In many cases, this results in unnecessarily traumatizing children by abruptly removing them from their families and placing them with strangers in foster homes or shelters, while doing little if anything to increase their safety. Most disturbingly of all, I have also seen too many instances in which the systemic weaknesses uncovered by investigations of child fatalities are identical to weaknesses exposed by previous child deaths in that same system. In other words, nothing much changes between catastrophes.

Why do our elected leaders allow this heinous cycle to continue? I have come to believe that the voting public's lack of interest in the functioning of the child welfare system accounts for much of the problem. Most Americans know little about what happens to the children in their state's system and seem to care even less; that is, until a horrific case like that of Jeremiah Oliver surfaces. This apathy is pervasive, even though the child welfare system is responsible for protecting hundreds of thousands of endangered children each year. This system identified 702,000 child victims of maltreatment in 2014 alone. Nearly half of those children were ages five and under, and 27%, or 189,540 victims of abuse and/or neglect, were babies and toddlers under the age of three.[6] These children are among the most vulnerable of all, yet they must rely on a system that is often underresourced and overwhelmed, one to which most Americans seem to turn a blind eye.

THE ROLE OF POVERTY

Perhaps the main source of widespread apathy regarding children in the child welfare system is that most of us don't readily identify with families affected by child abuse and neglect. We tend to view maltreatment as something that happens in families unlike our own. There is some reality to that perception; the majority of families ensnared in the child welfare system are low income and plagued by the multiple stressors that come with being poor. Research shows that children from families living in extreme poverty are as much as twenty-two times more likely to be victims of child abuse and/or neglect than children from nonpoor families.[7] One study found that more than one third of children born to low-income mothers had been reported to child welfare services by the time they were five years old; that's more than one in three low-income infants, toddlers, and preschoolers.[8]

Being poor contributes to risk for child abuse and neglect in multiple ways. As I explained in Chapter 4, poverty increases family stress, and high levels of stress contribute to child maltreatment; so does the extreme isolation experienced by families living in high-crime, low-resource neighborhoods. The often unsafe and overcrowded living quarters of poor families also put their children at risk for injuries. Moreover, without money to spend on child care, poor parents are sometimes forced to leave young children with inappropriate and sometimes dangerous caretakers. This helps to explain the too-common occurrence of young children being injured or killed by their mothers' boyfriends. Financial limitations also restrict parents' ability to provide enough nutritious food to their children, as well as toys and books that foster early learning. Another important factor is that poor parents, in comparison to middle-income parents, have less access to mental health services for themselves; these services are critical to addressing the substance abuse, depression, and psychological trauma that increase their risk for maltreating their children.

A fair discussion of the relationship between poverty, single parenthood, and child maltreatment must include a few caveats, the first being that although poverty is a potent risk factor for child abuse and neglect, most poor parents do not harm their children. Impoverished families who do, however, are more likely to come to the attention of child welfare authorities, as such families are more highly scrutinized by teachers and others who are legally mandated to report suspected child abuse and neglect.[9] This raises the suspicion that maltreatment among nonpoor families may be underreported and makes it difficult to accurately measure the relationship between family poverty and child maltreatment. I also want to point out that most single mothers do not maltreat their children; many are exemplary parents. However, families headed by single mothers are more likely than two-parent families to be poor, and single parents often have fewer supports than those who are married to buffer the stress of raising children. Decades of research show that social isolation, in combination with the stress and insufficient resources experienced by impoverished families, increases the risk of child abuse and neglect.[10]

To understand the role that poverty plays in child maltreatment, it is important to understand the distinctions between child abuse and child neglect. A large majority of the children served in the child welfare system are victims of neglect (75% of all cases in 2014) rather than abuse.[11] Unlike abuse, whereby a parent deliberately causes injury or other significant harm to a child, child neglect is defined as a parent's failure to protect his or her child from harm or to meet one or more of the child's basic needs. Of course, protecting children from harm and meeting their basic needs, such as providing safe and stable housing, poses a far greater challenge for parents who are poor than for those with adequate income. This reality and the fact that the majority of the children placed into foster care come from poor families reveals yet another way in which high rates of family poverty harm millions of children, and young children in particular. Recognizing the role of poverty in child neglect and the fact that a majority of all maltreatment cases are due to neglect tells us that the number of children experiencing the trauma and disrupted relationships, as well as the danger, of being removed from their parents and placed into foster care would decline if child poverty rates significantly decreased. Unfortunately, most policymakers, like most Americans, appear to be unaware of how consistently poverty funnels families into the child welfare system and children into foster care.

THE TANGLE OF POVERTY AND RACE

Given the persistence of racism in the United States, the widespread perception that a majority of families ensnared in the child welfare system are African American also appears to play a role in public indifference regarding how this system functions. Even some of my social work students express surprise in learning that the largest group of maltreated children are, in fact, white. In 2014, 44% of all child victims were white, 22% were Hispanic, and 21% were African American. Although larger numbers of white children are identified as maltreated, these percentages do not mean that white children are more likely than children of color to be identified as maltreated or to be placed in foster care. In fact, the numbers look quite different when we examine the rate of maltreatment for each of these racial groups.

In 2014, the child welfare system identified 8% of all white children, 9% of all Hispanic children, and 15% of all African American children as having been abused or neglected.[12] Why are African American children identified as maltreated at higher rates than are white or Hispanic children? It is reasonable to attribute these higher rates, at least in part, to similarly higher rates of poverty and single-parenthood among African American families. The facts that a majority of maltreatment cases involve neglect, and that child neglect is often a consequence of poverty, support this logic, as does the correlation between single-mother families and both poverty and child maltreatment. However, neither poverty rates nor family structure explain the disproportionately high rates at which the child welfare system places African American children into foster care, or the longer periods of time for which these children languish in the foster care system.

Although African American children make up only 14% of the children in the United States, they account for 26% of all children in foster care. Hispanic children, on the other hand, are slightly underrepresented, as they make up 24% of all U.S. children and only 21% of children in foster care. And white children are substantially underrepresented; 52% of all U.S. children are white, but white children account for only 42% of children in foster care. Even more difficult to explain is that on average, African American children remain in foster care for significantly longer periods of time than do white or Hispanic children.[13] Given the many ways in which placement into foster care and lengthy foster care stays can harm children's life chances (as I explain later in this chapter), these percentages show that African American children are more likely than other children to be exposed to such harms.

Too often, differences in how the child welfare system treats African American families begin at the investigation stage and persist throughout families' involvement in the system. A number of studies suggest that, all things being equal, child welfare workers are more likely to investigate rather than screen out reports of child maltreatment for African American families, and that investigations of black families are also more likely to result in the removal of children for placement in foster care. Moreover, studies comparing outcomes for children removed from African American, single-parent families to those removed from white or Hispanic single-parent families show that black children spend significantly longer periods of time in foster care before being reunited with their families.[14] The causes of these disparities are complex and hotly disputed; however, higher investigation and placement rates and longer stays in foster care for African American children demonstrate that, as in virtually every other aspect of our society, racial bias, conscious or otherwise, strongly affects decision making in our child welfare system.[15]

Although leaders of state child welfare agencies throughout the country have long been aware of disparities in the treatment of African American families, most states still have a long way to go in eliminating these inequities. In recent years, a number of states, led by the federal government and Casey Family Programs, have been experimenting with strategies aimed toward reducing disparities in how their systems serve families of color, African American families in particular. These efforts seem to be making a difference. Between 2002 and 2012, the number of children identified as "black" in foster care dropped by nearly 50%, the highest percentage reductions among children of all racial groups.

This is certainly a positive trend. However, we must temper our encouragement given that the number of children in foster care identified as "multi-racial" nearly doubled during that same period, and that mixed-race children were the only group for which foster care rates increased rather than declined. This suggests that at least some of the children previously categorized as "black" are now being identified as "multi-racial" and that reductions in the number of African American children in foster care may not be quite as substantial as reported.[16] We must also keep in mind that ingrained racial biases die hard and that the pace of progress in this area has been shamefully sluggish. It is for these same reasons that we should suspect that the erroneous perception that a majority of children in the child welfare system are African American continues to underlie some of the voting public's indifference to the functioning of this system. We have only to look at the American criminal justice system to find equally troubling race-based discrepancies in the treatment of individuals accused of a crime and similar levels of apathy among voters, and the officials they elect, regarding those inequities.[17]

Budget Cuts and Poor Oversight

The public's indifference to the plight of children in child welfare systems manifests itself in a number of ways that prevent sorely needed reforms from taking place. For example, Boston's media outlets provided limited coverage of Children's Rights' lawsuit on behalf of children harmed in Massachusetts' foster care system, a suit filed years before the disappearance of Jerimiah Oliver and the ensuing firestorm of criticism aimed toward DCF. They failed to regularly send reporters to cover the trial, in which witnesses vividly described the suffering of children in an underfunded, poorly monitored system.[18]

Between 2009 and 2014, Massachusetts lawmakers cut the DCF budget by nearly $130 million (adjusted for inflation), despite steadily growing numbers of families entering that system.[19] Even with additional state funding allocated to the agency after scathing reports on the deaths of young children under its supervision, DCF's inflation-adjusted budget for its 2014–2015 fiscal year was slated to be less than it was in 2007.[20] And Texas, whose system has the highest child death rate in the country, ranks forty-third among states for its per capita spending on child welfare services. In 2011, on its way out of the Great Recession, Texas cut, by $27 million, its budget for community-based services that help prevent child abuse and neglect from occurring in the first place.[21]

In Florida, the DCF budget shrank by $80 million in the seven years leading up to 2013, even though overall state spending increased by nearly $9 billion—a 13% increase—during that same time period. These cuts provide evidence that reducing funding has been less about economic hard times than a reflection of widespread indifference to the needs of the thousands of vulnerable children who rely upon the child welfare system to keep them safe. Need more evidence? As the *Miami Herald*'s exposé on the hundreds of children who died while under DCF supervision broke, Florida's child welfare system was slated for a further reduction of nearly $5 million for fiscal year 2014–2015—this despite the fact that a steadily improving economy had netted the state $1.2 billion in new revenue to spend in that same year. As stories of the suffering and deaths of hundreds of DCF children confronted Floridians in their morning papers, Senate President Don Gaetz stated the obvious: "I think in child welfare we have gone on the cheap, and I think that's been a mistake."[22]

These three states are hardly alone in going "on the cheap" when it comes to protecting vulnerable children. Between 2008 and 2010, in the depths of the recession, when disadvantaged families were experiencing even greater economic struggles and higher levels of stress than in the past, thirty-three states decreased spending on child welfare services, and three states froze their funding at prior levels. Deadlock in Washington made it worse. In passing the Budget Control Act of 2011, known as sequestration, Congress made its own cuts to services that help keep vulnerable children healthy and safe. Sequestration locked in reductions in federal funding to state child welfare systems, as well as in community-based supports for disadvantaged families with young children, programs that help prevent child abuse and neglect from occurring.[23] In an effort to offset those cuts and better protect endangered children, the Obama administration, in 2012 and again in 2013, proposed allocating $250 million a year to provide "incentive payments to states that demonstrate real, meaningful improvements" in service quality and outcomes for children in their child welfare systems. Congress failed to pass these measures in both years.

Trimming on Both Ends

Chronically insufficient resources and having one's career on the line every single day make leading a state child welfare system a thankless and nearly impossible job. It is no wonder, then, that states often end up hiring leaders who lack a thorough understanding of child welfare work and, therefore, make too many errors in setting priorities for allocating the inadequate resources available. Perhaps the greatest failure of some of the state leaders I've observed has been their reluctance to communicate, to their governors, legislatures, and the public, the myriad ways in which funding cuts erode their ability to protect vulnerable children. Granted, such communication is fraught with challenges, not the least of which is that those leaders serve at the pleasure of their governors, and state funding for child protection often becomes political fodder.

Adding to the challenge is the complex nature of child welfare work. News stories often focus on cases in which obvious signals of child endangerment were missed and basic procedures ignored, obscuring the fact that the protection of vulnerable children is a highly complicated endeavor. It is governed by a plethora of state and federal laws and regulations, yet requires, on a case-by-case basis, a great deal of human judgment, as it puts social workers and their supervisors in the position of trying to predict human behavior. Most governors and state legislators, like their constituents, have very little understanding of the complex balancing of children's needs, parental rights, family court jurisdiction, and resource availability that child welfare cases typically involve.

Despite this complexity, however, it is relatively easy to connect the dots between inadequate funding and its consequences for the children who rely on these systems. When it comes to advocating for the necessary resources, child welfare leaders too often shy away from their responsibilities to advocate on behalf of the thousands of endangered children their systems serve. For instance, in the throes of the DCF scandal in Florida, its interim director noted that "If what exists in the community is not adequate to keep a child safe in the home, the only answer is to remove that child from the home." "Maybe we got it backwards," she continued, "in that we tried to reduce out-of-home care before having those safety services that are needed."[24]

Reacting to frequent budget cuts in combination with increased demands on its system, Florida's DCF became increasingly focused on reducing the number of children it removed from their families, in order to reduce expenditures for costly foster home and residential care programs. Between 2003 and 2014, the number of children removed from their homes for maltreatment fell from 27,674 to 18,185, a 34% decrease. It is now clear that no one was paying attention to how that dramatic reduction impacted Florida's most vulnerable children.

Florida officials wrapped their efforts to reduce the numbers of children it placed into foster care in the rhetoric of family preservation, an approach that recognizes that being removed from even troubled families traumatizes children, and that children are sometimes emotionally and/or physically harmed while in foster care. Done properly, family preservation entails providing sufficient services and careful monitoring of vulnerable families in order to allow children to remain safely at home while professionals work with parents to improve their caregiving skills and other areas of concern. Moreover, it requires carefully assessing the level of risk in determining which families are appropriate for home-based services so that children are not left in dangerous situations. That's not what was taking place in Florida.

Instead, during the same period of time in which Florida's DCF drastically reduced the number of children it placed into foster care, it just as sharply reduced the number of children receiving protective services in their own homes, from 17,079 children in 2003 to 12,132 in 2014. As the *Miami Herald* discovered, Florida had been trimming its capacity to help endangered children on both ends: cutting back on its services to troubled families at the same time it was leaving far more children in such families. In fact, in 2013, the state was spending less on community-based services, the programs that help ensure that at-risk children are safely cared for in their own homes, than it had spent in 2007.[25] Given that thousands of mostly young children were left in families identified as being at high risk for maltreatment, without the necessary intensive services and close monitoring, it is surprising that the death toll in Florida wasn't even higher.

Florida's budget-cutting ax endangered DCF-involved children in other ways, including laying off 72% of its quality-assurance staff members. These professionals review case records to identify gaps and problems in the system so that they can be fixed before, instead of after, children are injured or killed. The state had also reduced spending for community-based services that are often critical to keeping children safe. For instance, in its review of the 477 child deaths, the *Herald* found that parents' drug and/or alcohol abuse was linked to at least 323 of these deaths.[26] The paper noted that many of these deaths occurred while Florida, like a number of other states, was cutting funds for substance abuse treatment programs. One does not have to be an expert in child welfare services or economics to identify the multiple connections here, between budget cuts and harm to children.

"Systems" Full of Gaping Holes

In Massachusetts, reports that a misplaced fax of a police alert may have played a role in DCF's failure to prevent the death of a young child sparked public outrage along with disbelief that in an era in which Google probably knows more details of our lives than do our closest friends, those entrusted with protecting children were relying upon communication by fax machine. Only in the aftermath of that outcry did the legislature approve funds to purchase 2,000 iPads for social workers to use while assessing and monitoring the safety of the children on their caseloads.[27] Ineffective and outdated technology is a problem in the child welfare systems across the country. It seems that in many states, motor vehicle departments obtain the technology necessary to efficiently process drivers' license renewals long before child welfare workers receive electronic tools for keeping closer track of endangered children. Every day, reliance on paper rather than electronic records, the use of outdated software, and other readily fixable problems impede the sharing of potentially life-saving information among child welfare workers and their supervisors, as well as with the police and court personnel. For example, only through a specially commissioned audit did the Massachusetts DCF discover that several children under its supervision, including children in two of its licensed foster homes, were living in households that contained registered sex offenders.[28]

Inadequate funding endangers children in other ways, including systems having fewer child welfare workers than needed to ensure children's safety. Across the nation, worker caseloads often become dangerously high. It does not take sophisticated knowledge to understand that if a total of fifteen families per worker is the maximum for being able to adequately monitor the safety and well-being of each of the children in those families, children are no longer safe when workers are responsible for twenty or thirty families, most of which contain more than one child. Why must it take a spate of child fatalities for officials to acknowledge the danger that high caseloads pose to children, and allocate funds to hire enough social workers?

A related concern, one that is rarely publicized, is that many states also cut corners by not requiring individuals hired as "social workers" to have a bachelor's or master's degree in social work. Estimates are that fewer than half of those providing social work services to our nation's most vulnerable children and their families have earned a social work degree.[29] It would surprise many to hear that there are no federal regulations that require states to hire only individuals with relevant college degrees to work with fragile children and families. Moreover, when states are unable to recruit qualified employees with social work degrees to work under the conditions and pay scale they set for their child welfare systems, they hire candidates with related college degrees like psychology or child development. Although individuals with these degrees are likely to have some expertise relevant to child protection work, most lack training in engaging troubled families and providing effective services to families from a wide range of different cultures. On-the-job training aimed toward building these skills is often lacking. Worse, there is nothing stopping systems in some states from hiring candidates with degrees in fields unrelated to child protection. This isn't terribly different than a hospital hiring history majors to perform open-heart surgery.

Neglecting the Special Needs of the Very Young

Another harmful consequence of underfunding and failing to adequately monitor child welfare systems is that most states lack procedures and specialized services for addressing the complex needs of infants and young children, despite the fact that nearly half the children identified each year as maltreated are ages five and under, and nearly 120,000 are infants.[30] A recent national survey revealed that most state systems are operating oblivious to the fact that children's social, emotional, and cognitive capacities develop most rapidly during their earliest years of life and that what happens in these first years has profound implications for the rest of their lives.[31] Although federal law mandates and a majority of states have policies requiring that children under the age of three in foster care be screened by professionals to identify serious developmental problems, less than one third have similar requirements for maltreated children who remain with their birth parents. Denying screenings to the latter group of children makes no sense because, as the survey's authors point out, "Young children who are not removed from their homes are just as vulnerable to developmental problems as those who are."[32]

Most states do not require that maltreated young children with significant health or developmental concerns be immediately referred to a specialist, and only three states require all their child welfare staff members to undergo training in meeting the special needs of infants and very young children. Given what we now know about early brain development, delays in identifying developmental problems in very young victims of maltreatment and in providing them with specialized care are unconscionable. By failing to be proactive in addressing such concerns, child welfare systems are missing critical but fleeting opportunities to ensure that highly vulnerable children develop as optimally as possible.

The same survey found that the policies and practices of most child welfare systems fail to reflect the importance of early life attachments between young children and caring adults. A majority of states do not require expedited case reviews and court hearings, or other processes designed to move young children out of temporary foster care and into a permanent family as rapidly as possible. Nor do most state systems require more frequent contact between babies and toddlers and their birth parents, in situations where children are likely to be returned home. Moreover, many fail to provide struggling birth parents ready access to the mental health, substance abuse treatment, and other services necessary for them to safely care for their children.

In failing to provide stability to infants and young children as early in life as possible, these systems are depriving them of opportunities to form vital, long-term attachments with caring adults, something crucial to lifelong emotional well-being. The longer children remain in temporary care—neither returned home nor placed with an adoptive family—the greater the odds that they will experience numerous broken attachments with adult caregivers. This happens because children who remain in foster care for long periods are more likely to be shuttled from foster home to foster home. Children who experience multiple foster placements are at high risk for developing serious behavior problems and other mental health disorders. Having such a disorder increases the likelihood of future foster care disruptions and makes children far less appealing to prospective adoptive parents, a vicious cycle all too familiar to child welfare professionals throughout the country.

Inappropriate and Potentially Harmful Interventions

An equally grave concern is the shortage of appropriate services, such as specialized therapy for children who have mental health problems stemming from the trauma of maltreatment and/or from having been abruptly removed from their families. These problems are especially acute in children who have been severely abused and those who have experienced numerous disrupted foster care placements. Child welfare workers seeking care for such children often confront long waiting lists and/or discover that local mental health providers lack the specialized expertise that helping such children requires.

The shortage of appropriate mental health services is partly to blame for the widespread practice of using drugs that were developed to treat the symptoms of adult mental illnesses to mute and control the troubling behaviors of traumatized children. Studies show that children in the child welfare system are far more likely to be given psychotropic medications than children with similar symptoms who are outside the system.[33] It is not uncommon for children in foster care to be taking a combination of three or four types of these powerful medications, many of which have never been tested on children, either separately or in combination with other drugs.

Health care practitioners are prescribing psychotropic drugs to maltreated children as young as age one, even though there is little evidence to show that young children benefit from these medications. Even more alarming, we know very little about the safety of these drugs and their long-term effects on the rapidly developing brains of the young children.[34] A 2014 report from an expert panel convened by the federal government to examine the biological effects of child maltreatment calls attention to this hazardous situation:

> Children and adolescents in foster care . . . are prescribed psychotropic medications at rates two to four times that seen in non-foster care Medicaid populations, with little evidence of improved mental health outcomes (Kutz, 2011). Whether these high rates of medication use reflect improper prescribing or are an appropriate reflection of need, data suggests that in addition to high usage rates of psychotropic medication, children in foster care are prescribed doses of the medications that exceed recommendations, [and] are more likely to be prescribed multiple psychotropic medications. In some cases infants and young children in whom there is no evidence of psychotropic medication efficacy are treated with medications (Billonci & Gleason, 2012).[35]

Serious questions remain regarding how these drugs impact the development of brain circuitry and the social, emotional, and learning capacities of children who are already extremely vulnerable. Yet there has been very little public outcry against what amounts to a dangerous experiment being conducted on the bodies and brains of thousands of America's most vulnerable children. Similar in some ways to the subjects of the infamous Tuskegee syphilis study in the middle of the last century, most of these children are from poor families and many are of color. And like the Tuskegee subjects, they have few advocates to protect them from the lasting harm this unregulated, ill-conceived experiment may cause.[36]

Abused and neglected children are also harmed when government goes "on the cheap" when it comes to funding other community-based services, especially for families affected by mental health problems, substance abuse, and/or domestic violence. As I explained in Chapter 4, these risk factors threaten the healthy development of young children and may diminish their lifelong capacity for emotional well-being and for learning. They also increase risk for child maltreatment and make it far more difficult for children in foster care to safely return home to their biological parents. Programs designed to address these and other risk factors are chronically underfunded and frequently land on both state and federal budget-chopping blocks.

Foster Care: Protection for Some, Serious Harm for Others

In the wake of the scandals, such as the death of Jeremiah Oliver, that occur after media reports of children being harmed or killed while living with their families, elected officials typically call for placing greater numbers of maltreated children in foster care. They view foster care as providing safety and stability to children at high risk for maltreatment by their birth parents—and for many children, it does just that. However, few outside the child welfare system realize that foster care, especially in severely underfunded systems, holds its own set of dangers to the safety and well-being of children, including risk for additional maltreatment, and emotional damage done by multiple changes in placements. This is especially true for babies and young children.

Forty percent of all children who entered foster care in 2014 were ages five and under, a total of about 166,000 young children. A large portion of these children were infants.[37] These facts raise grave concerns, given what we now know about how babies' and young children's capacities for learning and mental health are developing at their most rapid rate. Our concerns should be heightened by the fact that the average length of time children stay in foster care is about twenty-two months and that 30% of all children in state foster care systems remain there for two or more years.[38] These numbers tell us that many children are spending a large portion of their earliest years in temporary and often unstable care. And they are doing so at a time in which nurturing relationships, with frequent, consistent interaction with caring adults, are most critical to lifelong well-being. Although there is always hope to somehow make up for what was missed in the earliest years of life, not all aspects of what children are deprived of in these years can be offset by nurturing relationships later in life.

Few Americans realize how often children removed from their birth families by the child welfare system are shuttled between foster homes and, in many cases, group care facilities, such as group homes or residential treatment centers. More than 40% of all children placed in foster care are moved to a different foster home or care facility at least once during their first six months in state custody.[39] The longer a child remains in foster care, the more likely it is that he or she will experience a high number of moves. More than one third of children who remain in foster care between one and two years—the average length of stay—experience three or more changes of placement. Two thirds of children remaining in foster care for two years or longer are moved three or more times.[40] It is easy to understand the high rate of mental health and learning problems among children in foster care when we consider how a young and developing brain is affected by such frequent, dramatic disruptions in caregivers and relationships.

For a good portion of children, their time in the foster care system is punctuated with stays in shelters, psychiatric hospitals, and other institutions. In addition to the trauma of being removed from their families, these children must endure being taken from a foster home where they may have begun to feel safe and connected to foster parents and placed in a different foster home or facility. For too many children, this cycle is repeated multiple times, with dire consequences. A number of studies show that changes in placement often do children more harm than good, and that each change in foster placement decreases the likelihood that a child will return home or be adopted. Moreover, as I explained earlier in this chapter, multiple moves can harm children's life chances in a number of ways. Placement disruptions make it more difficult for children to form the healthy attachments that undergird social and emotional development. For many children, they contribute to severe, long-term behavior problems. Frequent moves also contribute to other mental health problems and poor performance in school and increase the odds that children will experience chronic unemployment and poverty in adulthood.[41]

To be fair, not all changes in children's placement are harmful, and some take place for the child's benefit. Examples of the latter include transferring a child out of a foster home and into a potential adoptive home or to the newly available home of a close family member. However, studies suggest that as many as 70% of placement changes have nothing to do with improving the well-being of the children moved. Instead, most changes in placement are made "to implement procedural, policy, and system mandates."[42] These bureaucracy-driven moves take place under a variety of scenarios, such as when child welfare workers fail to place siblings in the same foster home from the start and are later forced to move the children into a single foster home to comply with federal mandates regarding keeping brothers and sisters together. Placement moves also commonly occur when children are initially placed in a short-term foster home or shelter and must be moved to a long-term foster home. Both of these scenarios, like the majority of placement moves, indicate that state systems lack enough appropriate foster homes and care facilities to meet the diverse needs of the maltreated children in their custody.

Many children entering foster care already show symptoms of the developmental, learning, and/or behavior problems that often come with being cared for in poor, stressful environments. A large portion are also reeling from the trauma of being maltreated and from being abruptly removed from their homes. These children need foster parents who not only are warm and caring but also have the skills and support necessary to manage the challenges they present. The most troubled children need facilities, staffed by highly skilled professionals, where they can receive the specialized mental health and educational services necessary for them to recover and successfully live with an adoptive family.

How Going on the Cheap Perpetuates the Cycle

Meeting the needs of maltreated children requires considerable funding as well as time to create the appropriate resources and to recruit and provide adequate training to staff members and foster parents. With an adequate supply of the right kinds of settings, child welfare workers would have a much better chance of finding a foster home or care facility that could meet the needs of each of the children they place into care. Providing the right type of care in the first place would, no doubt, reduce the number of damaging moves children have to endure. The absence of such an array means that too often, child welfare workers are forced to choose from a meager selection of settings that they already know will be a poor fit for the children they must place. This is how so many children end up in overcrowded or substandard foster homes, or in group care facilities that are poorly suited to meet their needs. It is also how children come to be abused and/or neglected while in care and/or subjected to inappropriate treatments, including the use of psychotropic drugs that may be harmful to their developing minds and bodies.

STUCK IN THE SYSTEM

Children often become ensnared in the cycle when overburdened child welfare workers lack the time and resources necessary to keep children safe in their birth families, so greater numbers of children than necessary are placed into foster care. The absence of an adequate and diverse array of well-supported, closely monitored foster homes and care facilities results in children being placed in settings that are unsafe and/or fail to meet their needs. This, in turn, results in having to remove children from one setting and place them in another foster home or facility, one that may also be a poor fit.

This kind of instability, along with the trauma of being moved from place to place and the resultant broken attachments to caregivers, causes or worsens mental health problems in already vulnerable children. The presence of mental health problems, combined with a shortage of treatment resources, makes more changes in placement necessary and causes additional broken attachments and further emotional damage. Severe mental health problems decrease children's chances of reuniting with their birth family or being adopted by a new family. As a result, far too many children end up spending years stuck in a system that continues to inflict harm instead of protecting them and providing them with a safe, loving, and permanent family, something that most Americans would consider to be every child's birthright. These harms affect disproportionately higher numbers of African American children because, as I pointed out earlier in this chapter, these children are placed into foster care at higher rates than other children and languish there for longer periods of time.

What happens to children who become stuck in the child welfare system? Many of those who languish in foster care by the time they reach adolescence face a number of heartbreaking challenges. With few hopes of returning to their birth families or being adopted, these youths often engage in high-risk behaviors, including running away, using drugs and/or alcohol, and having unprotected sexual encounters. One consequence of this reckless behavior is that nearly half the girls in foster care report having been pregnant at least once.

Despite a steadily declining teen parenthood rate in the United States, the rate of teen parenthood among adolescents in the foster care system remains high. Girls in foster care are two and a half times more likely than their non–foster care peers to become pregnant by age nineteen. Moreover, research suggests that the more changes in foster placements a girl experiences, the more likely she is to become a teen parent.[43] Nearly half of adolescent boys in foster care report getting a girl pregnant, a rate double that of similar youths outside the system.[44] Not surprisingly, these teens report taking few if any measures to prevent pregnancy, and those who give birth indicate that having a child was, in large part, intentional. For many adolescents stuck in the foster care system, becoming a parent provides them with the ongoing family connection of which they have been deprived. Moreover, it confers, at least in their minds, a level of adult status they may not be able to find elsewhere, given their damaged prospects for a career and marriage.

Even more disturbing than high rates of too early parenthood are reports indicating that many teens in the foster care system become victims of human trafficking. Recent studies of sex-trafficking victims in California found that as many as 50% of these victims were foster children. It is easy to understand how teens who view themselves as belonging to no one and facing a bleak future become easy prey for those seeking to exploit them for financial gain.[45]

Far too many foster children languish in state custody until they become adults, at which point they are sent off to live on their own. This is known as "aging out" of the child welfare system, and it plays a central role in perpetuating the cycle of poverty. In 2014 alone, 22,319 youths aged out of foster care.[46] The vast majority of them were eighteen years old. Many of these young people have experienced multiple placements in foster homes and/or care facilities. Their case files are full of disrupted attachments to various foster parents and/or facility staff members, fragile, budding relationships that were suddenly terminated when the child was moved to a new placement. A history of chronic instability places these youths at greater risk for alcohol and drug abuse and other serious mental health problems. Moreover, it robs many of them of an adequate education, as children are typically pulled out of one school and put in another with each change of placement. To make matters worse, foster children typically have few, if any, adults to help with homework and encourage their learning. These factors explain why young adults aging out of foster care are typically several grades behind their non–foster care peers.

Despite their having grown up with such disadvantages, young adults are often discharged from the system with few resources or supports. It is ironic that in an era in which many middle-class and affluent parents deem their children not ready to be on their own at age eighteen or even older, and large numbers of young adults are still living in their parents' homes, so many of our most vulnerable young adults are being forced to fend for themselves. Unsurprisingly, they experience high rates of unemployment, poverty, and homelessness. Young adults who have aged out of the foster care system are also less likely than their non–foster care peers to complete college or earn a living wage and are more likely to use welfare and other government programs.[47]

Is it any wonder that as many as 30% of young women aging out of foster care become mothers by the age of twenty-one?[48] As is often the case for teens who become parents while in foster care, many unmarried young women who have left the system see few other prospects for being part of a family and realize that their chances for a successful career are remote. Becoming pregnant forces an indifferent system to pay attention to these young women, as they become eligible for subsidized food and health care that is aimed toward ensuring the health of their unborn child. They also have a better chance of finding a bed in a shelter or getting subsidized housing than nonpregnant homeless women. In the long run, however, early parenthood often seals the fate of poor women, because having one or more children creates additional, often insurmountable barriers to completing their education and finding adequate employment.[49] Here again, we see how gaping holes in the child welfare system funnel youths into lifelong poverty and maintain the cycle of intergenerational disadvantage.

Massive Human and Monetary Costs

Failing to adequately fund and monitor the child welfare system exacts an enormous cost in terms of the suffering of children and the lives and opportunities lost, as well as in taxpayers' dollars for remedial education, long-term mental health treatment, and juvenile and adult corrections. The fact that spending more, and spending more wisely, on families at risk for child abuse and neglect would decrease the amount spent on these more expensive costs seems to be lost on the majority of policymakers. Even those who appear to understand this reality tend to gravitate toward simple prevention programs that promise unrealistic outcomes "on the cheap," as I explain in the next chapter.

For every complex problem there is a solution that is simple, neat, and wrong.
H. L. MENCKEN

6 The Emperor's Old Clothes
THE FALSE PROMISE OF SIMPLE SOLUTIONS

OVER THE PAST DECADE, two significant trends have helped drive the search for early life interventions that improve the well-being and future prospects of disadvantaged young children. One is based in neuroscience. Relatively recent findings in brain development—several of which I discussed in Chapter 4— have focused policymakers' attention on the first years of life as an especially opportune stage for intervention. Early childhood program advocates often cite research showing that there are higher levels of malleability in the brains of infants and young children than in later stages of development and that much of the brain's circuitry or "hardwiring" takes place in early life, setting the stage for future learning and success. Policymakers and foundation leaders are becoming increasingly cognizant that although proper intervention can make a difference at any stage of life, intervening in the earliest stages holds particular promise for improving children's capacity to learn and succeed throughout life.

A second trend driving interest in early childhood interventions comes from the field of economics. Advocates of public investment in early childhood programs employ the "pay less now or pay much more later" argument to position these programs as cost-effective alternatives to the spiraling costs of special education, mental health treatment, and juvenile corrections, most of which are funded with public dollars. Moreover, they frequently make the point that the U.S. economy increasingly depends on a highly skilled workforce in order to compete in a globalized economic environment. The demand for higher levels of skill and expertise means that we really can't afford to leave any of our children behind, academically or otherwise. In advancing early childhood intervention as a means to close the school readiness gap between poor and nonpoor children, advocates also tap into widespread concern regarding the yawning gap in income between the wealthiest Americans and the rest of us, and fears regarding the disappearance of the nation's middle class.[1]

In this chapter, I discuss two major movements that dominate the discussion on improving the life chances of disadvantaged young children in the United States through programmatic interventions. The first advocates for widespread replication of certain home-visiting programs that target families during a child's first few years of life, including some that begin working with mothers during the prenatal stage. The second movement is the campaign to ensure that all children have access to preschool programs, at least by the time they are four years old. I illuminate a number of concerns related to wide-scale expansion of both types of programs, including some of the potential pitfalls of the often overzealous efforts to promote them as wise investments of public dollars.

The Home-Visiting Program Movement

One evening in the mid-1990s, an announcement on a national news broadcast that "gold has been discovered in California for the second time!" caught my attention. As I listened, I realized that the report was about the annual conference of the National Committee to Prevent Child Abuse, which happened to be held that year in California.[2] The recently discovered "gold" was promising results from a study of Healthy Families America (HFA), a program that provides home-based support to families with young children. The news anchor showed clips of jubilant advocates of HFA proclaiming that a major breakthrough had occurred in the prevention of child abuse and neglect. As the director of an organization focused on improving the life chances of vulnerable children, I was already familiar with HFA. The National Committee to Prevent Child Abuse had taken on expanding HFA across the country as a core aspect of its mission, and its Rhode Island affiliate had been lobbying state officials for funding to develop and expand the program throughout the state.

The notion of intervening early in the lives of vulnerable children to prevent problems such as child maltreatment and school failure is not new; it has been around at least since the establishment of New York Society for the Prevention of Cruelty to Children in 1875.[3] Until the past two or three decades, however, the United States had allocated relatively little funding to prevention programs for vulnerable children, while spending much larger amounts on programs aimed toward helping children once serious problems, such as child abuse, school failure, and delinquency, occur. Although this imbalance remains, things began to change in the early 1990s, when a number of foundations and the federal government stepped up their efforts to identify effective strategies for preventing child maltreatment and improving school readiness by intervening early in the lives of vulnerable children and their families.

The Packard Foundation played an important role with the publishing of its journal, *The Future of Children*. Two issues of the journal, published in 1993 and 1999, were especially influential in spotlighting home-visiting programs, such as HFA, as a promising strategy for improving outcomes for vulnerable young children. Four programs profiled in *The Future of Children* stood out from others as the most widely promoted and replicated:

- Nurse Family Partnership (NFP), in which nurses visit first-time new mothers from during pregnancy until the child turns two in an effort to improve the health and development of vulnerable children, and families' economic self-sufficiency
- HFA, in which paraprofessionals (nondegreed) and degreed staff members visit at-risk families with children from newborn to age five to promote effective parenting and prevent child abuse and neglect
- Parents as Teachers (PAT), in which paraprofessionals and degreed staff members visit pregnant women and children from newborn to age three in order to promote school readiness and develop partnerships between parents and schools, prevent child abuse, and increase parents' effectiveness
- Home Instruction for Parents of Preschool Youth (HIPPY), in which paraprofessionals visit families with preschool and kindergarten-age children to promote school readiness and school success, and encourage parents' involvement in their child's school and community.[4]

Although their goals and service delivery models vary somewhat, each of these home-visiting programs promotes its model as having some capacity for helping to break the cycle of intergenerational poverty by intervening early in the lives of young children and their families. The national headquarters of each of these programs promotes its program model and provides training and technical assistance to organizations seeking to replicate it.

THE MARKETING OF HOME-VISITING PROGRAMS

HFA was not the only program heralding its proven results and advocating for funding to expand throughout the country. For instance, at about the same time as the "gold discovery" report, a local family foundation was working to convince Rhode Island's school superintendents to establish HIPPY and PAT in their districts. The foundation's leaders were advocating for the replication of both home-visiting programs, which were already operating in a number of other states, because it believed that both had a "proven track record" of improving school readiness among disadvantaged young children. It was offering seed money to help start the programs on the condition that school districts commit to paying the entire cost of the programs once established. Not long after this, leaders of the local chapter of KidsCount, a national children's data-dissemination initiative funded by the Annie E. Casey Foundation, began campaigning for the establishment of NFP in Rhode Island, citing its proven effectiveness in reducing child maltreatment and improving long-term outcomes for vulnerable young children and their mothers.

During and since that time, leaders of nonprofit organizations and private foundations, as well as public policymakers all over the country, have been inundated with claims regarding the promising outcomes that various early childhood programs could be expected to achieve. Like them, I was intrigued by the promises made by the promoters of the four home-visiting programs and other similar programs. However, as I thought about the gravely disadvantaged families I encountered when I had been a frontline social worker, and those who were being served by Children's Friend, the agency I was leading, the purported results of these programs seemed too good to be true, especially given the barebones services they offered. Many of the family workers at our agency, as well as colleagues from other organizations that served highly vulnerable families, had similar doubts. Our skepticism came from observing the complex and chronic nature of the problems plaguing the poor families we saw every day. We tried to understand how a twice-monthly education session with a nurse or trained paraprofessional was anywhere near sufficient to address the educational deficits, mental health problems, and violence many of these families experienced, not to mention their struggles to meet basic needs such as food and housing. We saw how challenging it was to achieve change with these families even when we applied strategies that were far more comprehensive, more intensive, and longer-lasting than those provided by the models of home visiting that were being zealously promoted throughout our state and the nation.

Those of us in or near the trenches wondered how the results promised by these programs could be achieved by their one-size-fits-all approach, which offered mostly the same, predetermined services to all the families they served, especially if those families were experiencing multiple serious challenges and/or came from a wide variety of cultural traditions. We questioned how receptive a parent would be to a home visitor's lesson in how to teach her preschooler shapes or colors when that family had just received an eviction notice, or how a nurse could effectively teach a mother activities for stimulating learning in her infant when that mother was routinely being beaten by her boyfriend. Given their educational backgrounds—most were either nurses or paraprofessionals—home visitors in the four widely promoted programs were unlikely to have the advanced-level skills necessary to break through the terror and denial that accompanies domestic violence in order to convince a mother to get a restraining order against her boyfriend and move her family to a shelter. Moreover, none of these programs enabled their home visitors to take parents on searches for a decent place for their families to live, or to transport them to mental health counseling programs. We were equally puzzled as to how a program like NFP could dramatically reduce welfare use for the single-parent families it served without having the capacity for providing poor mothers with the education and job training services necessary for them to have a chance at becoming employed.

SEPARATING THE FACTS FROM THE HYPE

These questions led me on a journey to try to make sense of the promises being made by popular home-visiting programs, and how such claims could stand, given the apparent disconnect between the one-size-fits-all interventions that these programs offer and the multiple and longstanding challenges truly disadvantaged families face. What I learned from poring over dozens of sometimes convoluted and contradictory research reports published in academic journals and elsewhere is that each of the four prominent home-visiting programs I described above, and a number of similar, less well-known programs, have been shown to produce some desirable results for the children and families they serve. These results, however, are modest, and few appear to be long-lasting.[5] Given these facts, many early childhood development experts have reached the conclusion that home-visiting programs, at least by themselves, will not make enough of a difference to improve the life chances of vulnerable young children. This is especially so for children in families confronted by the complex challenges and dire stressors of intergenerational poverty.[6] Despite this consensus, numerous books, news magazines, and opinion pieces focusing on strategies to break the cycle of poverty continue to recommend expanding highly promoted home-visiting programs as central to this goal.

A majority of these publications cite one home-visiting program in particular, NFP, as having been proven to solve many of the problems plaguing poor families and improving the life chances of the young children in those families. Here are a few examples of plaudits for NFP from reasonably reliable sources of information.

From a 2009 *Time Magazine* story:

A 1997 study, also in JAMA [Journal of the American Medical Association], found that nurse home visits were associated with a nearly 50% drop in rates of substantiated child abuse or neglect in new families and that visits increased the amount of time between a mother's first and second pregnancies. Rates of hypertension, which is known to interfere with fetal brain development, were also reduced. And mothers spent less time on welfare and worked more.[7]

From the Governor of Delaware's website in 2014:

The initiative is based on over 37 years of research that has found amazing results: a decrease in pre-term deliveries for women who smoke and nearly a 50% reduction in child abuse and neglect cases ... The women are more likely to eat healthy, stop smoking, enroll in school, find work, and achieve better health outcomes for their children.[8]

From a 2009 book on promising strategies for breaking the cycle of poverty by a former U.S. Assistant Secretary of Education:

... the functional and economic benefits of the Nurse-Family partnership program have been, by far, greatest for the families at greatest risk. Tremendous cost savings accrue to the higher risk group ... Interpreting the pattern of results and cost benefits, the program helps to avert many of the most devastating outcomes for this at-risk population.[9]

These compelling testimonials, and dozens more in wide variety of publications, reflect some of the compelling lasting benefits attributed to NFP. The most persuasive benefit promised by the program is that it can save taxpayers large sums of money by reducing poor families' use of government benefits by moving impoverished mothers into the workforce as well by reducing spending associated with juvenile crime. A 2014 column that *New York Times* columnist Nicholas Kristof wrote with Sheryl WuDunn described NFP as "an anti-poverty program that is cheap, is backed by rigorous evidence and pays for itself several times over in reduced costs later on."[10] Claims such as these are widely believed, as they are said to have been proven through decades of rigorous scientific research, using randomized trials. The medical field's gold standard for evaluating the effects of interventions, randomized trials involve randomly assigning study participants to receive an intervention or to one or more control groups. It is also often reported that NFP works best with low-income families at the highest levels of risk.[11]

Through savvy messaging from the program's founder and chief evaluator, David Olds, a professor of pediatrics at the University of Colorado, these claims have made their way into the mainstream press, captured tens of millions of dollars from state and federal government and private foundations, and positioned NFP as a long-sought silver bullet, proven to achieve outcomes essential to breaking the cycle of intergenerational poverty. As a result, the program is being replicated with public funding across the United States at a rapid pace, and moving into other countries as well. Unfortunately, the facts, including those reported in scholarly papers by Olds and his team of NFP study authors, tell a different story. However, most of these facts are buried in the academic journals in which their papers are published. The discrepancies between what is commonly reported about the proven results achieved by NFP and what the studies actually say offer a cautionary tale about the over-zealous promotion of early childhood interventions and antipoverty programs.

Results from Only Three Studies

The claims that I quoted regarding outcomes achieved by NFP, and a plethora of similar claims posted elsewhere, are based on dozens of papers published in numerous academic journals, written by Olds and his team over the past thirty years. Some of these papers and spinoff articles in the mainstream press claim that the proven results of NFP are based on decades of research. What few of the program's most ardent advocates seem to understand, however, is that nearly all of the findings from NFP cited in these papers and articles are from the results of only three studies, one conducted in late 1970s and two studies conducted in the 1990s. The remainder of the research has consisted of follow-up assessments, conducted by Olds and his team, on the children and mothers in these same three studies.[12]

The Initial Study in Elmira

The most impressive results are those reported from the first study that took place in Elmira, New York, beginning in 1978. Olds and his teams enrolled 400 women, pregnant with their first child. Slightly more than a quarter of these women participated in a full course of NFP; they were visited by a nurse an average of once a month during pregnancy and in their child's first two years of life. Researchers divided the remaining mothers into three control groups in which participants received a minimal amount of other services instead of NFP.

Olds and his team tracked and measured numerous outcomes for mothers and children in the Elmira study until the children were nineteen years old. They reported encouraging results in a series of journal articles they published during the first few years after the study. In recent years, some of the conclusions Olds and his team reached regarding the meaning and implications of the results of their studies have been reinterpreted by independent experts, most notably those at the Coalition for Evidence-Based Policy (CEBP). The Coalition, whose mission "is to increase government effectiveness through the use of rigorous evidence about 'what works,'" reviewed the data and how the three studies were conducted. While lauding NFP as having been proven effective through the use of highly rigorous research design, CEBP found some of the conclusions that Olds and his team had trumpeted, such as NFP having conferred important benefits to families that were at higher levels of risk, to be "suggestive" rather than "proven."[13] Nonetheless, CEBP did confirm a number of promising results in its analysis of findings from the initial study of NFP.

CEBP analysts found that in the first study in Elmira, nurse-visited children were about half as likely to experience child abuse or neglect by the time they reached age fifteen compared to their peers in the control groups. These children also had less than half the number of lifetime arrests and criminal convictions by age nineteen. During the fifteen-year period after the birth of their first child, compared with those in the control groups, nurse-visited mothers in the study used welfare an average of three and a half weeks less per year, for a total of thirteen fewer months. These young mothers also reported experiencing 61% fewer arrests and 72% fewer criminal convictions than mothers in the control groups.

It's easy to see how results like these generated a great deal of enthusiasm for NFP. They created the perception that the program not only helps protect disadvantaged children from maltreatment but also saves taxpayers large sums by reducing the likelihood of children and their young mothers committing crimes. These findings also seemed to indicate that the program could achieve even bigger savings by reducing the number of additional births to poor women and increasing their employment, thereby reducing participating families' dependence on welfare and other government benefits.

A Second Study in Memphis

Despite its use of a highly regarded research design to demonstrate compelling results, the initial study of NFP left many unanswered questions. The most important has been whether NFP could be expected to show similar benefits for families who were facing greater numbers of risk factors and for children who were at higher levels of risk for rotten outcomes than those participating in the initial study. In response to these questions, Olds and his team conducted two additional studies of NFP, both in urban communities and with much larger samples of families. They again used gold standard research methods in these subsequent studies, randomly assigning pregnant women to either NFP or control groups.

In 1990, Olds' team enrolled 743 women in the second study of NFP that took place in Memphis, Tennessee. Unfortunately, NFP failed to produce lasting benefits for these mothers and their children that were nearly as persuasive as those reported for families in Elmira.[14] When the Memphis children were twelve years old, those whose families had participated in NFP and were determined to be at higher risk showed slightly higher scores on academic achievement tests and slightly higher grade-point averages.[15] However, these modest impacts did not translate into better educational or social outcomes for nurse-visited children in the Memphis study. As CEBP summarized: "there were no significant effects on these children's conduct outcomes (including arrests), mental health, grade retentions, special education placements, or ability to sustain attention."[16]

Equally disappointing, although there were fewer injuries to children during the period in which nurses were visiting their families, NFP failed to reduce child maltreatment rates over the first twelve years of life for children in the Memphis study.[17] Moreover, the program failed to produce any of the various other results Olds and his team had hoped for, as they noted in one of their journal articles: "We found no program effects on maternal involvement with the criminal justice system, child foster care or kinship care placements, or increased employment among nurse-visited mothers; in fact, the report of child foster care placements, as a trend, was higher in the nurse-visited than control families."[18]

Results for mothers in nurse-visited families in Memphis were also less compelling than those reported in the Elmira study. According to the CEBP's analysis, by the time their first child was twelve, the average amount of time that Memphis NFP mothers had used welfare and food stamps was about two weeks less per year than mothers in the control group.[19] And although participating in

NFP seemed to modestly reduce the number of additional children mothers had during the first six years of their first child's life, there were no significant differences in the number of subsequent births in families by the time the children were twelve.[20] The CEBP summarized the remaining results of the Memphis study of NFP: "There were no significant effects on mothers' time employed, likelihood of partnership with or marriage to the child's biological father, experience of intimate partner violence, substance use, arrests, incarcerations, psychological distress, or child foster care placements."[21]

A Third Study in Denver

Olds and his team conducted the third rigorous evaluation of NFP in the late 1990s, this time with 490 pregnant women in Denver, Colorado, whom they randomly assigned to participate in NFP or to a control group. These results were disappointing as well. Although children classified as being at higher risk showed some encouraging gains in development by age four, those benefits had faded by the time the children were six years old.[22] In follow-up assessments when these higher-risk children were six and nine years old, there were no significant differences between any of the nurse-visited and control-group children on any measure, including emotional and cognitive development, aggressive or rule-breaking behaviors, and school performance.[23]

Follow-up assessments of the Denver study mothers when their children were four years old found that although nurse-visited mothers delayed an average of four months longer before having a second child than did mothers in the control group, this delay had no significant effect on the number of additional births to these women.[24] As CEBP summarized, there were "no significant effects on most of the women's outcomes, including welfare receipt; employment; high school graduation; mental health; substance use; percent married or living with a partner; or number of subsequent births, abortions, miscarriages, or low birth weight newborns."[25]

FEWER BENEFITS FOR FAMILIES AT GREATER DISADVANTAGE

The shrinking benefits for families participating in NFP over the three trials naturally raise the question of why results from the second and third evaluations of the program were far less impressive than those reported for the original study in Elmira. What few of the most enthusiastic proponents of NFP seem to realize is that the families who participated in the first study were markedly different from the families in the other two studies. Approximately 40% of the families in the initial study were not low income and 40% of the mothers were married; 15% had no identified risk factors at all.[26] This tells us that a sizeable portion of families participating in the Elmira study were not struggling with grave economic disadvantages and/or the challenges of single parenthood. Families who participated in the first study starkly contrast with the families in the Memphis and Denver studies, in which nearly all the participating mothers were low income and unmarried. In Memphis, 85% of the mothers came from households with incomes at or below the poverty line, and 98% were unmarried; in Denver, 84% were unmarried and virtually all of the mothers were poor. Given these differences alone, the babies and toddlers in the initial Elmira study, as a group, were at less risk for child maltreatment, school failure, juvenile crime, and other rotten outcomes than were children in the subsequent two studies.

The families in the initial study were different in other ways. Approximately 90% of the mothers participating in the Elmira study were white and therefore didn't face the discrimination and other forms of oppression typically encountered by women of color, especially by those who are also poor. In contrast, 92% of the impoverished mothers in Memphis were African American, and 61% of those in the Denver study were either African American or Mexican American.

Different Environments and Different Eras

Olds and his team describe the section of Elmira in upstate New York where NFP was first tested as semirural. That means that living conditions were very different than for the families in the Memphis and Denver studies, who faced the overcrowded, violence-prone, economically and racially segregated conditions that characterize poor urban communities. It is also important to point out that the Elmira study of NFP was conducted more than thirty-five years ago, long before welfare reform and other policy changes unraveled the safety net for poor families. We can assume that even the more disadvantaged families in the initial study were spared the stress and hardship created by reduced access to government benefits experienced by families in subsequent eras. The first study also predated the flow of crack cocaine and other cheap drugs into poor urban neighborhoods, a development that has increased crime and child maltreatment rates and heightened the stress already experienced by families forced to live in such neighborhoods.

All of these factors help account for the contrasting results between the first study of NFP and those conducted more than fifteen years later in Memphis and Denver. The results of the three studies tell us that NFP worked much better for a group of families from an earlier era who faced minimal risk factors and had more resources than it did for families facing multiple challenges with fewer resources. Despite this fact, NFP continues to be heralded as a cheap and effective, if not miraculous, poverty-fighting strategy for vulnerable families in the current era and continues to garner significant amounts of public and private funding.

Disappearing Cost Savings

Much of this popularity is due to claims that NFP can sharply reduce government spending on welfare benefits for disadvantaged families, as well as on the costs of juvenile crime for both children and mothers. Such savings are unlikely to materialize for two important reasons. First, the more recent studies with much larger, poorer, and racially diverse groups of families found little to no evidence that NFP had any long-term impact on criminal behavior or on known precursors to criminal activity, such as behavior problems, for children or mothers.[27] Even the dazzling reductions in the numbers of arrests and criminal convictions reported for teens from the lower-risk families who had participated in the Elmira study of NFP lose some of their luster when we learn that these outcomes were for female children only; the program had no significant effect on the criminal behavior of boys. Given that boys are far more likely to be to be involved in the juvenile justice system, the reductions in youth crime apparently achieved by NFP in the Elmira study are less compelling.[28] These facts, in addition to NFP having failed, in the more recent Denver and Memphis studies, to demonstrate any significant reductions in known precursors to crime or to actual crimes committed by mothers and by children of either gender, mean that there is little reason to expect NFP to reduce crime and produce resultant cost savings in government spending.

The second reason is that the greatest savings to be realized for taxpayers, according to advocates for expansion of NFP, are in reduced use of government benefits (welfare cash assistance, food stamps, and Medicaid) by families who participate in the program. This is where widespread misunderstanding of the program's outcomes has created the most confusion. In examining the results of the Elmira study, CEBP reports, as I noted above, that by the time children in that study were age fifteen, families participating in NFP spent an average of about three and a half weeks less per year on welfare than did families in the control group.[29] For the more recent Memphis study, by the time their children were age twelve, the average amount of time that nurse-visited mothers had used welfare, food stamps, and Medicaid was about two weeks less per year than mothers in the control group.[30] CEBP calculated that for families in Memphis, participation in NFP resulted in $14,500 (in 2014 dollars) less government spending over twelve years on welfare and food stamps per family. It notes that this figure more than offsets the estimated $13,600 cost of providing NFP to a family.[31] This suggests that although providing NFP to poor families in the current era will not fulfill promises of large savings in government spending, the program would at least pay for itself and save a far more modest amount—about $900—when program costs are deducted from savings in the cost of government benefits.

However, even such a modest prediction of cost savings is unlikely to come true—and here's why. The Elmira study of NFP that showed large cost savings in welfare benefits was launched in the late 1970s, when poor women with young children could count on welfare cash assistance, food stamps, Medicaid, and other government benefits until their youngest child turned eighteen. Additional children born after the first child meant a corresponding increase in the amount of government benefits a family could expect. In this context, keeping large numbers of poor families off public assistance rolls meant substantially reduced government spending on these benefits.

After the Memphis study of NFP was launched in 1990, however, long-term reliance on public assistance was less of a sure thing for poor families, as calls for welfare reform became louder and more widespread. As I recounted in Chapter 3, once the Personal Responsibility and Work Opportunity Reconciliation Act (PRWORA or welfare reform) became law in 1996, states began creating policies to reduce the benefits that needy families could obtain and to limit the number of years a family could receive benefits. By the end of 1997, when children born to mothers in the Memphis study were six or seven years old, these policies had begun to take effect. In the following years, impoverished families in every state found their benefits reduced or eliminated as welfare reform was fully implemented.

We can see welfare reform's role in reducing government spending on poor families even more distinctly in the finding that there were no differences in the use of government assistance programs between nurse-visited and control-group families in the Denver study, which enrolled families in 1998, two years after the enactment of PRWORA. What ardent advocates for expanding NFP fail to realize is that the second and third studies demonstrated that not only will the program fail to save taxpayers' dollars by "paying for itself several times over in reduced costs later on," as Kristof and WuDunn were led to believe, any meaningful amounts of reduced government spending due to benefits from the program are unlikely.

Helping or Harming?

It is important to address one more widely held but mistaken belief about the "proven" cost-saving effects of NFP: that the program reduced families' dependence on government assistance by increasing the employment of participating mothers. This misconception likely stems from claims made by Olds and his team, including those in a 1999 article in *The Future of Children* in which they speculated that for mothers in the Elmira study, "It appears that the reduced rate of subsequent pregnancies positioned these mothers to eventually find work, become economically self-sufficient, and avoid substance abuse and criminal behavior" (p. 61).[32]

Neither in Elmira nor in the latter two studies of NFP did the program demonstrate significantly higher rates or longer durations of employment for nurse-visited mothers. In fact, Olds and his team reported in a journal article published eleven years after their *The Future of Children* paper that in the follow-up assessment of families participating in the Memphis study, they found that "in the 10–12-year period, nurse-visited mothers, as a trend, had *lower* rates of employment [italics mine] than did mothers in the control group" (p. 422).[33] The program failed to increase mothers' employment in the Denver study, and even for the lower-risk sample of families who participated in the initial Elmira study, the CEBP notes that NFP had no significant effect on the number of months participating mothers were employed.[34]

This rarely mentioned finding raises troubling questions not only about whether NFP helps families become self-sufficient (it clearly doesn't) but also about whether the program may have the unintended harmful side effect of discouraging poor mothers from accessing benefits for which their families are eligible. Cash assistance, food stamps, and other government programs such as WIC (a nutrition-supplement program for low-income pregnant women and their infants and young children) play a significant role in preventing hunger and malnutrition in babies and young children. As I pointed out in Chapter 4, not having enough to eat or eating the wrong kinds of food can impair young children's mental and physical development. This is but one of the potential negative consequences of poor families failing to access the government assistance available to them. Having fewer financial resources can also increase families' risk for homelessness and/or increase impoverished mothers' dependence on men who may cause harm to them and/or their children. Failing to access government assistance can increase the risk for child neglect in such families and for children being placed into foster care as a result of their parents being unable to meet their basic needs for housing, safety, and adequate nutrition. This may help explain why NFP-participating families in Memphis had higher rates of foster care placement than families in the control group.

Reductions in the use of government assistance can be beneficial to children in poor families only if they are more than offset by earnings from parents' employment. Otherwise, families using lower amounts of government assistance would likely subject their children to even more deprived upbringings. Not only would that be harmful to already vulnerable children, it could also contribute, ironically, to additional government spending on child maltreatment intervention and foster care, as well as on special education and other services often needed by school-age children who have been raised in severely deprived conditions. No one would argue that long-term dependence on government assistance is good for families; however, what remains of this assistance in the post–welfare reform era is, for many children, a lifeline that helps keep them fed, housed, and healthier and safer than they would be without such benefits.

The results of the Denver study, in which Olds and his team found NFP had no effects on reducing families' participation in government assistance programs, means that we can worry less that such a scenario is taking place for families currently participating in the hundreds of NFP programs throughout the country. However, these same results also further negate claims that the program will save taxpayers money by reducing impoverished families' need for government assistance.

HOW DID THIS HAPPEN?

You are probably wondering by now, as I once did, how there could be such a wide gulf between the significantly higher rates of maternal employment and lower rates of child abuse, the "prevention of devastating outcomes," and the "tremendous" cost savings NFP is widely expected to achieve and what research findings tell us about its actual potential to achieve these outcomes. This disconnect has a number of causes extending beyond the case of NFP that affect how the results from evaluations of a variety of early childhood programs are packaged and marketed.

The Quest for the Silver Bullet

Policymakers and the general public have a strong desire for cheap and simple solutions to complex, longstanding problems. The idea that home visits by a nurse during pregnancy and a child's first two years of life can substantially improve the odds that a poor family will become economically self-sufficient and their child will experience higher levels of school success and avoid criminal behavior is undeniably appealing. It is also farfetched, especially to anyone who works with truly disadvantaged families in the current context.

Such claims obscure the roles that a multitude of factors—as discussed throughout this book—play in maintaining poverty, including racial oppression and a shortage of education and job training programs for parents, and decent, affordable housing, transportation, child care, and mental health services for disadvantaged families, along with the chronic stress of living in violent, under-resourced neighborhoods. Rather than grapple with finding ways to address this complex array of challenges and improve the coordination, effectiveness, and accountability of various programs, elected officials and other policymakers often find it more expedient to buy into the promise of single-dimension programs like NFP, especially when they are convinced that such a program reduces crime and government spending on poor families. It is not surprising that the word "simple" often appears in descriptions of NFP's approach by those singing the program's praises.[35]

Ignoring the Powerful Influence of Context

Part of the reason that NFP is highly touted as a simple remedy for family poverty is that the program is highly standardized so that all participating families receive very similar services, delivered only by nurses, at predetermined intervals, and for a predetermined amount of time. NFP's headquarters allow very limited adaptation of their program model to address the unique characteristics and needs of each family served and of the communities in which the program operates. Instead, any organization wanting to develop an NFP program must agree to use the parent support and training curriculum developed by Olds and his team and deliver that curriculum in much the same way it was delivered in the three, decades-old studies.[36] This type of rigid replication has become known as maintaining fidelity to a program model. The thinking behind this concept is that we can expect a program that has been proven to work in a small number of settings to work as well in additional settings only if it is delivered, in each instance, in a near-identical manner.

The concept of fidelity makes sense in other fields, such as in medicine, whereby we can count on a certain dosage of a vaccine administered to a forty-pound child in Des Moines to provide a near-identical level of immunization when administered to a forty-pound child in Boston. However, such one-size-fits-all approaches are a poor fit for programs addressing problems as complex as intergenerational poverty. Every community has a unique array of resources such as social service, religious, educational, and recreational programs, and opportunities for employ-ment. Further, each disadvantaged community has its own array of challenges, such as high crime rates, housing shortages, and failing schools. As I explained in Chapter 4, these and many other factors affect a family's well-being and the life chances of their children. The context in which families live also affects the success of programs such as NFP, given that linking families with resources in their communities is a key service that these programs provide. The quantity and quality of community-based resources such as health and mental health clin-ics, food pantries, and adult education programs, to which nurses can link disad-vantaged families, helps determine outcomes for NFP-participating families and their children.

Context plays a role within families as well. Every family has its own unique array of resources and challenges. A range of characteristics, including families' religious and cultural identities and practices, the languages they speak, and parents' education levels, affect their participation in social service programs. Common sense tells us that to be effective, programs must be customized to be responsive to the specific needs and wants of the families they serve. A growing body of research tells us the same thing: that programs work best when parents are highly engaged in them, and that parents are more likely to be engaged in programs that closely address the needs important to their families.[37] These find-ings also provide some clues as to why NFP, with its requirement of fidelity (strict adherence to a prepackaged program model), failed to provide much in the way of substantial and lasting benefits to impoverished families in the Memphis and Denver studies.

Whether in health care, social services, or shopping, humans respond better when what is offered to them aligns with what they want. Even McDonald's, which built its empire on providing identical food items to customers all over the world, has been working, in recent years, to customize the interiors of its restau-rants and some of its menu items to match local and regional tastes.

Confusing Strong Research Design with Compelling Outcomes

An additional factor causing widespread misunderstanding of what can be ex-pected of NFP and similar rigorously evaluated programs is the current trend toward fetishizing rigorous research design to the point of failing to pay adequate attention to what the results of that research tell us. This dynamic manifested itself in a conversation I had a few years ago with the director of a family service agency who was enamored by the results promised by NFP. I tried to point out the inconsistent and declining results of the three studies, and concerns about whether worthwhile results could be expected in replication of the program in the post–welfare reform era, especially given the degree to which impoverished families vary, both within and across communities. The more concerns I raised, the more my colleague, nearly jumping up and down, repeated the mantra, "It has gold standard evidence! It has gold standard evidence!" As you might guess, this was not a very productive conversation; however, it helps illustrate the increasingly common tendency to fall so deeply in love with the evaluation methods used in a study that one becomes blinded to what the results actually say.

Unfortunately, this tendency has become widespread among policymakers and public and private funders of social service programs. They frequently misuse the mantra "evidence-based" for separating programs that are worth funding and expanding and those that are not. Within this context, the more rigorous and scientific the research design used to evaluate a given program, the more likely the results will be viewed as proven and the program as evidence-based. In the field of medicine, randomized trials, in which researchers randomly assign study participants to receive either a new treatment or a placebo, does represent a scientifically sound, gold standard method for such research. Of course, just as in medicine, we need to determine whether publicly funded antipoverty programs are effective. The narrow focus on randomized trials to evaluate these programs, however, is problematic for many reasons.

A number of prominent experts in early childhood program research as well as those well versed in program evaluation argue that the restrictions on the types of families to be served and strict adherence (fidelity) to a standardized, one-size-fits-all program model—key elements that lend themselves to evaluation by randomized trials—severely limit a study's applicability to a diverse array of families and contexts. They point out that these studies provide little guidance regarding what highly standardized programs like NFP can be expected to achieve in the current era for the diverse array of vulnerable families across the United States.[38] In a paper for a philanthropy journal, John Bare of the Arthur M. Blank Family Foundation criticized the Obama administration's narrow focus on such programs:

> ... there are no one-size-fits-all solutions to complex social issues. The accountability movement's inclination to codify "what works" and then require the approved protocol to be applied universally has led to the misuse of results of randomized trials and resulted in the failure to maximize impacts. In truth, there are no universal "what works" answers, at least when the programs involve human beings. Instead, sophisticated randomized trials yield evidence on what tends to work for whom, for

how long, under what circumstances, and so on. Every first-year methods student knows this. Yet these qualifications are dropped when account-ability champions, including the White House, look to use evaluation re-sults to select a single "what works" program to implement across the board.[39]

The Center for the Study of Social Policy's Lisbeth Schorr (who is also the former director of the Harvard Project on Effective Interventions) and Daniel Yankelovich (president of the policy think tank Public Agenda) make a similar argument:

> Unfortunately, evaluating complex social programs is not like testing a new drug. The interventions needed to rescue inner-city schools, strengthen families, and rebuild neighborhoods are not stable chemicals administered in standardized doses. Social programs are sprawling efforts with multiple components requiring constant mid-course corrections, the involvement of committed human beings, and flexible adaption to local circumstances. Paradoxically, the very nature of successful programs makes them almost impossible to evaluate as one would a new drug.[40]

Unlike the promising, multifaceted, flexible programs that Schorr has studied for much of her career, NFP is highly standardized, with few opportunities for adapting the program according to the needs of individual families. Because it is so tightly controlled, enrolling only first-time new mothers, delivering a stan-dardized set of services, and using only nurses to deliver the services, NFP lends itself to evaluation by randomized trials much more readily than do comprehen-sive, adaptable programs that address a much wider range of families' needs. Evaluating the latter entails grappling with variability in service providers' dis-ciplines and credentials, the makeup of the families served, and the frequency and duration of service delivery. These are just a few of the challenges inherent in evaluating the "sprawling efforts with multiple components" that characterize more promising, comprehensive programs. Unfortunately, these and other cau-tions have done little to slow the groundswell of support for replicating NFP's one-size-fits-all approach to addressing the needs of impoverished families with young children. Sadly, the rigor-of-study-design and return-on-investment arms race contributes little to our understanding of what type of interventions are likely to work for our most vulnerable young children and their families across a variety of contexts in the current era.

THE CONSEQUENCES OF PROMOTING INADEQUATE PROGRAMS

These dynamics have real-world consequences. For example, in 2009, the Obama administration's first budget blueprint included a provision to allocate up to $8 billion over ten years for NFP, as part of the stimulus package aimed toward pulling the country out of the Great Recession. The budget blueprint noted that the "program has been rigorously evaluated over time" and that "it produces a return on investment [of] between $3 and $6 per dollar invested." Touting their own rigorous studies, the leaders of other widespread home-visiting programs, including those I described earlier in this chapter, lobbied to include expansion of their program models as well. By the time the final budget was approved by Congress, the $8 billion line item for home-visiting programs had been eliminated. Instead, a much smaller but still significant allocation of $1.5 billion to be spent over five years on a variety of "evidence-based" home-visiting programs including NFP was written into the Affordable Care and Patient Protection Act ("Obamacare").[41]

More recently, New York State Senator Daniel Squadron, a Democrat, sought to garner $100 million in new state spending to expand NFP to a larger group of low-income families in that state beyond those already participating in the program. Squadron speculated that if half of the eligible families participated, "the state could save hundreds of millions of dollars."[42] What the article doesn't say, and what Senator Squadron probably didn't know, is that most of such calculations are based on findings reported in papers written by Olds and his team from the three studies with declining benefits that took place two to three decades ago.[43] Moreover, the senator is probably unaware that although the three studies show that NFP may have modest effects on the health and development of some very young children during the time the visits are occurring, the lasting results are even more modest, providing no indication that replicating the program will reduce poverty or result in substantial savings to taxpayers. Scenarios similar to what took place in New York have played out in state houses throughout the country as well as in Washington.[44]

Excluding Children at Higher Levels of Risk

These scenarios are especially unfortunate given that every dollar spent to deliver an inadequate program like NFP could be used to shore up and expand other, more promising approaches that offer customizable and more comprehensive services to a wider array of vulnerable families and to children at higher levels of risk than those NFP serves.[45] In addition to the lack of evidence that NFP is likely to provide much in the way of lasting benefits to families headed by poor, unmarried women in the current era, the program has not been tested on similar families in which mothers are expecting or already have a second or third child. From its inception to its current implementation, the program has limited its services to families of first-time new mothers. As one might expect, families headed by poor, single adolescents with more than one child are among those at the highest levels of risk, yet NFP excludes them from participation.[46] Moreover, as I explained in Chapter 4, young children in families headed by poor mothers who struggle with mental health and/or substance abuse problems and/or are victims of domestic violence are also at grave risk for rotten outcomes, and NFP has not been shown to benefit such children.

There are not nearly enough comprehensive, long-lasting programs to meet the needs of these highly vulnerable families, and funding to develop such programs is hard to come by; so are resources for developing and expanding programs that meet the unique needs of infants and toddlers in foster care, children who are also excluded from NFP.[47] Not only does spending on NFP and other narrowly focused programs draw funds away from expanding the inadequate number of existing programs that focus on these and other high-risk children and families, it also reduces the resources available for developing and rigorously evaluating new program models that hold greater promise.

Adding to the Chaos

In the 1990s, when advocates for NFP and the other home-visiting programs I mentioned at the beginning of this chapter began promoting their favorite program model in Rhode Island, my greatest concern was that bringing additional, inadequate programs to a state that already had several would only add to an already poorly coordinated, fragmented system. During those years, I saw many families of young children who were overwhelmed by various programs and service providers who sometimes provided duplicate services and worked at cross-purposes. I saw even more families who were unable to get any services at all, due to programs' long waiting lists and/or narrow criteria for participation. If things have changed at all in the years since then, they have only become worse, not only in Rhode Island but across the nation.

The causes of poorly functioning systems to support vulnerable families are similar to those that typically plague dysfunctional organizations: turf issues, insufficient expertise, and a lack of visionary leadership. These factors are endemic to government agencies at the federal and state levels. Even in the nation's smallest state, programs and resources for vulnerable families are strewn across several state agencies and poorly organized. This makes it difficult for families to access the services they need and makes the shortcomings and duplication of programs hard for policymakers to identify and fix. Instead of working to replace this chaos with a well-coordinated, transparent, and comprehensive system, public officials too often respond by piling yet another inadequate "program du jour" on top of the patchwork of programs their state already has.

The more fervently a given program is promoted as delivering proven results, the more likely elected officials like Senator Squadron and other policymakers are to believe that they are addressing deep-seated problems. This is not entirely their fault, given all the hype such programs generate and the challenges inherent in untangling the findings of complex research studies. Most of the champions of NFP and other highly promoted programs appear sincere in the desire to improve outcomes for young children in poverty, as well as to reduce government spending on poor outcomes. But when policymakers simply add another weak program to the array of existing programs with similar purposes without first determining whether the new program would complement what already exists, or how best to coordinate services to the families who most need them, it often exacerbates the chaos and dysfunction that characterize the current service system.

The Universal Preschool Movement

Like the home-visiting movement, the call to dramatically expand access to preschool in the United States is driven largely by concerns about growing inequality in young children's school readiness and chances for lifelong success, as well as those regarding the importance of the United States having a well-trained workforce. President Obama, as well as many prominent Democrats throughout the country, including those who ran for president in 2016, have championed proposals to make participation in a preschool program available to all four-year-olds in the United States, regardless of family income. On the surface, this seems like a commonsense proposal to address the inequities in school readiness between poor children and their higher-income peers, especially given that kindergarteners from affluent families are far more likely to have participated in a preschool program than their peers from lower-income families. Less than one half of four-year-olds and one third of three-year-olds in poverty are enrolled in a preschool program.[48] Advocates of universal preschool also cite the importance of improving school success for children across the income spectrum in order to keep up with rising demand for higher skills in the U.S. workforce.

UNIVERSAL OR TARGETED EXPANSION?

Upon close inspection, however, the cost of making preschool universal and its potential to close gaps in school readiness and achievement call into question whether it would be a good investment. Providing publicly funded preschool to all four-year-olds would require annual spending of $13 billion to $16 billion a year in addition to current levels of state spending on public preschool and federal and state spending on Head Start.[49] Making publicly funded preschool universal means that families who can well afford to pay for their child to be in preschool would no longer have to do so, because taxpayers would be shouldering this cost for all four-year-olds.

Advocates for universal preschool maintain that making the program available to all families regardless of income would cement public support for it, much like how the availability of free, taxpayer-funded K–12 education is rarely questioned. They note that universal access would make publicly funded preschool less vulnerable to budget cuts during economic downturns and would help ensure high quality for all by avoiding the all-too-common syndrome of poor programs for poor children. Moreover, advocates point to studies suggesting that children from disadvantaged families tend to do better in early education programs that include children from higher-income families than they do in programs in which all participating children are poor.[50]

Opponents of making publicly funded preschool universal—a group that includes many conservative politicians—cite the high cost, the less-than-compelling evidence of long-term benefits for children who attend Head Start and other publicly funded preschool programs, and what some of them see as further intrusion of government into providing what families should choose or choose not to provide for their children.

While this all-or-nothing debate plays out in Washington and in many state capitals, the more moderate voices advocating for providing publicly funded preschool for children from lower-income groups only are all but drowned out. Making publicly funded preschool available to children from families in the lowest 60% of income levels would require new public investments estimated to be $9.36 billion a year to enroll an additional 1.25 million four-year-olds.[51] This is substantially less than the $13 billion to $16 billion estimate for making free preschool available to all the nation's four-year-olds. The question most pertinent to the discussion here is: What can we expect the expansion of publicly funded preschool programs to achieve for young children from impoverished families?

Early research findings on publicly funded preschool programs suggest that high-quality programs tend to generate larger gains in learning than Head Start and that disadvantaged children may benefit slightly more from such programs than their nonpoor peers.[52] "High quality" is the important term in this discussion. It is extremely challenging for large-scale, publicly funded programs to offer the level of quality that can provide lasting benefits to children living in poverty. A recent study by Vanderbilt University highlights troubling concerns about the benefits of large-scale preschool programs for poor children. Researchers studied 1,076 low-income children in order to evaluate Tennessee's statewide preschool program for low-income children. The program, established to reduce inequities in early learning and school readiness for four-year-olds from low-income families, meets minimum accepted standards for quality, including appropriate student-to-teacher ratios and a well-regarded curriculum. Researchers followed children participating in the preschool program, and those in a control group of children who did not participate, into the third grade.

After a year of Tennessee's preschool program, participating children scored significantly higher on achievement tests in math, language, and literacy than children who did not participate in the program. Participating children also demonstrated higher levels of school readiness, the social and behavioral skills that support school success. However, these differences disappeared in kindergarten, and by the end of first grade, the only difference between children in the two groups was that children who had attended the preschool program demonstrated *lower* levels of school readiness than their control-group peers. Even more discouraging, by second grade, the low-income children who had attended preschool scored somewhat *lower* on most measures of academic achievement and school readiness than children in the control group.[53] These findings caused the study's authors to express caution regarding rapid expansion of preschool programs as a remedy for school readiness gaps between poor and nonpoor children:

> Pre-K intervention has been proposed as one way to address [poverty] and is expanding quickly in many states and with federal endorsement. However, the idea that pre-K can be scaled up quickly, cheaply, and without professional support or vision is certainly bound to be incorrect ... it is not at all obvious that the rush to implement pre-K programs widely without the necessary attention to the quality of the program provides worthwhile benefits to children living in those disadvantaged environments. (p. 42)[54]

HEAD START: PROMISING BEGINNINGS, DISAPPOINTING OUTCOMES

Any discussion of whether participation in preschool makes a difference for children from impoverished families must include an assessment of Head Start, the nation's largest and best-known preschool program for disadvantaged children. Launched in the 1960s as part of the Johnson administration's War on Poverty, Head Start was created to help break the cycle of poverty by providing low-income preschool-age children with "a comprehensive program to meet their emotional, social, health, nutritional and psychological needs."[55] The program was designed to engage not only children but also their parents and community members as stakeholders in the program's success by encouraging parents to volunteer to assist in Head Start classrooms and requiring in-kind resources from the local communities in which it operates. Today, Head Start provides preschool services to approximately 800,000 low-income children across the nation through a variety of models, including full-day, year-round programs, part-day programs, and a combination of home- and center-based programs.[56] The federal government spends around $8 billion annually on the program, with some states also contributing to program costs.

Results from rigorous evaluation of Head Start have been disappointing. Disadvantaged children who participate in Head Start perform better on IQ tests and assessments of academic skills than their non–Head Start peers; however, similar to the preschool program in Tennessee, follow-up studies show that these differences fade during the first few years of elementary school.[57] Various experts have put forth a number of theories regarding why these fadeouts occur. Perhaps the best known of these theories blames the poor quality of many of the elementary schools that low-income children attend after completing Head Start; proponents posit that it is nearly impossible to maintain gains in academic skills while attending underresourced schools with low-quality instruction and little individualized attention. Other theories include speculation that Head Start doesn't do enough to build the social and emotional skills that contribute to school readiness, and that improvements in the quality of child care that poor children receive enable those who haven't attended Head Start to perform similarly to those who do.[58]

After more than fifty years of its operation, the fact that we still have no solid evidence that Head Start makes a lasting difference in the lives of the millions of disadvantaged children it serves every year should be front-page news. I can't help but believe that were Head Start a preschool program for middle- and upper-income children, this lack of evidence certainly would be much better known. But similar to our underfunded and broken child welfare system, the failings of Head Start to substantially improve the life chances of poor children are only occasionally discussed outside of academic circles. When the media do report the program's lackluster outcomes, the progressive politicians who champion government funding for Head Start tend to look the other way, while conservatives who assail the program's shortcomings typically have little to say about improving the program or replacing it with something better.

It is not only public apathy toward programs for the poor that accounts for Head Start's steady expansion despite its disappointing results. In his book *The Sandbox Investment: The Preschool Movement and Kids-First Politics*, David Kirp, a professor of public policy at UC Berkeley, reports on how, similar to what happened with NFP, Head Start's popularity was greatly increased with some skillful marketing to media eager to trumpet relatively simple solutions to intergenerational poverty. Kirp recounts how in the 1970s, due to evaluation findings that most of the educational gains children made in Head Start faded in the early elementary school years, the program was on the federal chopping block, with its budget severely cut and enrollment halved. He speculates that Head Start may have been poised for elimination under the Reagan administration were it not for the publication of a report, *As the Twig Is Bent: Lasting Effects of Preschool Programs*.

The report was written by the Consortium for Longitudinal Studies, a group of researchers who were studying the effects of experimental preschool programs in various parts of the United States. Frustrated that compelling results achieved by some small programs "hadn't shaken the dominant belief that preschool was a proven failure,"[59] the researchers pooled the findings from all of their studies with that of Head Start, which was serving far larger numbers of disadvantaged children than the other programs. *The Twig Is Bent* included information about the fadeout of academic benefits for Head Start but emphasized the finding that across all the programs studied, children attending preschool were less likely than their peers to repeat a grade or be assigned to special education services.

This generally encouraging report had a significant positive impact on Head Start's image. What few outside of the early childhood education research community realized, however, was that among the programs profiled in the report, the one with the most impressive results was the Perry Preschool project, a small, more costly experimental program that served impoverished young children in Michigan. Kirp reports that "Soon enough, the media started attributing to Head Start the successes of Perry Preschool, even though the two programs were similar only in the fact that they both enrolled three- and four-year olds."[60] He shares quotes from various well-regarded mainstream publications touting the benefits of Head Start, including a 1984 *Washington Post* piece on the highly promising outcomes of Perry Preschool that referred to Perry as "a Michigan Head Start program," and this one from a 1987 *New York Times* article: "Head Start, one of the

jewels of the Great Society, has proven that high-quality early childhood education for the disadvantaged produces youngsters much more likely to finish high
school, hold a job, and avoid welfare and crime." In reality, these outcomes were
documented in the rigorous evaluation of Perry Preschool, not that of Head Start.

This second cautionary tale helps explain why, at least until the late 1990s,
when conservatives began figuring out the ruse, Head Start enjoyed hearty bipartisan support in Congress and with much of the American public. Even today, advocates often cite the impressive results of Perry Preschool and a few other small,
high-quality preschool programs in promoting public funding for expanding preschool programs, and even in promoting other early childhood programs such as
NFP, that serve children younger than preschool age. Unfortunately, what gets
lost in this messaging is the many dramatic ways in which the Perry Preschool
program differed not only from Head Start, but also from the vast majority of
preschool and other early childhood programs currently available to disadvantaged young children. Similar to what happened with NFP, an understanding of
the many changes in the context for such children in the fifty years since the
Perry program was piloted also has been lost in the hype.

WHAT IT TAKES TO ACHIEVE MEANINGFUL, LONG-TERM RESULTS

The Perry Preschool program was launched in Ypsilanti, Michigan, in 1961. Over
a four-year period, it enrolled approximately sixty three-year-old children into
an intensive, two-year program. All of the children were black and from impoverished families. As was the case with NFP and some similar home-visiting programs, the evaluation of the Perry Preschool program was noteworthy, as it used
randomized trials in which a group of children with similar characteristics were
randomly assigned either to attend Perry Preschool or to a control group. What
made this study truly remarkable, however, is that program evaluators followed
most of the participating children as well as their control-group peers into mid-
adulthood to age forty.

The outcomes for children who participated in Perry Preschool speak for themselves. In elementary and secondary school, they were significantly less likely to
repeat a grade or receive special education services, and their grade-point averages were consistently higher than their control-group possessive. Two thirds of
participating children graduated from high school compared to 45% of the children in the control group. At the age of forty, twice as many Perry participants
had completed college and 76% of them were employed, compared to 62% of those
in the control group. Participants earned 25% more income, were more likely to be
homeowners, and were less likely to have used welfare. Half as many of the Perry

participants had gone to prison or jail than did their control-group peers, and almost twice as many of them had raised their own children rather than having them raised by relatives or foster or adoptive parents.[61]

Small wonder that advocates of a plethora of early childhood programs wrap their programs in the mantle of Perry Preschool outcomes. What often goes unmentioned in the marketing efforts, however, is how Perry Preschool differed from the vast majority of today's preschool and other early childhood programs in important ways. Adjusted for inflation, this program cost about double per child than does Head Start. Funding at that level enabled the founders of Perry Preschool to hire teachers with college degrees, something relatively rare at the time, and pay them well. This contributed to the quality of what took place in classrooms and reduced the teacher turnover rate; this is a particularly important factor, given that high turnover is a common scourge of poorly funded programs. Class sizes were small to facilitate low student-to-teacher ratios and individualized learning, and the Perry curriculum was carefully constructed to focus on teaching children how to learn, rather than the "skill and drill" approach of many of today's programs. Moreover, the teachers made weekly visits to the children's homes in order to build strong school–family relationships and to encourage parents to read to their children and stimulate learning in a variety of other ways.[62]

ANOTHER EXAMPLE OF WHY CONTEXT MATTERS

There are a number of possible reasons—in addition to poorly paid teachers and large classroom sizes—why the current cadre of preschool programs aimed toward disadvantaged children is unlikely to achieve results anywhere near those of Perry Preschool. Some of these stem from the fact that the findings from the Perry Preschool study are more than fifty years old. As I noted earlier in this chapter regarding the three studies of NFP, the context for disadvantaged families has changed dramatically over the past few decades, much of it for the worst. This is especially so for families living in impoverished urban communities, where neighborhood segregation, crime rates, and the quality of housing have worsened, the availability of cheap drugs has increased, and decent-paying low-skilled jobs have all but disappeared.

In the absence of recent, rigorous studies, we have no way of knowing what results a program even as well designed and well resourced as Perry Preschool, by itself, would achieve in the face of these daunting risk factors. As is the case with home-visiting programs, the success of preschool programs targeting disadvantaged children depends in part upon the quality and availability of various other resources, such as education and job training programs for parents, health and mental health services, and affordable housing, to which these programs can link the families they serve. Their impacts also rely on the availability of early care and education programs for disadvantaged infants and toddlers in a given community, and the quality of learning that takes place for participating children well before they enter preschool. Moreover, given that it was tested only on African American children, there is no way to know how well a Perry Preschool–like program would work with poor white children or those from families who were among the waves of immigrants from Central and South America, parts of Africa, and Southeast Asia who have arrived in the United States in large numbers over the past fifty years.

As with NFP and the other home-visiting programs I discussed earlier in this chapter, these are among the many contextual factors that help determine a program's success in improving the life chances of the disadvantaged young children it targets. To use the medical metaphor one more time, unlike the protective effects of a vaccine, there is no way to adequately evaluate the effects of a human service program in isolation from the conditions and resources that surround its participants. How children fare and the level to which they benefit from a program depend in part on whatever additional resources are available to these children and what else is happening in their families, schools, and communities.

RESOURCES MATTER

Although we can expect—given all of these contextual factors—that outcomes for the Perry Preschool program, delivered in the same way it was in the 1960s, would vary from those achieved in the original study, the Perry study provides compelling evidence that a comprehensive, well-developed, properly funded early childhood program *can* make important lasting differences in the lives of highly disadvantaged children. So does another often-cited model, the Abecedarian Early Childhood Intervention Project that operated in Chapel Hill, North Carolina, in the 1970s. As with the Perry Preschool study, the evaluation of the Abecedarian program enrolled a relatively small group of poor children (fifty-seven), most of whom were black, and followed these children and a group of similar children for a number of years (to age twenty-one, compared to age forty for the Perry participants).[63]

The Abecedarian project provided services that were far more long-lasting and comprehensive than even those provided by Perry Preschool. Children were enrolled as infants and participated in the full-day, year-round early care and learning project for an average of five years. The program focused on all aspects of child development, provided transportation, and included regular visits to children's homes. In the classrooms, teacher–child ratios were one to three for infants and one to six for older children. Participants in the Abecedarian project scored significantly higher on achievement tests in math and science than their control-group peers throughout their elementary and secondary school years. At age twenty-one, they were nearly three times as likely to have attended college and half as likely to have become teen parents. Program participants were also far more likely to be working at a good job.[64]

It is not by happenstance that important and lasting outcomes from the Perry Preschool and Abecedarian projects correspond with the higher costs of these programs when compared with Head Start and other preschool programs. A year of Perry Preschool would now cost approximately $20,000 per child and the Abecedarian program anywhere from $16,000 to $40,000 per child, compared to approximately $8,000 per child taxpayers were spending for a year of Head Start.[65] Higher levels of per-child funding enabled the former two programs to offer more comprehensive services, hire and retain better-trained teachers, and keep teacher-to-student ratios much lower than in Head Start. In contrasting the Perry Preschool program to Head Start and other poorly funded preschool programs, Stephen Barnett, head of the National Institute for Early Education Research (NIEER), lamented to Kirp, "It's so far from what we do. Let me run a program where I get to hire two teachers for every twelve kids and pay them public school salaries. I'll bet my retirement plan on the outcome. Instead, we pay teachers a pittance, give them eighteen kids and an assistant who is just a high school graduate—and then there are complaints that the results haven't been replicated!"[66] (p. 58).

According to a report by NIEER, in 2013 and 2014, state-funded preschool programs served nearly 1.35 million three- and four-year-olds in the forty-one states that have such a program. Only eight of those states spent as much or more per child per year than the nearly $8,000 per child spent by Head Start for that same time period. It is also worth noting that eighteen states that fund some form of preschool cut funding to their programs in 2013. The situation in Florida demonstrates the public and political ambivalence attached to publicly funded preschool. After voters approved a measure to create a statewide universal program, the Florida legislature eliminated a high-quality preschool program serving disadvantaged children and replaced it with a much weaker program available to all children. Lawmakers allocated a pitifully small per-child expenditure to its universal program that amounted to $2,238 in 2013. In that same year, Florida cut funding to the program by almost $13 million.[67] We should be skeptical regarding the levels of quality that can be expected of publicly funded preschool programs unless the government adequately funds them and establishes and enforces strict quality standards.

REDUCING OR EXTENDING DISPARITIES?

There are other troubling questions regarding the potential impacts of universal preschool as a strategy for closing the achievement gap. Given the racial and economic segregation of neighborhoods in our impoverished inner cities and the poor quality of many of the schools in such neighborhoods, what can we expect regarding the quality of publicly funded preschool programs offered in those communities? As is the case with most public schools, would the quality of the preschool programs and the level of school readiness they impart be determined by a child's address? And what would happen to Head Start? Using public funds to provide higher-quality preschool programs while permitting Head Start to continue as is, serving large numbers of poor children with a track record of modest benefits, most of which appear to fade in elementary school, would likely expand rather than narrow the school-readiness gap between poor and nonpoor children.

To be clear: Publicly funded universal preschool may hold promise for improving the overall academic achievement of American schoolchildren, thus helping the nation compete in the global marketplace. But the large-scale models that exist in various states and those being advanced by many advocates of universal preschool do *not* appear to hold promise as a remedy to the wide gaps in school readiness and achievement between poor and nonpoor children. Follow-up studies of children participating in Perry Preschool, the Abecedarian project, and other intensive programs carefully designed to meet the needs of disadvantaged children and their families, suggest that such programs—adapted for families in the current era—may provide important, lasting benefits to disadvantaged children. They tell us that the most effective programs are likely to be those that go well beyond a narrow focus on raising test scores, by helping young children learn how to learn and by engaging families in their children's education.

Unfortunately, universal preschool, as it is currently being promoted, appears to represent a form of trickle-down education, providing a modest boost to everyone in hopes that those at the bottom will be boosted as well. Although some studies suggest that disadvantaged children may benefit slightly more than other children, we have reason to doubt whether those benefits will last and whether large-scale preschool programs can be expected to have meaningful impacts on preventing poor outcomes for children from the most disadvantaged families. Based on what we know so far, implementing universal preschool runs the risk of mainly pushing down, from age five to age four, the existing school-readiness gap between poor and nonpoor children.

An equally grave concern is that putting most of our early childhood intervention dollars in the universal preschool basket is likely to perpetuate our nation's neglect of the prenatal period through the first three years of disadvantaged children's lives as starting points for intervention and support. The lackluster results of NFP and the other home-visiting programs discussed earlier in this chapter, compared to the meaningful and lasting results of the much more long-term and comprehensive Abecedarian program, tell us that there is much work to be done in this area. Yet funding remains scarce to develop new, comprehensive models of early childhood intervention programs that target infants and young children from highly disadvantaged families, and to test these models in the current era and over time, much like the founders of the Abecedarian project were able to do. So do resources to shore up more promising but still inadequate models of early childhood intervention like Early Head Start, which I discuss in the next chapter. This will not change as long as the American public, the media, and policymakers are being led to believe that yawning gaps between the life chances of poor and nonpoor children can be closed by simple solutions, among them universal preschool and the current cadre of popular home-visiting programs.

Fueling Cynicism

As I've noted previously, a large portion of the public and many politicians are highly skeptical of both antipoverty and early childhood programs. Conservative politicians often cite the modest and fleeting outcomes of Head Start—which, like NFP, is promoted as both an antipoverty and early childhood development program—as evidence that government funding of such programs is a waste of taxpayers' money. Elected officials too often exploit the mantra about the wastefulness of "throwing money" at ineffective programs for the poor to justify cutting or eliminating antipoverty programs. Any new initiatives to help poor families, including those I propose in the next chapter, must overcome this cynicism among both policymakers and voters in order to attract adequate government support. This is a very high hurdle. It is hard to watch the mythmaking regarding NFP follow a similar trajectory to that of Head Start, the poster-child program for what many conservatives have come to see as wasteful spending on antipoverty programs for families with young children.

It's well past time to heed the cautionary tales of Head Start, NFP, and other early childhood programs whose results fail to match what policymakers and the public expect them to accomplish. Overhyping the modest benefits to be expected from home-visiting programs, universal preschool, and other programs can only contribute to the widely held belief that nothing works in breaking the cycle of intergenerational poverty. The wide gap between the relatively small and often-fleeting benefits of such programs and the lasting, transformative outcomes they promise gives those intent on eliminating resources and supports for poor families additional justification for doing so. These discrepancies also make it more challenging to access public funding for developing and bringing to scale new programs that hold greater promise for improving the life chances of vulnerable young children in the current era.

In the next chapter, I provide a description of what such programs should offer vulnerable children and their families and how these services and supports should be delivered, drawing upon what we have learned from the evaluations of Head Start, universal preschool, and home-visiting programs, including NFP.

7 We're Gonna Need a Bigger Boat

STRONGER, BETTER PROGRAMS FOR BREAKING THE CYCLE

GIVEN THAT MOST of what maintains high rates of child and family poverty in the United States is structural—that is, it stems from ineffective, outdated, and/or oppressive policies—much of what needs to be done lies in the policy arena. In the final chapter I discuss a range of policy changes necessary to get at the roots of poverty and make significant inroads toward eliminating its shameful presence in our nation. Before doing so, however, I believe it's important to explore what can be done at the programmatic level to ensure that resources aimed at improving the life chances of impoverished young children are spent in a way that ensures the best possible results for these children and their families.

In this chapter, I examine strategies for building, expanding, and evaluating programs that hold greater promise for improving the well-being and life chances of young children growing up in poverty than programs currently in place. These extra-strength approaches utilize findings from brain development and other areas of research, along with what we have learned from newer approaches to delivering services designed to meet the complex needs of these children and their families in the current era. I also discuss strategies for funding these approaches and examine the issue of accountability. In accomplishing the latter, I present recommendations for shifting away from our current overreliance upon and misuse of randomized trials as the imprimatur of evidence of a program's value and toward an expanded array of evaluation methods that are a better match for the multipronged programmatic approaches that breaking the stubborn cycle of poverty requires.

How We Got Here

By now it should be clear that what stands in the way of making progress in building effective programs that help break the cycle of intergenerational poverty is another cycle that seems nearly as intractable. This one is characterized by the insistence that there are simple, cheap fixes for the complex array of interconnected problems poor families face; the fetishizing of medical-model, randomized trials to determine which programs work; rising levels of public and political cynicism regarding antipoverty interventions; and the miserly allocation of funding for identifying and building real solutions. While each aspect of this cycle reinforces and propels the others, our child poverty rate remains stubbornly high, with millions of young children left on the path toward rotten outcomes. Instead of a functional system that addresses the complexity of chronic poverty and of the lives of the children and families it ensnares, impoverished families must rely, in most communities, on a patchwork of disconnected programs and initiatives, each with its own eligibility criteria and each focusing on one or just a few aspects of the problem.

This disconnect helps maintain poverty and high levels of child and family vulnerability. For example, young, single parents may obtain food stamps to help feed their families, but without transportation to a grocery store and help with learning how to make nutritious meals on a tight budget, they have no better option than to squander them on overpriced junk food at the local convenience store. Such a mother may be referred to a work readiness program but find herself unable to access mental health services for treating the severe depression that makes it nearly impossible for her to get out of bed. Another such mother may enroll in a GED program to complete her high school studies in order to get a job, only to lose her GED slot while the state takes weeks to approve a child care voucher for her two young children. As I was describing these and other scenarios commonly inflicted on impoverished families by the disjointed, inadequate array of services that passes for a system in most communities, a friend observed, "That's like giving a family a car—one part at a time." Unfortunately, the analogy is an apt one. Just as obtaining a series of auto parts would leave all but the most gifted mechanic among us without the means to drive anywhere, the erratic trickle of disconnected services and resources available to disadvantaged families doesn't add up to a coherent means for escaping poverty's stubborn grasp.

There are a number of reasons for this unfortunate state of affairs. We can place considerable blame on the funding siloes in Washington and in every state, whereby resources aimed toward disadvantaged families with young children are administered by a labyrinth of separate departments with poor coordination and limited oversight. Another major problem is that state and federal government agencies and private foundations are focusing too much attention and resources on hoped-for silver bullets—standardized, single-service antipoverty and child development approaches that easily lend themselves to replication and "gold standard" evaluation. This leaves few resources available for the development of innovative, comprehensive models that build on the strengths present in even the most vulnerable families and that address multiple needs simultaneously rather than piece by piece.

The academic world contributes to the problem by overemphasizing randomized trials in evaluating one-size-fits-all program models, models that lend themselves to publishable research papers but fail to do enough to improve the long-term prospects of many of the families these programs target. Moreover, experts analyzing the results of such programs haven't done enough to inform policymakers and foundation leaders about the inadequate results, compared with the level of need in the most vulnerable families, that many of these models produce. Adding to the problem is the little space granted for the perspectives of practitioners on the front lines of service delivery, who witness the daily struggles of poor families amidst a chaotic and inadequate service and resource "system." These professionals have a great deal to contribute to the planning and evaluation of the programs in which they labor, but they are often sidelined as capable of offering only nonscientific, anecdotal information about how their programs operate. Equally unfortunate is that the voices, needs, and preferences of families targeted by various antipoverty and child development initiatives—if they are heard at all—play a very small role in determining the shape and scope of such programs.

Time for a New Approach

It is well past time for a different approach, one that recognizes the inadequacy of the current piecemeal array of programs and services for making meaningful and lasting differences for children and families with extreme and multiple needs. We must move beyond reflexively embracing any intervention that has evidence of even paltry benefits for vulnerable children and families as the remedy for meeting these complex needs. This means digging beneath the headlines touting relatively cheap, simple solutions in order to understand what those benefits were, under what conditions they occurred, and for which children and families. Most importantly, we must understand that a program that has been shown, even through gold standard evaluation methods, to benefit disadvantaged children and families in past eras and/or produce benefits that do not lead to improved life chances is not necessarily a better investment than a newer, more promising approach that is being rigorously evaluated with methods other than randomized trials.

USING WHAT WE KNOW TO INFORM WHAT WE DO

Over the past fifteen years, consensus has deepened among practitioners working with families in impoverished communities across the country, as well as experts studying the effects of programs targeting such families, regarding the need for more powerful and comprehensive approaches to addressing these challenges. In its seminal 2000 report *From Neurons to Neighborhoods*, the National Research Council called for a fundamental rethinking of our approach to the needs of vulnerable young children and their families. It noted that many of the prominent programs in place at that time had been created in previous eras, achieved relatively modest results, and utilized little of what research had to say regarding the more powerful types of interventions that should be developed. Ten years later, lamenting the slow progress in this area, Jack Shonkoff, one of the report's two editors, observed that

> . . . *large numbers of young children and families who are at greatest risk, particularly those experiencing toxic stress associated with persistent poverty complicated by child maltreatment, maternal depression, parental substance abuse, and / or interpersonal violence, do not appear to benefit significantly from existing programs* [Shonkoff's italics]. Highly disorganized parents are less likely to seek services and more likely to drop out of programs when they do enroll. When they are successfully engaged, the needs of families facing exceedingly complex social and economic disruptions typically overwhelm conventional early childhood program staff whose expertise is restricted to child development and parenting education. Consequently, the evaluation literature on interventions for children in highly distressed families, such as programs for children who have been victims of abuse or neglect, reveals relatively limited evidence of success (MacMillan et al., 2007). (p. 361)[1]

Shonkoff, along with a growing number of his colleagues, are calling for innovation and experimentation to create and test programmatic strategies that respond to the needs of the most vulnerable children and families in order to "close the gap between what we know and what we do right now" (p. 362).[2] What do we know? Research tells us that relationships—between service providers and parents, and parents and their children—matter greatly, and that the quality of caregiving a young child receives affects his or her life-long physical and emotional health, and that when caregivers—be they parents, foster parents, or child care teachers—have the support and assistance they need, they are much better equipped to nurture the children in their care. Research findings also confirm what practice experience, along with common sense, tell us: that chronic and complex problems require long-term and multifaceted interventions

In a 2014 report entitled *An Evidence Framework to Improve Results,* the Center for the Study of Social Policy's Lisbeth Schorr and its director, Frank Farrow, along with Joshua Sparrow of Boston's Brazelton Touchpoints Center, echo Shonkoff's call for better solutions and cite a number of initiatives across the nation that are employing multiple interventions in carefully coordinated ways to address the needs of those most vulnerable. They synthesized research findings and the observations of those working on the frontlines providing services to such families to identify common attributes of what they call complex interventions—those that hold promise for addressing the tougher problems faced by so many of today's highly vulnerable families:

- They are not targeted only on individuals, but aim to change families, neighborhoods, larger communities, norms, and systems.
- They pursue multiple, intertwined, and even unanticipated goals.
- They involve collaboration across professional and organizational boundaries.
- They seek to reform systems to respond to the complex environments and cultures that influence outcomes.
- They rely on subtle and hard-to-measure effectiveness factors, including trusting and respectful relationships.
- They deal with issues not inherent within a program model.
- They devise solutions uniquely suited to their particular time, place, and participants.
- They integrate proven and promising practices with ongoing activities. (p. 5)[3]

Programs that embody most of these attributes are a far cry from tightly controlled, one-size-fits-all interventions such as the home-visiting programs I examined in Chapter 6 and what's typically offered in universal preschool programs. Because they were developed more recently and offer a wide range of services that adapt to the needs of those they set out to serve, the programs Schorr and her colleagues highlight are not nearly as well known as NFP and similar home visiting programs or Perry Preschool. And because they offer a multifaceted response to the complexities that characterize the lives of the individuals and families they target, we probably won't see them written up in newspapers and magazines as cheap, simple solutions to poverty or the other problems these programs target. Moreover, the expectation that such programs will be adapted and customized when transferred to other communities beyond those for which they were originally developed makes it challenging for economists to conduct elegant return-on-investment analysis on them.

And so we have a situation in which the very characteristics that make programs promising are the same characteristics that make it difficult to bring these approaches to prominence. It's important that we overcome this dilemma. In efforts to do so, Shonkoff, Schorr and her colleagues, and a number of other experts are working to inform public policymakers as well as leaders of major foundations regarding the importance of supporting innovation and experimentation in building and testing more powerful programmatic approaches aimed toward breaking the cycle.[4]

TARGETING YOUNG CHILDREN AT GREATEST RISK

There is no reason to believe that a preschool or other type of program designed to meet the needs of nonpoor children will have the capacity to substantially improve the prospects of children living in the midst of the extreme stress and hardship that poverty creates.[5] If the past few decades of breakthroughs in research tell us anything, it is that the needs of the latter group of children are far more extensive than those in the general population, and outstrip the capacity of most existing early intervention programs. Shonkoff and others have concluded that a key reason the current cadre of popular programs are largely ineffective with highly vulnerable children and families is because they fail to take into account lessons from recent research on the multiple ways in which poverty affects and harms young children.

Those advocating for making programs universal as a way to protect them from being underfunded or eliminated, as is often the case for initiatives targeting only those who are disadvantaged, offer some compelling arguments. However, it is time to challenge the conventional wisdom that the voting public will not support high-quality programs unless they are available to poor and nonpoor children alike. It is well worth considering that it may not be the lack of universal availability that dooms programs aimed toward helping the poor, but rather the lack of evidence that such programs make real and lasting differences in lives of the individuals and families they target.

I believe there is a good chance that a larger segment of the public would support investments in programs aimed toward impoverished children and their families if these programs were to demonstrate their effectiveness is making lasting, meaningful differences in outcomes for children in these families. Of course, in an ideal world (or at least in a more collectively oriented, less individualistic nation), there wouldn't be a choice of whether to make further investments on behalf of all children or only those who are most vulnerable. We *should* have publicly funded preschool available for all children and a range of supports for any family that needs them, along with far more intensive interventions for those at greatest risk. However, given that the portion of public dollars aimed toward improving the lives of children and their families will always be relatively small—at least in comparison to, say, the hundreds of billions we spend each year on defense—it makes the most sense to tightly target these resources toward significantly reducing the number of poor children who experience lousy outcomes.

This means casting a laser-like focus on the challenges faced by the most vulnerable children and families—those living in extreme poverty and/or at risk for or experiencing child maltreatment, and those headed by poor parents struggling with substance abuse and other mental health problems and/or domestic violence. It is also important to target fragile families headed by young teens who have few social and economic supports, and the families of young parents who have aged out of the foster care system. There is plenty of evidence to show that the future outlook for young children in these families is especially grim. What's needed are intervention strategies that are up to the task of addressing the chronic and severe challenges such families face in order to help improve outcomes for their children.

Follow-up evaluation of well-crafted early childhood and family support programs from past eras—such as Perry Preschool and the Abecedarian project—tell us that such programs can improve the lives of such children and their families. They also tell us that we need stronger programs to address the longstanding and multiple problems confronting today's highly vulnerable families. As Shonkoff points out, "All available information points to the same conclusion: intervention in the early years can make an important difference, and the magnitude of policy and program impacts must be increased" (p. 365).[6]

Building and Sustaining Stronger Approaches

How do we go about increasing "the magnitude of policy and program impacts" for the most vulnerable young children and families? We can begin by making adequate investments in the development and testing of far more substantial intervention strategies. I call these more extensive and intensive, and carefully coordinated services "extra-strength" approaches in order to distinguish them from the unidimensional "services lite" typically offered by most of our early care and education and family support programs. The term extra-strength also signifies that the most promising strategies recognize and build upon the strengths to be found in even the most vulnerable families, rather than incorporate the deficits-based approach present in too many of the current cadre of programs.

I offer recommendations for two programmatic approaches for making truly substantial progress in breaking the cycle of disadvantage:

1. Develop and test comprehensive and customizable extra-strength family support programs that hold promise for making meaningful and lasting improvements in the lives of highly vulnerable young children and their parents.
2. Develop and test a cadre of extra-strength early care and education programs, including specialized preschool programs for highly vulnerable children, specifically designed to help such children overcome the disadvantages of early life poverty and build resilience.

I provide a brief description here of each of these proposed program initiatives, highlighting key elements that enhance the likelihood of effectiveness with today's impoverished families.

Extra-Strength Family Support Programs

Family support programs are those that help parents nurture their children, support early learning and development, and help families with a range of needs and challenges. Most of these programs deliver services during visits to the homes of participating families, and many include opportunities for the families served to come together periodically for mutual learning and support. Over the past two decades, consensus among program practitioners and other experts has grown regarding many of the key principles and characteristics that family support programs should employ to help break the cycle of poverty among highly vulnerable families with young children.[7] I have integrated these into a set of elements that define extra-strength family support programs. These programs:

- *Target the needs of both young children and their parents, going far beyond addressing parents primarily as their child's caregiver and first teacher to assist parents with their own physical and mental health needs, as well as their educational and employment needs.* Like NFP, most of current cadre of large-scale family support programs engage parents primarily in their child caring role and fail to adequately address the multiple challenges poor parents face, including substance abuse and other physical and mental health problems, unemployment, and domestic violence. There is good reason to believe that this omission plays a significant role in the failure of many of these programs to produce meaningful and lasting benefits to children in the families they serve. To improve the life chances of vulnerable young children, programs must also help parents overcome their own impairments and address their educational and work readiness needs. Such an approach acknowledges the obvious: that children are more likely to do well when cared for by parents whose own needs are met, are physically and mentally healthy, have adequate social support, and are either financially self-sufficient or working toward becoming so.
- *Focus on helping parents understand their children's physical, social, emotional, and cognitive development, and offer customized support and training to parents in how best to promote their child's learning and emotional health.* Every parent and every child is unique. Instead of offering a predetermined curriculum to train parents on how best to nurture their children, programs should include an assessment of parents' strengths and needs in their role as their child's first teacher. This enables service providers and parents to create a customized plan for building on parents' strengths in helping them learn how to support optimal development for their children. It is important that these efforts work to strengthen both the quality and the quantity of nurturance parents provide to their babies and young children.
- *Screen young children for the effects of trauma and for signs of developmental delays and ensure that those affected receive appropriate services at the earliest possible point.* Trauma is common among children who have witnessed family and/or community violence, and especially among maltreated children who have been in foster care. Programs must ensure that affected

children receive specialized mental health services designed to help protect them from the lasting harm that experiencing trauma, especially early in life, can cause.[8] Family support programs must also ensure that children are screened for signs of delays and other problems in their development and are linked to the early intervention services to which children with disabilities are entitled, under federal law, during their first three years of life. Such services, when delivered early in life and over an extended period of time, can play a significant role in reducing or preventing the harmful lifelong impacts of disabilities.

- *Help families access high-quality early care and education programs and encourage good communication between parents and their children's early care and education teachers.* High-quality care, when combined with the comprehensive services of an extra-strength family support program, is essential to the healthy development of impoverished young children whose parents work or are participating in education or job training programs. Moreover, positive and productive communication between parents and their child's early care and education teachers helps optimize children's learning and development.

- *Take the time to learn about these and other characteristics of each family before services are planned and initiated.* Asking parents about their needs, goals, and desires and paying attention to their responses help parents to engage and commit to participating in family support programs. Moreover, such an approach avoids the confusion and stress that occur when families are inundated with services they neither want nor need, as well as the wasteful duplication of services provided to families by multiple, similarly focused programs.

- *Demonstrate respect for parents as the leaders of their families and acknowledging that the majority of even the most troubled parents want to do the best possible job in caring for and raising their children*

- This includes actively engaging fathers, regardless of whether they reside in the same home as their children, as well as grandparents and other adults acting in a parenting role. Studies show that parents participate more enthusiastically in services when they feel respected and heard by service providers, when their strengths are acknowledged, and when the needs they identify are being addressed. Research also links high levels of parent engagement in services with positive outcomes for their children.[9]

- *Honor and respect families' ethnic, cultural, and religious traditions; identify sources of support and resilience within these traditions; and tailor interventions accordingly.* Families feel respected when practitioners treat differences in these characteristics as potential sources of strength rather than deficits that must be overcome. Demonstrating respect also means providing services in the language family members are most comfortable using, and taking the time to understand a family's relationship with their church, clan, tribe, civic organizations, and similar groups to which family members may belong.

- *Offer a range of services customized to each family's unique needs, strengths, resources, and desires.* This array would typically include mentoring, counseling, and employment training and assistance for parents; linkage to quality early care and education for children; demonstrating activities that encourage healthy development for children; and providing crisis intervention, advocacy, and linkage to a wide range of additional services. The needs and resources of each family should determine the amount of time program practitioners spend delivering these and other services to a given family. Programs must be sufficiently flexible to spend more time with families in the midst of crises, such as when a family is being evicted from their home, than they do with families during periods of relative stability.

- *Provide services to families in their own homes whenever possible to ensure that families have access to assistance in an environment that is comfortable for them.* Some parents find the offices of social service agencies to be intimidating, and many impoverished families lack reliable, hassle-free transportation, making it difficult to arrive at appointments on time. For these reasons, and also because families are typically more relaxed in their own homes, family support services are most effectively delivered there. Extra-strength family support programs should augment home visits with opportunities for parents to come together so that the individualized parent training and mentoring they provide is reinforced by opportunities for social support and mutual learning with other parents.

- *Maximize the benefits of resources available in a family's community by helping families access needed services, and carefully coordinate all services to ensure that they are beneficial to each family served.* It is usually not enough to simply give impoverished parents the phone number of a program or other resource they need, as many service providers do. Many disadvantaged parents are ill equipped to work their way through the maze of recorded messages and menus and the various barriers that prevent them from accessing these resources. Low levels of education and limited English-speaking ability make this process even more intimidating for a large portion of poor parents. That is why it's important to assist parents who face such challenges by helping to make phone calls, set up appointments, and arrange transportation. Service providers must also be willing to advocate on families' behalf to ensure they have access to the resources they need. Close collaboration with those providing additional services to families helps ensure that all service providers are on the same page and that young children, particularly those who are most vulnerable, do not fall through the cracks that separate various programs and services.

- *Have the capacity to work with families on a long-term basis to generate the many positive changes that productive and trusting relationships between parents and service providers can yield.* A dearth of reliable and responsive relationships and chronically unmet needs underlie many of the challenges highly vulnerable parents face. Because of this, it is not possible to address these challenges and help troubled families get on a steady path of well-being and financial stability through short-term intervention. Therefore, programs must commit to working with these families for the long haul. Equally important, parents who lack supportive and encouraging relationships are far less able to provide essential nurturance to their young children than parents whose needs for support are met. Given what we know about how important warm, nurturing parent–child relationships are to healthy child development, programs must do all that they can to ensure that vulnerable parents have adequate social and emotional support—something that can only be accomplished over a substantial period of time.

- *Utilize multidisciplinary teams in order to offer an array of services that can be customized for each family served*

- Given that every family has a unique set of needs and resources and that the difficulty of the challenges each family faces varies even among highly vulnerable families, programs must have teams of service providers with diverse skills and expertise available to effectively address those challenges. Master's-level social workers typically are best prepared for addressing domestic violence as well as substance abuse and mental health problems in both children and parents. Nurses bring skills for teaching parents about adequate nutrition and ways to safely care for their children. Early childhood educators help parents understand their children's development and support and encourage optimal development of social and learning capacities. Paraprofessionals can provide informal support and mentoring to troubled and/or overwhelmed parents, especially parents who are very young or have learning limitations of their own.

Having such a cadre of practitioners enables extra-strength programs to deploy multidisciplinary teams customized to the needs of each family they serve.

- *Carefully select, train, and support all program staff members.* Working with disadvantaged and vulnerable families requires high levels of skill and persistence and is often stressful. Providing services in families' homes can be isolating, and the conditions of poor neighborhoods, including high crime rates, can add to the stress that frontline service providers experience. High staff turnover, common in programs that serve those at high levels of disadvantage, disrupts the critical relationships that service providers in extra-strength programs develop with the families they serve. Therefore, programs must invest in providing high-quality training and mentoring to frontline staff members on an ongoing basis. These activities support service providers in doing their best work with troubled and challenging families and can help reduce staff turnover.

- *Allow plenty of room for adapting promising models of intervention to best fit the unique strengths, needs, and characteristics of families served*

- Because families are always changing, it is important that programs are flexible and can meet the changing needs of the families they serve. It is also important for programs to support ongoing innovation in the tools and approaches they utilize to address the multiple challenges impoverished families face. Extra-strength programs look to integrate new, carefully evaluated interventions that show promise in reducing families' risk for child maltreatment and improving the quality of nurturance parents give to their young children. They also incorporate interventions that have been shown to help reduce behavior problems in young children.[10] Extra-strength programs are explicit in placing value on service innovation and creating opportunities for the families they serve as well as for service providers to contribute to ongoing program improvement efforts, embodied in the systematic learning process discussed later in this chapter.

AN EXAMPLE OF AN EXTRA-STRENGTH PROGRAM

Many of these extra-strength elements, which incorporate the characteristics of successful programs identified in Schorr's 1988 book *Within Our Reach: Breaking the Cycle of Disadvantage* and in her more recent paper with Farrow and Sparrow, are being embraced by organizations setting out to build a bigger and better boat: stronger, more comprehensive services for the most vulnerable families.[11]

Child FIRST, a home-based program for vulnerable families with young children that was initiated a half-dozen years ago in Bridgeport, Connecticut, is a good example of an extra-strength program that is nearly as comprehensive as what I am describing here. This program is built on a strong foundation of respecting the strengths and priorities of the parents and the uniqueness of each of the families it serves. Child FIRST employs a team of service coordinators and graduate-level mental health counselors to deliver an array of services customized to meet the needs of each family enrolled in the program. Instead of sticking to a predetermined curriculum for working with parents and young children, service providers offer individually tailored parent support and training, as well as mental health counseling and linkages to additional resources in the community. To ensure that the program is delivered with consistent levels of quality, staff members must deliver services according to a strong set of standards that reflect the core principals of the program.[12]

Rigorous evaluation of Child FIRST shows promising results in reducing risk for child maltreatment and problems with language development and behavior, although long-term follow-up information is not yet available.[13] Unfortunately, Child FIRST, like most programs incorporating the elements of extra-strength programs, is small and provides services in only a few geographic areas. This is because—as one might surmise—these strategies for serving highly vulnerable families are relatively costly in terms of both the amount of funding and the herculean efforts building such programs require. Because they are multifaceted, these programs also require extraordinary coordination across service providers, resources, and organizations. As I explain later in this chapter, programs that incorporate extra-strength strategies are also more challenging and often more expensive to evaluate than simpler approaches. These factors make it very difficult to obtain and hold on to funding awarded by government and foundation decision makers, many of whom continue to be attracted to programs that are simpler, cheaper, and easier to replicate and evaluate, despite clear evidence that such programs are insufficient for improving long-term outcomes for highly vulnerable children and their families.

LESSONS FROM EARLY HEAD START

We must find ways to overcome these obstacles and build and bring to scale programs that hold real promise for improving the life chances of young children in highly vulnerable families. The most efficient way may be to build upon the framework of Early Head Start (EHS), the only large-scale family support program in the United States designed to provide something close to the extra-strength strategy I have outlined here. EHS was established by Congress in 1994 and is administered by the federal government. Although EHS is overseen by the federal Head Start Bureau and incorporates many of the values upon which Head Start is based, the program differs from Head Start in a number of ways, most notably that it serves younger children (those from newborn to age three). Moreover, services to families can last for more than three years, as EHS has the capacity to enroll poor pregnant women to help ensure that these women receive prenatal care and other services aimed toward improving the odds for having a healthy newborn, and can continue serving families until the child's third birthday.

EHS was built on principles established by the Advisory Committee on Services for Families with Infants and Toddlers, convened by the U.S. Department of Health and Human Services in the early 1990s. The committee called for a high-quality, comprehensive program that focused on families' strengths and would "support and enhance strong, caring, continuous relationships which nurture the child, parents, family, and caregiving staff."[14] It emphasized the importance of supporting parents as the primary nurturers of their children and addressing parents' growth and goals, including economic self-sufficiency; honoring and respecting the culture and other unique qualities of each family; delivering services that are sufficiently comprehensive and intensive with flexibility and responsiveness to families' needs; facilitating effective transitions for children into Head Start and other preschool programs; and collaboration with other organizations, including churches, civic groups, and community-based service providers. Based on these principles, which are reflected in the elements of extra-strength services I outlined, the Advisory Committee identified four cornerstones—later known as building blocks—as the key elements of EHS services:

- Child Development—enhancing each child's development by providing individualized support that honors the unique characteristics and pace of early development, including cognitive, social, emotional, language, and physical development, with an emphasis on building strong, nurturing relationships between babies, toddlers and their parents
- Family Development—collaborating with parents to create individualized family development plans for the provision of a full range of services to help and support parents, expectant parents, siblings, and extended family members whose well-being plays a role in the development of the family and very young child
- Community Building—serving as a catalyst for creating a community that helps support the healthy development of its young children, in part by "ensuring a comprehensive network of services and supports for

young children and their families which are culturally responsive," beginning with an in-depth needs and resource assessment, followed by a community-wide planning process

- Staff Development—selecting staff members who, together as a team, possess the spectrum of skills and expertise necessary to provide high-quality, family-centered services; engaging in supportive caregiving relationships with infants and toddlers; and developing respectful, productive, and empowering relationships with families and coworkers, and ensuring that these staff members receive ongoing training and support.[15]

Today, EHS serves about 110,000 children, approximately 4% of the 2.7 million infants and toddlers living in poverty.[16] Unlike NFP, which restricts its services to first-time new mothers, EHS serves poor families with infants and toddlers regardless of whether there are additional children in these families. It is also far more flexible, tailoring the services it delivers, who delivers them, and how and where it delivers them according to the needs of each family served. Communities establishing EHS can customize their program with a choice of three different models of intervention: programs that primarily work with families in their own homes, programs that provide center-based early learning services to children, and programs that use a combination of the first two models, providing both center- and home-based services.

Important but Modest Impacts

Shortly after EHS was launched, the federal government commissioned an ambitious evaluation of the program, using a combination of instruments and approaches in a randomized trial. Three thousand pregnant women and families with infants and toddlers were randomly assigned to participate in EHS at one of seventeen program sites across the country, or to a control group that did not participate in EHS. A wide range of impacts were measured when the children were ages three and five, and later, when they had entered grade five. This multi-faceted evaluation approach yielded a plethora of information not only about the benefits of EHS, but also about the children and families who appeared to benefit most and least, as well as program characteristics that seemed to produce the strongest benefits.[17]

Although a number of the results from the evaluation of EHS are encouraging, especially for African American children and their families, they indicate that EHS still has a distance to go in its efforts to make lasting improvements in outcomes for the children and families the program targets. Some of the benefits of EHS faded over time, and the program appeared to be less effective with families deemed to be at high levels of risk for poor outcomes.[18]

Levels of Funding and Oversight Matter

Having overseen the development and operation of an EHS program at Children's Friend nearly fifteen years ago and closely observing the expansion of the program since that time, I have some ideas as to why some of its key benefits were not as widespread and lasting as one would hope. EHS is an example—one that is too common—of a program that is built on principles that call for the delivery of extra-strength services but often fails in doing so. This failure results from insufficient funding and inadequate enforcement of standards that require programs to consistently deliver all of their services in an extra-strength–like manner. EHS study findings that benefits were greatest for families participating in EHS programs that had more fully implemented the program, rather than those that offered a less broad and potent array of services, provide some evidence for this. To its credit, the Obama administration took a number of steps to strengthen oversight to ensure that EHS programs are meeting federal performance standards, at least to the degree that current funding levels allow. These efforts will go only so far, however, as long as the program lacks the necessary financial resources to fully implement its four-building-blocks approach.

As they are currently funded, EHS programs are seldom able to deliver more than weekly visits to families experiencing a crisis or those who are in such dire straits that they need more intensive services in order to make headway in overcoming the challenges confronting them. Inadequate resources have also forced programs to focus largely on activities aimed toward promoting child development, delivering fewer services to improve the well-being and employment prospects of vulnerable parents. For EHS families in deepest poverty, current program funding levels fail to account for how labor-intensive it is to assist deeply troubled and poorly educated parents in making real progress toward self-sufficiency while supporting optimal development for their children.

LEARNING FROM EXPERIENCE TO CREATE BETTER STRATEGIES

Despite the current shortcomings in the implementation of EHS, the principles that undergirded the program's creation make it a promising platform for developing and testing a true extra-strength program for highly vulnerable young children and their families. Merging the funding silo that contains EHS, for which the government spends approximately $1.5 billion per year, with the siloes in Obamacare and other federal agencies, as well as in states, that hold more than $400 million to fund NFP and similar home-visiting programs would provide a pool of more than $1.9 billion to build such a program. This could be combined with additional funding drawn from the approximately $8 billion that funds Head Start. An efficient way to implement the stronger, enriched model would be to use the infrastructure currently in place at EHS sites across the country and phase out the current version of EHS while launching a new extra-strength version with more resources focused on improving outcomes for both children and parents in highly vulnerable families. Improved standards and oversight would be just as important as ensuring that the new version of EHS has sufficient funding to deliver services in extra-strength ways. Program sites would need sufficient time to upgrade to the stronger version, and it would be important that they do so in a way that meets the new higher standards of quality. Sites that fail to fully implement all aspects of the new version within a reasonable amount of time should be defunded and the funding granted to another organization that demonstrates its capacity to develop a full-strength version of the program in a reasonable amount of time.

Embracing All Four Building Blocks

Utilizing the funds now allocated to Head Start and EHS, the extra-strength version of EHS would serve pregnant women and children to age five, like Head Start currently does, rather than just to age three, as EHS currently does. Most services would be provided in families' homes, and they would address a full range of needs. To maximize its chances of success, this new initiative would fully incorporate the four EHS building blocks of supporting optimal development for children, strengthening their families and communities, and providing ongoing training and support for those delivering program services. The extra-strength initiative I am proposing would help parents in fostering the social, emotional, and cognitive development of their children. Equally important, it would have the capacity to help prepare impoverished parents for employment that pays a wage adequate for supporting their families. For some parents, this means linking them with appropriate job training programs; for many others, it means addressing their physical and mental health problems, as well as basic educational needs, such as literacy, English-language skills, and/or high school equivalency. The most highly disadvantaged parents must have access to these foundational education services so that they can acquire the basic competencies necessary to participate in job training and other work readiness programs.

In areas that lack an adequate supply of these resources, program leaders would engage in EHS-style community building: working with other community stakeholders and government officials to ensure access for any parent who needs education and employment resources. They would also work to ensure that an adequate supply of affordable, high-quality child care is available, and that both children and adults in their target communities have access to quality health and mental health care, domestic violence services, and other essential resources. In addition, program leaders would collaborate with state, federal, and community-based housing agencies to help address the shortage of safe, adequate housing for families with young children.

Responsiveness and Continuity Are Important

This type of long-term strategy is promising in part because, as both service providers working in family-based programs and participating parents know, it's the *relationships* between service providers and families that hold power to change lives, rather than any cadre of interventions alone. Many vulnerable parents carry with them a history of negative interactions with programs and institutions, including their own school failure, and traumatic, shaming, and/or disappointing encounters with child protective, law enforcement, and public assistance officials. It takes time for these parents to develop the strong, trusting relationships with service providers that are necessary to create lasting significant change for themselves and their families.

Some researchers question whether highly vulnerable parents would shun participating in extra-strength programs, based on the high dropout rates for such parents in existing home-visiting programs. The experiences of the service providers I know, who are on the frontlines of this work, confirm what a number of studies on parent engagement show: that when parents feel respected by service providers who demonstrate interest in addressing their most pressing concerns, they typically grab on to such programs and hold on to them for dear life. It is also important to recognize that the conditions in which many of our most fragile families find themselves are the culmination of generations of deprivation and living in the margins of society. The skills and knowledge that it takes to become financially self-sufficient as well as meet the needs of one's children—competencies middle-class parents take for granted—require a great deal of time and support for disadvantaged and troubled parents to develop. Programs that terminate services to highly vulnerable families after a few months of involvement often pull the rug out from under the tenuous progress these families may have achieved—something that happens all too often and likely plays a key role in the fading of program benefits for children over time.

Fostering Productive Relationships, Not Dependency

Some will view what I am proposing here as just another way of encouraging what they see as already too much dependence among poor families on outside resources, a dependence that stands in the way of these families becoming self-sufficient. To see the holes in this logic, we need only to look at the dismal results of most less intensive, short-term strategies. Of course, families who are drowning in the effects of chronic disadvantage and have little in the way of social support come to rely on the lifeline well-designed programs can offer, something that could be considered to be dependence. Instead of prematurely forcing these families to fend for themselves, however, I am advocating for strengthening that lifeline and encouraging parents to hold on to it while they work to achieve the levels of stability and competence necessary to nurture their children and move toward becoming economically self-sufficient. This longer-term approach would facilitate the building of strong, productive relationships between service providers and parents, relationships that are essential to helping parents develop critical nurturing relationships with their young children. It would help ensure that families achieve their goals and that the tightly intertwined physical, emotional, and learning needs of vulnerable children in these families are met during the crucial early stages of development.

Such an approach is important for reaching many of today's young parents who were themselves raised in impoverished conditions, and those who have aged out of our child welfare system. As children, many of these parents missed out on being consistently nurtured, had spotty educational experiences, and/or have endured highly traumatic experiences, something that often leads to substance abuse and other physical and mental health problems. Helping troubled parents overcome these struggles is a necessary step, and a time-consuming one, toward making real progress in interrupting the cycle of intergenerational poverty.

Extra-Strength Early Care and Education Programs

Another critical programmatic strategy is to ensure that young children in highly disadvantaged families have access to extra-strength early care and education programs. This includes high-quality, comprehensive care for babies and toddlers whose parents work or are participating in an education program, and preschool programs for children ages three and four.

BOTH QUALITY AND COMPREHENSIVENESS MATTER

Results from the follow-up evaluations of Perry Preschool provide encouragement that a similarly comprehensive approach may produce lasting benefits for disadvantaged preschool-age children in the current era. So do those from Chicago's Child-Parent Centers (CPCs), which have been providing preschool and other services to disadvantaged children for more than forty years. Like Perry Preschool, CPCs were designed to provide children with plenty of individualized attention and to engage parents as well as children in the learning process. Although not as pervasive as those achieved by Perry, the benefits for children participating in a CPC preschool were found to be considerable and lasted into adulthood. Sadly, like too many other early childhood programs designed to provide intensive and comprehensive services, the CPCs fell victim to funding cuts a number of years ago, as Chicago pushed to provide preschool experiences for higher numbers of children. Expanding the number of children served without providing for the same per-child spending forced the CPCs to reduce and/or eliminate many of the elements essential to their success. By 2000, evaluation of the diminished program showed that participating children experienced fewer benefits than in the past, a finding that should surprise no one.[19]

Lessons from the evaluation of the Chicago CPCs confirm those from the decades-old Perry Preschool study in informing us about what it takes for preschool programs to make lasting and meaningful differences for disadvantaged children. Similarly encouraging findings from the Abecedarian project point to the same essential elements in programs that provide care and early learning opportunities for infants and toddlers. These elements include the following:

- Well-qualified and trained teachers who receive ongoing support and mentoring and earn salaries that reflect the skill, expertise, and hard work their jobs require
- Small class sizes and small teacher-to-child ratios that provide opportunities for individualized attention, customized learning, and quality teacher–child interaction
- Classroom environments with a wide variety of learning tools and resources to engage children at a variety of stages of development and with a range of capacities
- High-quality teaching and learning that takes place in a creative, language-rich environment and focuses on the development of learning capacities, such as decision making rather than test-driven, "skill and drill" techniques

- A holistic approach that recognizes the intertwining of cognitive, social, and emotional learning and integrates practices that promote healthy social and emotional development
- Inclusion of staff or consultants with expertise in early childhood mental health to help identify and address children's emotional and behavioral challenges and to ensure that the needs of children affected by psychological trauma are addressed
- A set of effective parent engagement practices, including home visits and opportunities for mutual parent support, that recognize parents' strengths as well as the daunting day-to-day challenges most poor parents face
- Capacity for serving children and families from a broad range of ethnic and cultural backgrounds that is reflected in the composition and practices of program staff, the availability of services in languages spoken in the local community, and activities that honor and celebrate various types of diversity
- Effective collaboration with child welfare agencies to address the often complex needs of young children involved in that system, and similarly close collaboration with providers of early intervention services under Part C of the American with Disabilities Act for children with disabilities
- Capacity to effectively link disadvantaged families with a wide range of resources, including health care and nutrition programs, mental health services, and housing programs.

Each of these elements plays a key role in programs' effectiveness with highly vulnerable children, whether these programs are infant–toddler child care centers or preschools attached to public schools or run by private organizations.

"EARLY LEARNING THAT STICKS"

We now have evidence to show that carefully designed, high-quality publicly funded preschool programs can help poor young children achieve sizeable, lasting gains in school readiness, learning capacity, and proficiency in a number of subject areas. A 2013 Bill and Melinda Gates Foundation report by Jim Minervino, leader of the advocacy group Ready On Day One, and the University of Virginia's Robert Pianta highlights studies of four well-established publicly funded preschool programs that target primarily poor children in New Jersey, North Carolina, Maryland, and Boston. Gains achieved by participating children in all four locales persisted through grade three, and gains for children in the

North Carolina and Maryland programs persisted through grades four and five respectively.[20]

The authors refer to these four preschool programs as "early learning that sticks" to differentiate their results from the fading of early gains found in disadvantaged children who had participated in the studies of Head Start, publicly funded preschool in Tennessee, and elsewhere. They note that the successes of the four programs confirm what a growing body of research has found: the quality of teaching is the most powerful single factor contributing to children's learning and to the durability of that learning. Moreover, Minervino and Pianta point to teachers providing social and emotional support and helping children to development skills for *how* to learn as components of the teaching process that play a critical role in producing lasting gains in the learning capacities of poor preschoolers. They note that the four successful programs demonstrate a commitment to quality across a wide array of characteristics, including classroom size and teacher–student ratios, curriculum, assessment, and staff development.

FUNDING MATTERS HERE, TOO

Early care and education programs that incorporate extra-strength elements are likely to be significantly more expensive than most existing child care and preschool programs. For instance, annual costs (in 2013 dollars) for the four publicly funded preschool programs targeting poor children that were featured in the Gates Foundation report range from about $8,500 in North Carolina to upwards of $12,000 in New Jersey (which has a higher cost of living). High-quality care for infants and toddlers with better-trained teachers and extra supports for vulnerable children and their parents built in would also be considerably more expensive than the programs in which most poor babies and very young children currently participate.

Similar to funding extra-strength family support programs, existing federal funding streams could be repurposed to support the development of extra-strength early care and education programs for young children at high risk for poor outcomes. The federal government currently spends upwards of $20 billion a year on child care and preschool programs, including Head Start (but not including EHS) through a patchwork of programs with varying eligibility criteria and rules.[21] Nearly a quarter of that funding goes directly to states through the Child Care and Development Block Grant program, where it is used for a wide variety of purposes with little accountability for demonstrated improvements in the quality of early care and education poor children receive.[22] States are also using millions of dollars of their own revenue to help subsidize child care for low-wage families, to expand access to preschool programs, and to fund quality-improvement initiatives. Given that all this spending has not done enough to narrow gaps in school readiness and achievement, it makes good sense to repurpose a significant portion of these funds to develop targeted, intensive, and comprehensive approaches to early care and education for our most vulnerable young children.

Minervino and Pianta's analysis shows that the high-quality publicly funded preschool programs currently operating in Boston and New Jersey could be delivered at an average cost of about $8,000 to $10,000 per child, per year, in thirty and twenty other states respectively, given lower wage and benefit structures in those states where there is a lower cost of living. This cost is higher than the average $7,800 (in 2013 dollars) per child spent by state-run preschools, but not by much.[23] These numbers present a compelling case for repurposing funds currently spent on Head Start and other preschool programs to craft new programs for disadvantaged children, programs that embrace levels of quality similar to the four programs profiled by Minervino and Pianta. To further increase the odds of delivering early learning that sticks for highly vulnerable preschoolers, policymakers should strongly consider incorporating extra-strength parent support and engagement strategies and support for children with a wide range of behavioral, emotional, and developmental challenges. I realize that doing so would raise the cost per child even further above current preschool costs in most states. However, unless we find ways to cover the costs of key elements of extra-strength preschool programs, we cannot expect results similar to those of comprehensive programs like the Perry Preschool program.

Funding Better Approaches to Early Childhood Poverty

Scaling up the two initiatives I describe here, extra-strength family support and early-care and education programs, would require additional investments of public and private funding in addition to what we are already spending. To those who object to additional expenditures for this purpose, I would point out that the myriad weak, poorly coordinated programs and initiatives currently in place are costing us dearly, and not only from the fiscal standpoint of spending considerable funds and achieving only modest benefits. Tragic human costs are incurred when programs fail to make enough of a difference for the individuals and families at which they are targeted. We have had enough tinkering in the margins: delivering programs "on the cheap" while watching poor children move along pathways toward lousy outcomes, unable to escape the never-ending cycle of disadvantage.

To be clear, I am not calling for the allocation of large amounts of new funding as the only means to support the new strategies proposed here. Instead, I propose pooling and repurposing a large portion of the funds already being spent on impoverished young children and their families, and especially funds that support programs with unsatisfactory results. We should reallocate these resources and augment them with additional, carefully targeted funding to develop and test these and other strategies that hold greater promise than those currently in place in most communities.

Accountability in Extra-Strength Programs

Documenting program results is a critical part of the comprehensive strategies I've proposed in this chapter and for similar approaches to helping disadvantaged families, especially given how evaluation methodology and the concept of return on the investment of public dollars now drives the development and expansion of human service programs. Many policymakers seem to believe that they must choose between relying heavily on evidence produced by randomized trials and tolerating low levels of accountability in publicly funded programs, but this is a false dichotomy. Identifying and being accountable for the results achieved by intervention strategies is more important than ever. But, as I explained in the previous chapter, depending on a single, often poorly suited approach to evaluating these strategies won't ensure that policymakers make well-informed choices in selecting programs to support. Instead, such reliance privileges tightly controlled, single-focus program models like NFP for laying claim to having "proven" effectiveness and garnering a disproportionate share of available resources, even though such programs are likely to achieve only modest and fleeting benefits for poor families in the current era.

A small but steadily growing consensus among experts in the research arena, a number of foundation leaders, and those at the helm of community-based programs is that we need to utilize a wider range of evaluation tools for understanding the highly challenging and complex problems facing today's vulnerable families, and the effectiveness of the multifaceted approaches these problems require.[24] As Schorr and her colleagues point out,

We need a new evidence framework to respond to changing times: we are tackling tougher problems, the results of many past interventions have been disappointing, and our new ways of working require new and continuous ways of learning and generating knowledge that can, in turn, lay the foundation for further progress. (p. 1)[25]

They cite a number of programs around the country that utilize multifaceted approaches to working with individuals and families facing multiple challenges, and employ evaluation methods that are also multifaceted and fit well with the interventions being provided.

Child FIRST, which I described earlier in this chapter, is such a program. The evaluation of Child FIRST demonstrates that it is possible to evaluate a flexible, multifaceted, customizable set of family support interventions using an array of rigorous methods, including, in this case, randomized trials. Although families were randomly assigned to intervention and control groups, program results were also measured across a number of dimensions related to effective parenting and child safety and well-being. The use of multiple measures enabled the program to evaluate its effectiveness even though the type and intensity of services varied according to each family's individual strengths and needs.[26] Because their services are continually shifting in response to the needs of the families they serve and their effectiveness typically relies on hard-to-measure factors, including trusting relationships between service providers and parents, evaluating programs like Child FIRST is more complex than evaluating standardized, one-size-fits-all models of intervention.

SYSTEMATIC LEARNING TO IMPROVE PROGRAM OUTCOMES

To meet such challenges, Schorr and her colleagues call for wide endorsement of a "sturdier evidence framework" in which programs and interventions are identified as evidence-based through the use of multiple methods to understand them and the results they produce, rather than solely on randomized trials. A key aspect of this framework is what they refer to as *systematic learning*, an approach to evaluation that focuses on how and why a program works, for whom it does and doesn't work, and the circumstances under which it works. Like the Continuous Quality Improvement (CQI) systems already in use in many organizations, this process generates valuable information that program leaders can use to continuously strengthen their program and improve its effectiveness with the individuals or families it targets.[27]

Moving beyond CQI, systematic learning enables program developers and leaders to identify the core components of the program—those essential to its effectiveness—that can be transported and applied to other communities and organizations, allowing room for adapting the program to the unique conditions of each setting. Organizations establishing the program in a new setting assess the program's potential fit with the characteristics and needs of the communities, individuals, and/or families they intend to serve. They use the results of this assessment to adapt the program as necessary to help ensure its fit and effectiveness within its new setting. This approach is a significant departure from the requirement of fidelity—near-slavish adherence to the original model of a program—such as that which happens with each replication of NFP and other highly standardized programs. Instead, systematic learning systems work to identify core components of a program's success in order to increase the likelihood of positive results when transplanting it to other settings.

Widespread use of a systematic learning approach to program accountability and expansion could play a powerful role in improving the quality of child- and family-serving programs across the nation. Unfortunately, however, there is not enough funding available to support ongoing opportunities for innovation and information sharing among the providers of these services. Without funds to support these activities, it is usually impossible for programs to use ongoing evaluation findings for systematic learning and the sharing of lessons learned across systems and locations. This is a missed opportunity, given that those laboring in the fields of child welfare, early childhood care and education, and family support are starving for expertise and capacity for meeting the needs of families with tougher, more complex needs and improving outcomes for vulnerable young children.

Much like what Schorr observed in *Within Our Reach* nearly twenty-five years ago, pockets of innovative work with highly vulnerable families being done in communities across the country are underpublicized. Even the development of the Internet—a source of information that was in its infancy when Schorr published her book—hasn't done enough to change that. Consequently, lessons from the evaluations of such programs are greatly underutilized as sources of knowledge regarding what works in helping to break the cycle for poor families. Today, we still have far too few mechanisms in place for the mutual learning and capacity building that a systematic learning approach to program accountability entails. Shifting the focus of public policymakers and foundation leaders away from the futile search for simple, easy-to-evaluate solutions to intergenerational poverty and toward a systematic learning approach that embraces the complexity of this problem would go a long way toward helping identify what it really takes, from a programmatic standpoint, to make meaningful inroads in interrupting poverty's cycle.

There is good reason to expect that such a shift, along with the policy prescriptions I describe in the next chapter, constitute what it will really take to break that cycle for millions of America's children.

8 From Neurons to National Policy
POLICY PRESCRIPTIONS FOR ENDING
INTERGENERATIONAL POVERTY

BY NOW IT should be clear that intergenerational poverty in the United States is a multifaceted problem caused and perpetuated by the interplay of a variety of economic, political, programmatic, and policy factors. I hope that it is equally apparent that no single-focus silver-bullet solution exists to a problem as chronic and complicated as this one. The lack of simple solutions should not stand in the way of making substantial progress toward interrupting the cycle of poverty, nor should we allow the complex, stubborn nature of this problem to be used as an excuse for doing nothing to improve the life chances of our nation's most vulnerable young children. Instead, we must use the lessons learned during the past fifty years of antipoverty programs and policies in the U.S. and from initiatives in other countries, along with research findings in brain science, early childhood development, and other fields, to guide new approaches to this recalcitrant problem.

Perhaps the most important lesson is that by themselves, neither income supports nor social service programs are sufficient to break the cycle. Putting more money in the hands of poor families is critical to their well-being and the healthy development of their young children. However, additional income alone will not overcome the physical and mental health problems, family and community violence, educational deficits, and impaired parenting that generations of neglect have visited on families stuck at the bottom of our economy and cut off from mainstream society. Conversely, although well-designed extra-strength family support and early care and education programs hold promise for improving the odds of poor children succeeding in school and in life, even the best programs will have muted effects if families don't have enough income to meet their basic needs and are continually harmed by discriminatory and oppressive policies.

A Comprehensive, Multifaceted Strategy

This tells us that we need to mount a carefully crafted, comprehensive policy strategy for ensuring that far fewer American children experience the lousy outcomes that family poverty causes and perpetuates, especially if it occurs early in a child's life. We must address the economic factors that keep families stuck in poverty's stubborn clutches and at the same time foster the development of stronger, more effective programmatic approaches for helping impoverished families with young children succeed. Further, we must reform and improve the systems that play a significant role in maintaining and/or perpetuating intergenerational disadvantage. This means making significant changes to our early care and education, child welfare, and criminal justice systems. The success of such a strategy requires us to give up our attraction to quick fixes and easily measured results and to understand that a problem as chronic and complex as intergenerational poverty will require a multifaceted approach and a much more long-term perspective. As Patrick Sharkey observes,

> to confront the problem of multigenerational disadvantage requires policies that have the potential to reach multiple generations of family members, to generate a lasting impact on families and to be sustained over time. Point in time investments, even if they are based on promising ideas and strong theory, are unlikely to have transformative impacts on families that have lived in disadvantaged communities over decades and generations. (p. 12)[1]

It is well past time to focus on the transformative impacts Sharkey and other experts recognize as necessary instead of continuing to tinker in the margins with inadequate, fragmented approaches. Such an enterprise will require the support of political leaders of both major parties and a good portion of the American public, which is something difficult to imagine given the harsh rhetoric and "blame the poor" ideology so prevalent in the current environment. Countering these forces means building a national movement to change the way Americans think about impoverished families. Shifting our response to poor families from one of blaming to one of understanding and compassion will be necessary in order to create the political will necessary to ensure significantly better outcomes for our most vulnerable children.

In this concluding chapter, I describe a number of policy prescriptions that in combination would give today's impoverished babies, toddlers, and preschoolers a much better shot at a healthy and successful life. These recommendations address local, state, and national policies that play a role in determining what happens to these children. I also call for a national movement that puts our most vulnerable children at the top rather than the bottom of our national agenda. In closing, I call upon our elected officials and other policymakers, as well as members of the media and every citizen, to make ending child poverty a defining cause of our time.

Policy Prescriptions for Breaking the Cycle

Less wealthy nations with poverty rates substantially lower than those of the United States have been deliberate in crafting policies that support families, especially while their children are in their youngest, most vulnerable years. Most of Europe and other countries, including Australia and Japan, focus on meeting the needs of young children by offering paid parental leave and providing high-quality early care and education for children from families at the lowest income levels, as well as many other family-friendly initiatives.[2] These and most other developed nations also do a better job of addressing teen pregnancy, juvenile crime, and other lousy outcomes when they do occur, giving vulnerable young people opportunities to build a successful life despite having been born into troubled families and/or having made serious errors in judgment. As I noted earlier in this book, the U.S. response to most of these problems and to poor families in general is strongly punitive, an approach that too often increases the hardships of those in need while ensuring that problems become entrenched and increasingly costly in both human and financial terms. We must learn from the achievements of other nations as well as the unsatisfactory results of many of our past and current approaches and create a policy agenda that holds real promise for breaking poverty's intransigent cycle. I will outline eight areas upon which that agenda should focus.

RAISE THE MINIMUM WAGE AND ENSURE AN EFFECTIVE SAFETY
NET FOR FAMILIES WITH PARENTS WORKING AT LOW-WAGE JOBS

Politicians and commentators on both sides of the aisle like to repeat the adage, "the best social program is a job." Unfortunately, for millions of America's families, having a parent with a full-time job is not enough to escape many of poverty's ills. The 3.2 million workers who earn the federal minimum wage of $7.25 per hour or less do not bring home enough money to meet the basic needs of a typical family, nor do millions more who earn slightly above the minimum wage, especially those living in areas with high costs of living.[3] Moreover, many low-wage employers do not provide health care benefits or sick and vacation time to the parents who work for them, or help with the cost of child care.

Government benefits, such as food stamps and subsidized health care and child care, subsidize low-wage–paying businesses by helping to fill some important gaps for impoverished families with parents who are employed. Yet the American public tends to demonize working families who must rely on these and other benefits rather than blaming the fast-food chains and big-box stores that get away with paying poverty wages with few or no benefits. It is well past time to shine a bright light on this situation, one that provides perhaps the strongest argument for raising the federal minimum wage to an hourly amount that can support a family. Such an increase is the most effective way to reduce the number of working families who must rely on taxpayer-funded benefits in order to get by.

Until those at the bottom of our economy can count on earning a living wage, we must ensure a strong safety net for low-wage families with young children. The fact that children under the age of six—a stage in which rapid brain development occurs—are more likely to be poor than any other age group should be of concern to every American. There is nothing mysterious about what young children need for healthy development and to be prepared to learn and succeed in school: nurturing relationships, safe and stable housing, good nutrition and health care, and multiple opportunities for early learning pretty much sums it up. Yet millions of parents working full-time, low-wage jobs are finding it impossible to provide these basics for their children. As a result, too many young children arrive at school with multiple barriers to learning and find themselves already on the path to the lousy outcomes that almost guarantee a life of poverty.

Any strategy for changing these harmful trajectories must include providing low-wage families with additional resources. The federal Earned Income Tax Credit (EITC) offsets payroll and income taxes and puts additional cash into the hands of low-wage families with children. According to the Center on Budget and Policy Priorities (CBPP), 27 million low-wage earners received a federal EITC for the 2013 tax year. The average credit for a family with children was $3,074, which averages out to a monthly wage boost of $256. Since its inception, the EITC has enjoyed bipartisan support because it supplements the incomes of low-wage earners and rewards work.

Studies show that the credit provides incentives for low-income parents to maintain employment and helps raise incomes above the poverty level for millions of disadvantaged children and their families.[4] Additional research shows a connection between increased income through the EITC in families with young children and better school performance and higher earnings for those children when they grow up.[5] Despite these and other benefits, important provisions of the EITC, along with the broader federal Child Tax Credit (CTC), were set to expire in 2017. Fortunately, Congress recently acted to prevent 8 million low-income children from experiencing deeper levels of poverty despite having at least one parent in the work force.[6]

In addition to preventing the erosion of EITC, Congress should expand the CTC to include the lowest-wage families. Currently, families earning between $30,000 and $110,000 are ensured the full benefit of this credit. Because it only benefits families who pay a certain amount in taxes, a family earning $100,000 is eligible for the full credit, while a single mother earning $12,000 and her young child receive no benefit at all.[7] Extending the CTC to lower-income families is a simple way to supplement the incomes of working families at the very bottom of the income scale and put more cash into the hands of those who need it the most.

Moreover, Congress should expand the amounts of both the EITC and CTC for low-wage families with children ages six and under, in recognition of the especially devastating impacts of poverty on children in the most critical stages of development. This would help protect and support the healthy development of millions of vulnerable children. and offset some of the harm caused by our lack of commitment to ensuring that workers at the bottom of the pay scale earn enough to support a family. In the absence of an adequate minimum wage, we must also to ensure that low-wage families have access to food stamps (SNAP), the Women Infants and Children (WIC) nutrition programs, and subsidized health care and child care in order to give their children a better shot at a healthy and successful future.

RESTORE AND ENHANCE THE SAFETY NET FOR FAMILIES WITH HIGHLY
VULNERABLE PARENTS WHO ARE UNABLE TO WORK

A large portion of the backlash against families who utilize government benefits seems to focus on those in which the parent is unemployed. As I pointed out in Chapter 3, part of our national narrative is a constant diatribe against families who are "chronically dependent on government handouts" and who are "takers, not makers." The prime target of this invective seems to be the relatively small portion of families headed by a single parent who is unemployed. Few Americans seem to understand that a majority of these parents are unable to hold a job due to chronic physical and/or mental health problems, physical or mental disabilities, and/or inadequate levels of education. Even fewer realize that a significant number of these parents were subjected to years of instability in the foster care system and that, in addition to the physical and emotional scars inflicted upon them, many are hobbled by disastrous education histories that have left them with a very limited capacity for employment.

Families headed by such parents often need a substantial amount of resources delivered over an extended period of time to help ensure that the young children being raised in them are not doomed to grow up with similar prospects to those of their parents. In addition to the basic safety net benefits (minus the tax credits, for which nonworking families are ineligible) that I listed for working-poor families, these highly disadvantaged families typically need many of the extra-strength family support services I described in the previous chapter. These programs would provide intensive mental health, remedial education, and work readiness services to vulnerable parents who have the potential to become employed, while service providers partner with parents to help ensure the healthy development and school readiness of their young children. They would offer fragile families assistance with obtaining and maintaining safe and stable housing and adequate health care, resources necessary to the optimal development of children and to the well-being and, therefore, future employability of their parents.

Although expansion of Medicaid, especially under the Affordable Care Act, has brought physical and mental health coverage to many previously uninsured parents and their children, many low-income families still lack coverage and those with coverage often struggle to find care, especially for addressing mental health and complex medical problems.[8] Ensuring that poor families access food stamps (SNAP) and WIC is also important, especially given what research suggests about the long-term benefits these nutrition programs confer to young children in poverty. A number of studies show that children in poor families who used food stamps to supplement their diets were less likely to have stunted growth, and in adulthood to be diagnosed with heart disease, or to become obese. They also were more likely to graduate from high school.[9]

Some will calculate the costs of these services and supports for highly vulnerable families and conclude that the children (as well as taxpayers) would be better off if they were removed from their indigent parents and placed into foster care—or, as Newt Gingrich would have it, orphanages. I have studied enough case records of young children who entered the foster system due to the effects of family poverty and emerged as young adults with serious mental health problems and low educational attainment to know that that is a foolish answer. Most of the children in long-term foster care whose records I've read had spent time in residential programs or group homes—today's orphanages—where their problems failed to improve; in many cases they became worse. And then there are the monetary consequences: the cost of a year of foster care is about $40,000, and residential care is easily triple that amount.

In many but not all cases, it would be better to utilize public funding to support neglected children in their own homes rather than separate them from their families and put them into our chaotic and underresourced foster care system, a system in which they may languish and experience multiple disrupted relationships and school failure. The funds that would have been spent on foster and residential care for children neglected due to family poverty could be used instead to help their families obtain safe and stable housing, get help for their mental health needs, and take better care of their children. A portion of these funds could also pay for intensive remedial education and work readiness services for parents that could lead to employment and less dependence on government benefits. This is a far better strategy than the current one that attempts to punish vulnerable parents into the workplace by severely restricting benefits; this approach harms young children and all but ensures that the cycle of intergenerational poverty continues.

PROVIDE THE CHILD WELFARE SYSTEM WITH ADEQUATE FUNDING AND OVERSIGHT

As the stories and examples in Chapter 5 illustrate, gaps and poor practices in state child protective systems across the country play a significant role in maintaining poverty, as well as endangering the safety and well-being of millions of our most vulnerable babies, toddlers, and preschoolers. This is one of the most shameful aspects of the nation's neglect of poor families. Dangerously high caseloads, gaps in expertise, and a severe shortage of high-quality foster homes and community-based programs for maltreated children and families at risk for maltreatment threaten the safety and life chances of millions of children, and the youngest children most of all. As I have explained, these conditions are the result of chronically underfunding state systems as well as failing to provide adequate oversight to ensure that these systems utilize best practices to protect and nurture the children whose lives depend on them.

Lower Caseloads and More Training Mean Safer Children

How should additional funding be used? Despite the complex nature of child welfare work, the answers are relatively straightforward. The not uncommon scenario of child welfare workers carrying caseloads of thirty to forty families when national standards range from twelve to seventeen families per worker tells us that we must provide state systems with the resources necessary to hire enough social workers to keep caseloads manageable.[10] This would help ensure that each child and family receives the services and monitoring necessary to keep children safe and to help families stay together when that is in the children's best interest. It would also help prevent children from getting lost in the foster care system, in which each passing month and each change of placement reduces a child's chances of being raised in a stable, permanent family. The fact that adolescents who languish in foster care are far more likely to become single parents with poor prospects for earning a living tells us that reducing foster care drift is an important cycle-breaking strategy.

A number of states are working to ensure that the caseloads of child welfare workers are manageable and are improving their practices for serving families as well.[11] Unfortunately, much of this work is driven either by lawsuits filed on behalf of children who have been harmed by oversized caseloads and other poor practices, or by public scandals that have broken in the wake of children dying because of such poor practices. It is well past time to become proactive in protecting our most vulnerable children rather than reacting only to lawsuits and children's deaths.

Improving the training and education of those charged with protecting maltreated children from further harm and promoting their well-being is another facet of improving outcomes for these children. The hiring of child protective workers without relevant degrees and the inconsistent levels of on-the-job training states and regions of states provide is of grave concern, given that these individuals make life-and-death decisions regarding highly vulnerable children on a daily basis. Requiring proper educational backgrounds and ensuring that all child welfare personnel receive the training and supervision necessary to make these decisions with high levels of expertise would go a long way toward promoting safety, well-being, and permanency for such children.

Better Foster Homes for Better Child Outcomes

State systems also need additional resources to improve the recruitment, training, and support of foster parents and to maintain an adequate supply of safe and caring homes for children who must be placed into foster care. Foster parents in such homes play a critical role in nurturing the physical and mental health and well-being of maltreated children. In too many instances, however, child welfare workers are forced to place children in settings that not only fail to meet the children's needs but are only marginally better than the homes from which the children were removed. I have seen too many cases like those described in Chapter 5 in which children would have likely fared better had they been left in the care of their neglectful biological parents rather than having been placed in unsafe and unstable foster homes. Providing child welfare systems with adequate resources to recruit and support a sufficient number of good-quality foster homes would enable states to eliminate homes that provide marginal-quality care and, most importantly, those that endanger children. This is essential to the safety and well-being of the extremely vulnerable children who need foster care, and very young children most of all.

Improving the quality of foster care would also help prevent rotten outcomes among the more than 400,000 children in foster care, nearly half of whom are aged six and under.[12] Equally important, child welfare systems must improve their capacities for assisting troubled families who, with the proper resources and supports, can safely care for their children at home. They must also improve their capacity for identifying suitable adoptive parents and accelerating the adoption process for children whose biological parents are unable to raise them. Taken together, all of these strategies hold great promise for reducing the number of children who are harmed and whose life chances are diminished while languishing in foster care.[13]

Meeting Children's Needs and Reducing Racial Disparities

Another important strategy is to ensure that all children in the child welfare system, and young children in particular, receive the specialized services they need to overcome the harmful effects of the trauma and broken relationships many of these children have endured. When delivered in a timely manner, high-quality psychotherapy and caregiver training hold promise for helping children cope, strengthening their resilience, and improving their capacities for engaging in close, nurturing relationships.[14] In addition to ensuring appropriate mental health treatment is readily available, states must do a better job in ensuring that all infants and toddlers are linked to pediatric heath care and receive timely screening for disabilities, and that those diagnosed with disabilities receive the early intervention services they need. This is critical given that children in these systems are far more likely to have physical and learning disabilities, and interventions work best when they begin early in a child's life.

Although federal legislation passed in 2003 under reauthorization of the Child Abuse Prevention and Treatment Act requires such timely screening and access to services, there is much room for improvement in compliance in most states.[15] Moreover, most states provide early intervention services only to young children with a diagnosed disability, and not to those who show signs of being *at risk* for disabilities. Congress should mandate that all young children under the age of three who are involved in the child welfare system and identified as being at risk for disabilities receive early intervention services aimed toward reducing that risk and should provide states with the funding necessary to do so.[16]

State child welfare agencies should focus more attention on the other needs of the very young children within their systems. This includes recognizing the powerful impacts of early attachments by ensuring that babies, toddlers, and preschoolers are able to develop and maintain stable, nurturing relationships with their parents. In cases where such relationships with parents are not possible, child protective workers must ensure that young children have opportunities to develop close, continuous bonds with other caregivers, be they foster parents, adoptive parents, and/or early care and education providers. Ensuring stable, nurturing relationships means facilitating frequent visits with biological family members (when appropriate), minimizing the number of placements children experience, and putting more effort and resources into recruiting the best possible foster and adoptive parents for these children. It also means expediting court reviews to reduce the amount of time young children languish in the system.

The federal government must also provide states with additional resources and stronger mandates aimed toward eliminating racial disparities in the treatment of children and families in the child welfare system. As I explained in Chapter 5, regardless of whether they are intentional, some of the practices of child welfare agencies and family and juvenile courts create additional disadvantages to children of color, and African American children in particular. Despite efforts at the federal level and in some states, along with those of a number of private organizations, racial disparities continue to exist in the rates in which children are removed from their parents and placed into foster care and in the amount of time children languish in care. This is morally wrong and must be stopped. We need a nationwide initiative to sensitize and train child welfare and court personnel at all levels regarding this issue and to instill practices aimed toward eliminating race-based disparities that contribute to disproportionate rates of poor outcomes among black children. We must hold states accountable for ensuring that decision making in child welfare is based on what is in the best interest of each and every child, regardless of his or her family's race.

Oversight Matters as Much as Funding

These and other important reforms require additional allocations of funds to state child welfare agencies; however, money alone will not improve the system. As the examples in Chapter 5 painfully illustrate, these agencies also need more oversight—at the state and federal levels—than what is currently in place. We must break the cycle of chronic indifference toward this system, one that is punctuated by outrage and calls for reform when yet another child falls through the cracks and dies, and then returns to indifference a few months later—until the next tragedy strikes. To do so requires improving capacity at the federal and state levels for ongoing monitoring, as well as support for system-wide improvements that take place at times other than in the wake of a scandal caused by the needless death of a child.

Congress should find ways to strengthen the Child and Family Services Review that is periodically conducted by the federal government to assess each state's performance in the areas of child safety, permanency, and well-being.[17] Increasing the frequency of reviews and the resources and oversight dedicated to ensuring that states make needed improvements in a timely manner would help improve the functioning of child welfare systems and save children's lives. So would careful examination of federal review findings and monitoring of the improvement process by state legislatures, along with consistent media attention to their state's progress in this area. We also need—and this is another place where members of the media play an important role—better ways of informing the public about the fragile nature of the children and families involved in the child welfare system, the complex and often volatile nature of this work, and the consequences of failing to invest sufficient funding and oversight to ensure that this system works as well as it possibly can.

MAKE HIGH-QUALITY EARLY CARE AND EDUCATION AVAILABLE TO ALL DISADVANTAGED INFANTS, TODDLERS, AND PRESCHOOLERS

Despite large-scale efforts and millions of dollars spent in recent years to raise the quality of the early care and education programs available to families across the nation, "poor care for poor children" is still too often the norm in many low-income communities. This is largely due to the obscenely low wages paid to teachers working in child care and preschool programs in these communities. The field of early care and education is a low-paying one to begin with, with salaries well below those of most other professions. The problem is even worse in communities with high numbers of low-wage–earning parents who must rely on government subsidies to help pay for the cost of child care. In many communities, these subsidies are not enough to enable child care centers and preschool programs to hire well-qualified teachers and to provide them with the support they need in order to nurture and promote the optimal development of the children in their care. And they are not nearly enough to attract and keep teachers who are equipped to address the multiple challenges—such as higher incidences of behavior problems and disabilities—typically found among young children being raised in poverty. These circumstances result in a situation in which the children who most need skillful nurturing and learning opportunities typically get considerable less than their less-vulnerable peers. Whenever this situation occurs, child care reinforces, rather than reverses, the disadvantages that come with being born to poor parents.

The broader issue of low salaries for early care and education teachers is a complex one, affected by both market forces (what parents are willing and/or able to pay) and cultural ones (undervaluing caregiving work done by a predominantly female workforce), and not something to be solved here. However, by taking a targeted approach, we can do substantially more to raise the quality of care for the babies, toddlers, and preschoolers who are most in need of high-quality care and early education in order to develop optimally. This means ensuring an adequate supply, in impoverished communities, of early care and education programs that encompass the extra-strength elements I described in the previous chapter. Well-prepared, adequately compensated teachers are the lynchpin of such programs, and improved salaries, supports, and training are the tools necessary to attract and retain high-caliber teachers in the programs in which they are most needed.[18] All of the elements of quality care I described in Chapter 7 are important; the best place to start is finding the ways and means to hire and retain the best teachers.

BREAK DOWN SILOS CONTAINING FEDERAL AND STATE AGENCIES WHOSE
MISSIONS INCLUDE IMPROVING THE WELL-BEING OF FRAGILE FAMILIES AND
THE LIFE CHANCES OF VULNERABLE CHILDREN AND YOUTH

One of the greatest barriers to creating and sustaining programs that effectively support vulnerable families and improve outcomes for the young children in these families is the poorly coordinated array of funding streams dedicated to these efforts. At both the state and federal levels, resources are siloed in agencies focused on children's and adult mental health, child protection, early care and education, early childhood disabilities intervention, school readiness, parent education and employment, nutrition support, cash assistance, and more. Each state and federal agency and the funding initiatives they put forth have their own set of eligibility criteria, standards, goals, and objectives. Poor coordination between states and the federal government and the often haphazard ways in which various states use federal block grant funds add to the confusion. This makes for highly inefficient deployment of the scarce resources allocated to fighting poverty and improving children's life chances. Further, it causes the phenomenon I mentioned in the previous chapter that is analogous to giving struggling families a car one part at a time instead of providing an entire car, something that would be infinitely more useful.

Part of the problem is one of scarcity: state and federal agencies focused on addressing human needs are chronically underfunded. However, rather than just calling for more resources, we must find better, more efficient ways to use the resources currently allocated for addressing poverty and improving outcomes for children. The work being done in building early childhood systems that is under way in a number of states, supported by the federal government, offers some hope; however, it is important that these systems include close coordination of programs that policymakers typically see as tangential to child development.[19] These include adult mental health, adult literacy, and job training services, along with child protection and family preservation programs. Close coordination of these programs with those that provide early care and education, early intervention, and early childhood mental health services is essential to ensure that all services in which a given family participates are well coordinated and effective in helping that family reach its goals.

What individual states can accomplish in the areas of systems building depends largely on how resources are distributed at the federal level. To maximize their effectiveness, resources for adult education programs, job readiness and training programs, and mental health and substance services must be closely aligned with those focused on meeting the needs of young children and also with the child welfare system. By merging resources from relevant federal agencies and creating pools of funding to develop extra-strength family support and early care and education programs, the federal government could make the development of these programs far more feasible and expeditious. Rather than creating more block grants, which are often subject to misuse by states, this strategy would channel funds to states for developing extra-strength family support and early care and education programs that meet high universal standards for quality and comprehensiveness.

This would mean drawing funds from federal agencies as disparate as the Children's Bureau, the Substance Abuse and Mental Services Administration, and the Departments of Education and Labor, and systematically channeling these funds to states or directly to communities to build stronger, far more comprehensive community-based programs. The latter approach (channeling funds directly to communities) is similar to how the federal government currently funds EHS and may well be an effective way to build upon current EHS programs as a platform for extra-strength services. Of course, funds pooled for this purpose would be dollars withdrawn from current federally funded programs, and such a process would likely create a political firestorm fueled by entities that would be losing some of the funding they currently count on. However, the pay-offs from structuring and delivering services to our most vulnerable children and their families in a coherent and comprehensive way—one that holds far greater promise than what takes place through existing funding mechanisms—are likely to be well worth the Herculean efforts and substantial political fortitude such an undertaking would require.

MAKE WISE INVESTMENTS IN IMPROVING THE LIFE CHANCES OF DISADVANTAGED TEENS AND YOUNG ADULTS

Although obvious, it bears repeating that children are poor because their parents are poor. As I have outlined so far in this chapter and in the previous chapter, there are a number of ways in which the United States can improve the well-being of its most vulnerable young children and their families. In doing so, we can short-circuit the trajectory of poverty by helping to ensure better outcomes for these children, including reducing the risk of their becoming poor and dysfunctional parents. If we want to begin interrupting the cycle as soon as possible, we must do a better job of meeting the needs of adolescents and young adults who are already at risk for lousy outcomes. These are youths being raised by poor parents in struggling families, many of whom live in disadvantaged, often violent neighborhoods. They are the teens and young men and women I described to Governor Carcieri in Chapter 3 who grew up in poverty's clutches and arrived at school already well behind their nonpoor peers. Many of these youths are trying to cope with the consequences of the trauma and stress in their early years as well as in their current living situation. Most are living and going to school in our economically and racially segregated urban cores, where quality educational experiences and positive mentors are scarce and violence is a part of everyday life. A large portion of these youths will not graduate high school; poor students are five times more likely to drop out than their nonpoor peers.[20]

As NYU's Lawrence Aber and the Urban Institute's Ajay Chaudry point out, like very young children, youths in their late teens and early twenties are transitioning through a critical developmental stage that has important implications for their future life chances. They note, however, that just as with children who are in their first four years of life, government spends far less to help support healthy, positive outcomes for young adults than it does for children ages five through seventeen.[21] Neglecting the needs of disadvantaged individuals during the stages at which they are most vulnerable is wrongheaded public policy. It costs the nation billions of dollars in addressing crime, homelessness, chronic physical and mental health conditions, and too early parenthood, not to mention the human costs of lives with little hope.

Breaking the Cycle Through Better Services for Disadvantaged Youths

We must do all that we can to see that the current cohort of disadvantaged teens and young adults have a decent shot at a productive and healthy future. This means investing in education, job training, mentoring, specialized mental health counseling, and other services critical to improving the life chances of these youths. The expansion of Medicaid under the Affordable Care Act that extended coverage to poor adults is a step in the right direction, providing health care coverage to a population that has been historically underserved. Much more should be done. Programs like Year Up, which offers intensive training, mentoring, internships, and job placement assistance, should be expanded to serve higher numbers of disadvantaged young adults. This represents a good investment, given than 80% of Year Up's participants are employed or in school full time four months after graduating from the program.[22]

We should also further develop and expand programs that provide similar services to teens who have dropped out of school as well as those in danger of dropping out. Long Beach, California's school system offers a promising approach to curbing dropout and encouraging higher education among its predominantly low-income students, many of them from immigrant families. Through a partnership with local public colleges, Long Beach high school students are guaranteed a full-tuition scholarship for their first year of college, as long as they meet admissions standards. The school system offers students as much help as they need to boost their academic performance in order to meet these standards and succeed in college. This partnership is increasing both the number of disadvantaged students going to college and college graduation rates for these students.[23]

Given the undeniably strong connection between early single parenthood and chronic poverty, we should expand high-quality, comprehensive programs that work with disadvantaged girls in their teens to help prevent teen parenthood. With its mantra that "the best contraceptive is hope," the Carrera Adolescent Pregnancy Prevention Program at New York's Children's Aid Society provides an extra-strength approach with promising results. The program works with girls throughout their high school years, offering tutoring, sports and arts programs, help with applying to college, career advising, and other services. Staff members work to form caring relationships with not only the girls but their families as well. The Carrera program has demonstrated impressive results in delaying initial sexual encounters, increasing condom and contraceptive use, and reducing pregnancy rates.[24] Similarly intensive and comprehensive programs should be made available at every high school in impoverished communities across the nation. This is a far more promising approach to the problem of too-early parenthood than the shaming, blaming, and punishing of teen parents that too often substitutes for effective teen pregnancy prevention in many states.

Special Attention to the Needs of Youths Exiting Foster Care

Adolescents and young adults who have grown up stuck in our dysfunctional foster care system warrant special attention. As I described in Chapter 5, the approximately 26,000 youths aging out of foster care each year represent a population at particularly high risk for poor outcomes.[25] The authors of a recent study on youths leaving foster care summed up the challenges they face:

> In comparison with their peers, they are, on average, less likely to have a high school diploma, less likely to be pursuing higher education, less likely to be earning a living wage, more likely to have experienced economic hardships, more likely to have had a child outside of wedlock, and more likely to have become involved with the criminal justice system.[26]

Many of these youths are also struggling with the mental health problems brought on by the traumatic experiences and multiple disrupted attachments children in foster care often experience.

We must explore ways to better equip state child welfare systems to do right by these youths, who are often pushed out by these systems with little in the way of supportive relationships, adequate education, or basic life skills. This means providing intensive case-management services to ensure that young adults aging out of foster care receive the counseling, remedial education, job training, and life skills mentoring they need. It also means working to reduce shamefully high rates of homelessness among this population by providing long-term housing subsidies for youths who have left foster care, and supervised housing for those unable to live on their own. We should offer a program similar to the Carrera Adolescent Pregnancy Prevention to all adolescent girls in foster care to help these young women see a future for themselves other than too-early parenthood and the lifelong poverty it typically brings. A few states have experimented with pregnancy prevention efforts in their foster care programs; however, these initiatives lacked the relationship-based, customized approach of programs like Carrera, one that holds far greater promise for changing the odds for highly vulnerable adolescents.[27]

REFORM OUR UNJUST, FAMILY-DESTROYING CRIMINAL JUSTICE SYSTEM

Among the many ways in which the astoundingly high rate of incarceration in the United States harms this nation are its impacts on child poverty. A majority of the 2 million adults in state and federal prisons have children under the age of eighteen. Studies show that children of incarcerated parents are less likely to have their basic needs met and are more prone to social and emotional problems than their peers.[28] Incarceration deprives hundreds of thousands of children of the presence and care of at least one of their parents, and families of the potential earnings of the incarcerated father or mother. Moreover, it pushes thousands of children into foster care.[29] These problems compound the effects of poverty, given that the vast majority of inmates come from families who are already poor. Of course, the additional hardships brought about by the incarceration of parents hit African American families especially hard, given that blacks are far more likely than whites to be sentenced to prison, even when convicted on similar charges.[30]

This reality points to reforming our criminal justice system as another important aspect of reducing child poverty in the United States. Although the complexities of such reform are well beyond the scope of this book, mass incarceration plays too big a role in maintaining intergenerational poverty, especially among nonwhites, to not at least acknowledge the urgent need for change. We must recognize that among the many harms of mass incarceration is that it not only deprives children of their parents, it also makes it far more difficult for parents to support their families, given how having a criminal record damages employment prospects.

To be truly effective, criminal justice reform must take place on a number of levels, from the ways in which police officers interact with individuals of color, sentencing guidelines and mandatory sentences, probation and parole policies, and many aspects of the ill-conceived War on Drugs. A number of recent developments offer some hope for reform, from the Black Lives Matter movement and changes in drug sentencing policies in a number of states, to signals from members of Congress in both parties that fixing our broken criminal justice system will get more than the lip service it has gotten so far.[31]

Similar to what happens in our criminal justice system, the U.S. immigration system destroys families and diminishes the life chances of hundreds of thousands of children. A majority of young children who are undocumented and those living with undocumented parents live in deep poverty and are at particularly high risk for lousy outcomes. In addition to the various hardships and long-term adverse consequences of early life poverty, fear of arrest and deportation heightens levels of stress in the families of these children.[32] This exposes young children to toxic levels of stress and increases the likelihood of maltreatment, both of which harm children's chances for success in school and in life.

If we truly care about ending child poverty, we must change these shameful, family-destroying policies. In November 2014, President Obama signed an executive order for an initiative called Deferred Action for Parents of Americans and Lawful Permanent Residents (DAPA). This initiative is aimed at the parents of American citizens who are themselves in the country illegally but can document that they have been law-abiding residents of the United States since 2010. On a case-by-case basis, these parents would be able to apply for a work permit and driver's license and a chance to remain in the United States for renewable two-year increments. Although this executive order does not address undocumented children, it could have significant favorable impacts on the millions of citizen children being raised by undocumented parents.

We must take on the powerful forces that work against reforms to our immigration policies. In a June 2016 vote, the Supreme Court blocked DAPA and related measures.[33] The rhetoric of all the leading Republican candidates for president in the 2016 race and the power of Tea Party members in Congress, along with hostile courts, dim the likelihood of meaningful immigration reforms, including those that would improve the life chances of millions of American children.

Building a National Movement

It has been heartening, over the past few years, to find the subject of high rates of poverty in the world's richest country back on the national agenda, however marginal its position among other policy topics. Prominent leaders, including President Obama, House Speaker Paul Ryan, and Pope Francis, have shone new light on this shameful phenomenon. Unfortunately, most of the public discourse on reducing poverty either lacks specifics or still focuses on creating harsher penalties for families ensnared in poverty. Meanwhile, millions of America's youngest, most vulnerable children are forced to watch their chances for a happy, healthy, and successful future diminish.

More than twenty-five years ago, Lisbeth Schorr wrote,

> Considering the wealth of our knowledge about the dangers of growing up in areas of concentrated poverty—areas now readily identified—and our knowledge about interventions that can change outcomes even for the most disadvantaged children, it becomes unconscionable not to take whatever action is needed to make these interventions available. (p. 288)[34]

Today, our failing to take action is even more unconscionable, given all that we've learned over the past three decades about just how pervasive, devastating, and long-lasting the effects of early life poverty can be. We've also learned so much more about what does and doesn't work to help lift families out of poverty and improve the future prospects of young children in poor families.

WISE INVESTMENTS AND A LONG-TERM VIEW

Given our stalled progress in putting these lessons to work, it is clear that it will take nothing less than a widespread, multifaceted national movement to break the cycle of poverty and improve the life chances of poor young children. Such a movement must be based on a realization of how challenging and long-term a task this will be, and it must avoid the pitfall of seeking cheap, single-focus solutions to this deep-rooted and complicated problem. We must also understand that it will require intervening on a number of different levels at the same time. As presidential candidate Barack Obama put it in 2007, "If poverty is a disease that infects the entire community in the form of unemployment and violence, failing schools and broken homes, then we can't just treat those symptoms in isolation. We have to heal that entire community."[35] Nine years later, much of this work still remains to be done.

The policy and programmatic initiatives I've described in these last two chapters offer a blueprint for making real progress in reducing poverty and advancing opportunity in our nation. To do so will take the commitment and concerted efforts of Americans in a wide variety of roles, from foster parents, teachers, health care professionals, and social workers to foundation administrators, government officials, and our elected leaders. Even with broad public support and involvement, it will take time before we see results and even more time before we will be able to confirm that those results are making a lasting difference in the life chances of our most disadvantaged children. Identifying the impacts of these efforts will require the use of wide array of evaluation methods, and ensuring that our strategies are the best they can be will require an investment in systematic learning at both the policy and programmatic levels.

We must come to terms with the fact that reducing poverty and improving outcomes for poor children will require spending additional public money in addition to reallocating much of what we're already spending. To be clear: I am not calling for the allocation of new government funding for less than highly promising, well-designed strategies or for strategies with low levels of accountability. We can't afford to waste public credibility any more than we can afford to waste poverty-fighting dollars. However, the fact that funding aimed toward addressing poverty is so scarce, compared to so many other government expenditures, helps drive the wrong-headed search for ways to do so on the cheap. As I explained earlier in this book, this perpetuates another damaging cycle, in which funding goes to inexpensive, inadequate strategies promising unrealistic results, with public and political cynicism escalating when those strategies fail to deliver the lofty results they promised. We need higher levels of *both* financial support and accountability in programs and policies aimed toward reducing child poverty.

LESSONS FROM GREAT BRITAIN

To succeed, we must also counter the widespread belief that nothing works, that intergenerational poverty is an inescapable byproduct of capitalism. Americans need only look across the pond to Great Britain to see that this pessimism is unwarranted. Launched in 1999 under Prime Minister Tony Blair and his Labour Party, Britain's war on poverty reduced its child poverty rate by nearly 50% over a ten-year period.[36] The British strategy employed three components: (1) encouraging work and making work pay, (2) increasing financial support for families with children, including those headed by an unemployed single parent, and (3) investing in programs that supported the optimal development, school readiness, and school success of poor children.[37] Unlike in the United States, Britain's leaders understood that it would take additional government funding as well as a multipronged approach to substantially reduce its child poverty rate.

In tackling child poverty, Britain not only increased its minimum wage to one that was relatively higher than in the United States but also created tax credits that put additional money into the hands of working parents throughout the year, unlike the once-yearly payout of our EITC.[38] The British developed programs that encourage single mothers to work by using relationship-based strategies, including ongoing mentoring and work readiness programs. Unlike welfare reform in the United States, Britain does not force single mothers of young children into working by slashing benefits or imposing time limits on those receiving welfare benefits. In fact, a central component of the British antipoverty strategy was to increase the size of its Child Benefit subsidies. The Child Benefit is paid throughout the year to all but the wealthiest families to help defray the costs of raising children, regardless of whether parents are employed.[39] This policy reveals the core differences in approaches to poverty in the two countries: Britain's welfare reform initiative set out to end child poverty, while the United States focused on "ending welfare as we know it," with reductions in child poverty as a hoped-for byproduct. The result of the U.S. approach, as we now can see it, was to diminish our safety net while our child poverty rate has remained the highest among similarly developed nations.

The third component of Britain's strategy was to invest in programs that promote healthy development and school success, with a special focus on young children. To improve the odds for all its children, it enacted universal preschool and extended paid parental leave for all families. For disadvantaged young children, Britain created free child care programs for two-year-olds and increased the hours of preschool provided to impoverished three- and four-year-olds. For children ages newborn to three living in the poorest communities, the government established Sure Start, a program that provides a wide range of customized services to these children and families in their homes as well as through family resource centers. The latter are "one-stop shopping" centers created in child care centers and other locales, offering parent training, breastfeeding support, help with overcoming barriers to benefits, and other services to disadvantaged families.[40] To help ensure that children sustained the progress made through participating in early childhood programs, Britain launched a number of initiatives designed to improve the quality of instruction in its primary and secondary schools, reduce its dropout rate, and offer vocational training and work readiness support to disadvantaged youths.[41]

Sadly, with a shift in the political winds in Britain over the past few years, the government began reducing the funding allocated to its antipoverty initiatives. Not surprisingly, progress on further lowering its child poverty rate has stalled and is in danger of rolling backward.[42] Despite these discouraging developments, the results of the British initiative demonstrate that it is possible to substantially reduce the child poverty rate in a highly developed nation that embraces capitalism. They also tell us that doing so requires a multifaceted approach—one that ensures that work pays, helps single mothers become employable, provides supports for families with children regardless of parental employment, and invests in high-quality programs that begin in the first years of children's lives.

THE CRITICAL ROLE OF WIDESPREAD PUBLIC SUPPORT

There is another, equally important lesson we can learn from Britain's war on poverty. The stalling of gains for British children in the wake of budget cuts demonstrates the importance of broad public and political buy-in across ideologies and over time in order to sustain progress. Alison Garnham, a key figure in Britain's successful initiative, cites the failure of Blair and his Labour Party leaders to adequately educate the general public about their poverty-fighting strategy and the remarkable results it was achieving. Blair and his party were "doing good by stealth," according to Garnham, in not ensuring that the British public understood the centrality of reducing child poverty to the nation's economic success, and the goals, methods, and accomplishments of its poverty-fighting initiative. Events in Britain have convinced Garnham and the Childhood Poverty Action Group she now leads that an effective media and communications strategy is essential to any large-scale government effort to reduce childhood poverty.[43]

If attaining public buy-in regarding the importance of eliminating childhood poverty and of government's role in doing so is an uphill climb in Great Britain, the climb is far steeper and more daunting in the United States. As we saw from the many examples I provided in Chapter 3, bashing poor families and government programs that assist these families has become deeply rooted in the culture of a large segment of the American public. To build a comprehensive strategy that truly holds promise for substantially reducing child poverty and sustaining our progress in doing so, we need to change the conversation regarding America's poor families. We can begin by calling out politicians and members of the media who consistently take cheap shots at individuals and families who rely on what's left of our shrinking safety net and sensationalize the relatively rare incidents of misuse of government benefits. We must also recognize and confront the racialized nature of much of this rhetoric and the damage it does in a nation whose racist history continues to play out in its policies and its politics.

We must find ways to educate the public, members of the media, and elected officials at all levels about the alarming rate of child poverty in our nation as well as the moral and economic costs of allowing millions of children to grow up with their needs for nurturance, safety, learning, and physical and mental health unmet. A good place to start is by helping all Americans see that rather than subscribing to a mythical culture of dependence, most highly disadvantaged families are headed by a parent who was ill served in our dysfunctional public systems. We must show how the life trajectories of many of today's poor parents are, at least in part, symptomatic of failures in our child welfare, mental health, education, criminal justice, and immigration systems.

This tells us that intergenerational poverty is a structural problem rather than a cultural one and that we must reform these and other systems in order to give today's highly disadvantaged babies and toddlers a better start in life than their parents had.

Lastly, it is important that we counter the mythmaking generated by the media when they feature the story of an individual from an extremely disadvantaged background who has grown up to become wildly successful. Although inspiring, the danger of such narratives is that they imply that anyone can succeed through hard work, regardless of the disadvantages into which he or she is born—our much-treasured Horatio Alger, rags-to-riches stories. The life stories of most Americans tell us otherwise: the vast majority of us who have experienced success in life came from backgrounds that nurtured and advanced our life chances and provided us with opportunity in many ways, some of which we may not even realize. If more Americans understood this reality, it would be less difficult to garner public support for helping poor families and to heed the conclusions of famed journalist Malcom Gladwell from the years he spent studying successful individuals:

> We overlook just how large a role we all play—and by "we" I mean society— in determining who makes it and who doesn't. . ... To build a better world we need to replace the patchwork of lucky breaks and arbitrary advantages today that determine success—the fortunate birth dates and the happy accidents of history—with a society that provides opportunities for all.[44]

Notes

CHAPTER 1

1. Schorr, L. B., & Schorr, D. (1988). *Within our reach: Breaking the cycle of disadvantage.* New York: Anchor Press/Doubleday.

2. Shonkoff, J. P., & Bales, S. N. (2011). Science does not speak for itself: Translating child development research for the public and its policymakers. *Child Development*, 82(1), 17–32.

CHAPTER 2

1. Edelman, P. (2013). *So rich, so poor: Why it's so hard to end poverty in America.* New York: The New Press.

2. *Ibid.*

3. Center on Budget and Policy Priorities (2014). Chart book: The War on Poverty at 50, overview. Retrieved from http://www.cbpp.org/research/chart-book-the-war-on-poverty-at-50-overview; U.S. Census Bureau (2015). Income, poverty and health insurance coverage in the United States: 2014. Retrieved from https://www.census.gov/newsroom/press-releases/2015/cb15-157.html.

4. Center on Budget and Policy Priorities (2014). Greenstein testimony before House Budget Committee on poverty and the safety net. Retrieved from http://www.cbpp.org/greenstein-testimony-before-house-budget-committee-on-poverty-and-the-safety-net.

5. As the EPI notes: "The relative poverty rate is defined here as the share of individuals living in households with income below half of household-size-adjusted median income. Poverty rates are based on income after taxes and transfers."

6. Center on Budget and Policy Priorities (2014). Greenstein testimony before House Budget Committee on poverty and the safety net. Retrieved from http://www.cbpp.org/greenstein-testimony-before-house-budget-committee-on-poverty-and-the-safety-net.

7. National Center for Children in Poverty (2016). Basic facts about low-income children: Children under 18 years, 2014. "Above low-income is defined as at or above 200% of the federal poverty threshold (FPT), poor is defined as below 100% of FPT, and near poor is between 100% and 199% of the FPT. The low-income category includes both the poor and near-poor." Retrieved from http://www.National Center for Children in Poverty.org/publications/pub_1145.html.

8. National Center for Children in Poverty (2016). Basic facts about low-income children: Children under 18 years, 2014. Retrieved from http://www.National Center for Children in Poverty.org/publications/pub_1145.html.

9. National Center for Children in Poverty (2015). Basic facts about low-income children: Children under 6 years, 2013. Retrieved from http://www.National Center for Children in Poverty.org/publications/pub_1096.html.

10. National Center for Children in Poverty (2012). Young children at risk: National and state prevalence of risk factors. Retrieved from http://www.National Center for Children in Poverty.org/publications/pub_1073.html.

11. National Center for Children in Poverty (2016). Young children in deep poverty. Retrieved from http://www.nccp.org/publications/pub_1133.html

12. Maholmes, V., & King, R. B. (Eds.) (2012). *The Oxford handbook of poverty and child development*. New York: Oxford University Press.

13. Duncan, G. J., Yeung, W. J., Brooks-Gunn, J., & Smith, J. R. (1998). How much does childhood poverty affect the life chances of children? *American Sociological Review*, 63(3), 406–423; Maholmes, V., & King, R. B. (Eds.) (2012). *The Oxford handbook of poverty and child development*. New York: Oxford University Press.

14. National Center for Children in Poverty (2012). Young children at risk: National and state prevalence of risk factors. Retrieved from http://www.National Center for Children in Poverty.org/publications/pub_1073.html; Duncan, G. J., Yeung, W. J., Brooks-Gunn, J., & Smith, J. R. (1998). How much does childhood poverty affect the life chances of children? *American Sociological Review*, 63(3), 406–423.

15. Gillham, B., Tanner, G., Cheyne, B., Freeman, I., Rooney, M., & Lambie, A. (1998). Unemployment rates, single parent density, and indices of child poverty: Their relationship to different categories of child abuse and neglect. *Child Abuse & Neglect*, 22(2), 79–90.

16. U.S. Department of Health and Human Services, Administration for Children and Families, Administration on Children, Youth and Families, Children's Bureau (2015). Child maltreatment, 2014. Retrieved from: http://www.acf.hhs.gov/programs/cb/resource/child-maltreatment-2014

17. Herrnstein, R., & Murray, C. (1994). *The bell curve: Intelligence and class structure in American life*. New York: Free Press.

18. I discuss this aspect of American racism in the next chapter and show how it plays a role in maintaining the cycle of poverty among families of color.

19. Krein, S. F., & Beller, A. H. (1988). Educational attainment of children from single-parent families: Differences by exposure, gender, and race. *Demography*, 25(2), 221–234; Bianchi, S. M. (1994). The changing demographic and socioeconomic characteristics of single parent families. *Marriage & Family Review*, 20(1-2), 71–97.

20. Massey, D., & Denton, N. (1993). *American apartheid: Segregation and the making of the underclass*. Cambridge, MA: Harvard University Press.

21. National Center for Children in Poverty (n.d.). Child poverty pervasive in large American cities, new census data show. Retrieved from http://www.National Center for Children in Poverty.org/media/releases/release_162.html.

22. Sharkey, P. (2013). *Stuck in place: Urban neighborhoods and the end of progress toward racial equality*. Chicago: University of Chicago Press.

23. Alexander, M. (2012). *The new Jim Crow: Mass incarceration in the age of colorblindness*. New York: The New Press; HighBeam Research (2015, March 4). Cardin calls DOJ report on Ferguson police deeply troubling and cause to ban racial profiling by all law enforcement. *States News Service*. Retrieved from http://www.highbeam.com/doc/1G1-403994005.html?.

24. Mauer, M. (2006). *Race to incarcerate* (rev. ed.). New York: The New Press.

25. Alexander, M. (2012). *The new Jim Crow: Mass incarceration in the age of colorblindness*. New York: The New Press, p. 6.

26. *Ibid.*, p. 7.

27. Downey, M. (March 21, 2014). New federal report: Racial disparities in school discipline begin in preschool. *Atlanta Journal Constitution*. Retrieved from http://www.ajc.com/weblogs/get-schooled/2014/mar/21/new-federal-report-racial-disparities-school-disci/.

28. Sarche, M., & Spicer, P. (2008). Poverty and health disparities for American Indian and Alaska Native children. *Annals of the New York Academy of Sciences*, 1136(1), 126–136.

29. *Ibid.*

30. Dreby, J. (2012). How today's immigration enforcement policies impact children, families, and communities: A view from the ground. Retrieved from https://cdn.americanprogress.org/wp-content/uploads/2012/08/DrebyImmigrationFamiliesFINAL.pdf; Suárez-Orozco, C. (July 15, 2010). In the best interest of our children: Examining our immigration enforcement policy. Retrieved from http://www.apa.org/about/gr/issues/cyf/immigration-enforcement.aspx.

31. *Ibid.*

32. Urban Institute (2010). Facing our future. Retrieved from http://www.urban.org/research/publication/facing-our-future.

33. *Ibid.*

34. Duncan, G. J., & Brooks-Gunn, J. (1999). *Consequences of growing up poor*. New York: Russell Sage Foundation; Holzer, H. J., Whitmore Schanzenbach, D., Duncan, G. J., & Ludwig, J. (2008). The economic costs of childhood poverty in the United States. *Journal of Children and Poverty*, 14(1), 41–61; Heckman, J. (2006). Skill formation and the economics of investing in disadvantaged children. *Science*, 312(5782), 1900–1902.

35. Holzer, H. J., Whitmore Schanzenbach, D., Duncan, G. J., & Ludwig, J. (2008). The economic costs of childhood poverty in the United States. *Journal of Children and Poverty*, 14(1), 41–61.

36. Heckman, J. (2006). Skill formation and the economics of investing in disadvantaged children. *Science*, 312(5782), 1900–1902.

37. Center on Budget and Policy Priorities (2014). Greenstein testimony before House Budget Committee on poverty and the safety net. Retrieved from http://www.cbpp.org/greenstein-testimony-before-house-budget-committee-on-poverty-and-the-safety-net.

38. *Ibid.*

39. Shaefer, H. L., & Edin, K. (2013). Rising extreme poverty in the United States and the response of federal means-tested transfer programs. *Social Service Review*, 87(2), 250–268.

40. National Campaign to Prevent Teen and Unplanned Pregnancies (2014). Six reasons teen births are plummeting. Retrieved from http://thenationalcampaign.org/.

41. *Ibid.*

42. Hetzner, N. M. P., & Brooks-Gunn, J. (2012). Employment in low-income families. In V. Malholmes & R. B. King (Eds.), *The Oxford handbook of poverty and child development.* New York: Oxford University Press, pp. 240–259.

43. Mincy, R. B., Jethwani, M., & Klempin, S. (2015). *Failing our fathers: Confronting the crisis of economically vulnerable nonresident fathers.* New York: Oxford University Press.

44. Johnson, W. E. Jr. (2000). Work preparation and labor market experiences among urban, poor, non-resident fathers. In S. Danzinger & A. C. Lin (Eds.), *Coping with poverty: The social contexts of neighborhood, work and family in the African American community.* Ann Arbor: University of Michigan Press, pp. 224–261.

45. Mincy, R. B., Jethwani, M., & Klempin, S. (2015). *Failing our fathers: Confronting the crisis of economically vulnerable nonresident fathers.* New York: Oxford University Press; Johnson, W. (2000). Work preparation and labor market experiences among urban, poor, non-resident fathers. In S. Danzinger & A. C. Lin (Eds.), *Coping with poverty: The social contexts of neighborhood, work and family in the African American community,* pp. 224–261.

46. Center on Budget and Policy Priorities (2014). Greenstein testimony before House Budget Committee on poverty and the safety net. Retrieved from http://www.cbpp.org/greenstein-testimony-before-house-budget-committee-on-poverty-and-the-safety-net.

47. Sherman, A., Greenstein, R., & Parrott, S. (2014). Policies to reduce poverty: Supporting family income as an investment in children's futures. In K. McCartney, H. Yoshikawa, & L. B. Forcier (Eds.), *Improving the odds for America's children: Future directions in policy and practice.* Cambridge, MA: Harvard University Press, pp.189–202.

48. CBPP. Countdown day three: Top ten facts about Social Security. Retrieved from http://www.cbpp.org/blog/countdown-day-3-top-ten-facts-about-social-security.

49. CBPP (n.d.) Safety net programs kept millions out of poverty in 2014. Retrieved from http://www.cbpp.org/safety-net-programs-kept-millions-out-of-poverty-in-2014.

50. National Center for Children in Poverty (2015). SNAP kept 4.7 million Americans out of poverty last year. Retrieved from http://www.cbpp.org/blog/snap-kept-47-million-americans-out-of-poverty-last-year.

51. Center on Budget and Policy Priorities (2014). Greenstein testimony before House Budget Committee on poverty and the safety net. Retrieved from http://www.cbpp.org/greenstein-testimony-before-house-budget-committee-on-poverty-and-the-safety-net.

52. Center on Budget and Policy Priorities (2014). Chart book: The War on Poverty at 50, overview. Retrieved from http://www.cbpp.org/research/chart-book-the-war-on-poverty-at-50-overview.

53. National Center for Children in Poverty (2015). Basic facts about low-income children: Children under 6 years, 2013. Retrieved from http://www.National Center for Children in Poverty.org/publications/pub_1096.html

54. National Center for Children in Poverty (2008). Measuring poverty in the United States. Retrieved from http://www.nccp.org/publications/pub_825.html.

55. Center on Budget and Policy Priorities (2014). Greenstein testimony before House Budget Committee on poverty and the safety net. Retrieved from http://www.cbpp.org/greenstein-testimony-before-house-budget-committee-on-poverty-and-the-safety-net.

56. Sharkey, P. (2013). *Stuck in place: Urban neighborhoods and the end of progress toward racial equality.* Chicago: University of Chicago Press; Lindsey, D. (Ed.) (2009). *Child*

poverty and inequality: Securing a better future for America's children. New York: Oxford University Press.

57. Maholmes, V. & King, R. B. (Eds.) (2012). *The Oxford handbook of poverty and child development.* New York: Oxford University Press

58. Sharkey, P. (2013). *Stuck in place: Urban neighborhoods and the end of progress toward racial equality.* Chicago: University of Chicago Press; Lindsey, D. (Ed.) (2009). *Child poverty and inequality: Securing a better future for America's children.* New York: Oxford University Press.

59. National Center for Children in Poverty (2009). Homeless children and youth: Causes and consequences. Retrieved from http://National Center for Children in Poverty.org/publications/pub_888.html; Duncan, G. J., & Murnane, R. J. (2014). *Restoring opportunity: The crisis of inequality and the challenges for American education.* Cambridge, MA: Harvard Education Press.

60. Duncan, G. J. & Murnane, R. J. (2014). *Restoring opportunity: The crisis of inequality and the challenges for American education.* Cambridge, MA: Harvard Education Press, p. 5.

61. Magnuson, K., & Duncan, G. J. (October 2014). Can early childhood interventions decrease inequality of economic opportunity? Prepared for the Federal Reserve Bank of Boston Conference, Inequality of Economic Opportunity in the United States. Retrieved from http://www.bostonfed.org/inequality2014/papers/magnusun-duncan.pdf.

CHAPTER 3

1. Davis, M. (2005). Despite job spurt, R.I. sees wage disparities. *Providence Business News,* Retrieved from: http://pbn.com/Study-Despite-job-spurt-RI-sees-wage-disparities,18609

American Civil Liberties Union, Rhode Island Affiliate (2007). The politics of division: Governor Donald Carcieri's record on civil rights during his second term in office. Retrieved from: http://riaclu.org/images/uploads/The_Politics_of_Division_Report_2007.pdf

Murray, C. (1993). The coming white underclass. *Wall Street Journal,* 29, A14.

2. The Republican "Contract with America." Retrieved from http://wps.prenhall.com/wps/media/objects/434/445252/DocumentsLibrary/docs/contract.htm.

3. Coley, R. L., & Chase-Lansdale, P. L. (1998). Adolescent pregnancy and parenthood: Recent evidence and future directions. *American Psychologist,* 53(2), 152; Gershenson, H. P., Musick, J. S., Ruch-Ross, H. S., Magee, V., Rubino, K. K., & Rosenberg, D. (1989). The prevalence of coercive sexual experience among teenage mothers. *Journal of Interpersonal Violence,* 4(2), 204–219.

4. Kearney, M. S., & Levine, P. B. (2012). Why is the teen birth rate in the United States so high and why does it matter? NBER Working Paper No. 17965. Retrieved from http://www.nber.org/papers/w17965.

5. Annie E. Casey Foundation (2015). The 2015 Kids Count data book. Retrieved from http://www.aecf.org/resources/the-2015-kids-count-data-book/.

6. National Campaign to Prevent Teen and Unplanned Pregnancy (2013). Why it matters: Teen childbearing and child welfare. Retrieved from https://thenationalcampaign.org/resource/why-it-matters-teen-childbearing-and-child-welfare.

7. Coley, R. L., & Chase-Lansdale, P. L. (1998). Adolescent pregnancy and parenthood: Recent evidence and future directions. *American Psychologist,* 53(2), 152.

8. Thornberry, T. P., Smith, C. A., & Howard, G. J. (1997). Risk factors for teenage fatherhood. *Journal of Marriage and the Family,* 59(3), 505–522.

9. Bill O'Reilly (2014). Happy 50th birthday war on poverty. Retrieved from http://www.foxnews.com/transcript/2014/01/10/bill-oreilly-happy-50th-birthday-war-poverty/.

10. American Press Institute (2014). How Americans get their news. Retrieved from http://www.americanpressinstitute.org/publications/reports/survey-research/how-americans-get-news/.

11. Blake, A. (January 23, 2014). Huckabee: Dems think women can't control their libido. *Washington Post*. Retrieved from https://www.washingtonpost.com/news/post-politics/wp/2014/01/23/huckabee-dems-think-women-cant-control-their-libido/.

12. Huffington Post (March 12, 2014). Paul Ryan laments inner-city culture of not working. Retrieved from http://www.huffingtonpost.com/2014/03/12/paul-ryan-inner-cities_n_4949165.html.

13. CNN (March 13, 2014). Ryan's inner-city comments sparking backlash. Retrieved from http://politicalticker.blogs.cnn.com/2014/03/13/ryans-inner-city-comments-sparking-backlash/.

14. Ryan apologized for some of his comments two years later. Retrieved from: http://www.jsonline.com/news/opinion/paul-ryan-apologizes-for-poor-remarks-b99699688z1-375098021.html

15. King, M. L. Jr. (1967). *Where do we go from here: Chaos or community?* New York: Harper and Row.

16. Kristof, N. (March 1, 2014). The compassion gap. *New York Times*. Retrieved from http://www.nytimes.com/2014/03/02/opinion/sunday/kristof-the-compassion-gap.html.

17. Kessler, A. (July 9, 2013). Homeless shelter volunteers are the real cause of homelessness. *Wall Street Journal*.

18. Blow, C. M. (March 22, 2014). Paul Ryan, culture and poverty. *New York Times*. Retrieved from http://www.nytimes.com/2014/03/22/opinion/blow-paul-ryan-culture-and-poverty.html.

19. Shonkoff, J. P., & Bales, S. N. (2011). Science does not speak for itself: Translating child development research for the public and its policymakers. *Child Development*, 82(1), 17–32.

20. U.S. Government Office of Accountability (2010). Supplemental nutrition assistance program: Payment errors and trafficking have declined, but challenges remain. Statement of Kay E. Brown, Director: Education, Workforce, and Income Security Issues: GAO-10-956T. Retrieved from http://www.gao.gov/assets/130/125136.html.

21. Bennett, J. T. (October 23, 2011). Lawmakers push Defense fraud, waste report to influence supercommittee cuts. *The Hill*. Retrieved from http://thehill.com/news-by-subject/defense-homeland-security/189247-lawmakers-push-report-highlighting-11t-in-defense-spending-waste-fraud.

22. Lardner, R. (August 30, 2011) Military spending waste: Up to $60 billion in Iraq, Afghanistan war funds lost to poor planning, oversight, fraud. *Huffington Post*. Retrieved from http://www.huffingtonpost.com/2011/08/30/military-spending-waste_n_942723.html.

23. U.S. Internal Revenue Service (2011). IRS releases new tax gap estimates: Compliance rates remain statistically unchanged from previous study. Retrieved from https://www.irs.gov/uac/IRS-Releases-New-Tax-Gap-Estimates%3B-Compliance-Rates-Remain-Statistically-Unchanged-From-Previous-Study.

24. Yahoo News (August 9, 2012). USDA unveils steps to fight food stamp fraud. Retrieved from http://news.yahoo.com/usda-unveils-steps-fight-food-stamp-fraud-202649946.htm.

25. U.S. Department of Health and Human Services (2012). Office of Inspector General semiannual report to Congress. April 1, 2012–September 30, 2012. Retrieved from: https://oig.hhs.gov/reports-and-publications/archives/semiannual/2012/fall/sar-f12-fulltext.pdf.

26. Bernstein, N. (September 6, 2012). Long-term care looms as rising Medicaid cost. *New York Times*. Retrieved from http://www.nytimes.com/2012/09/07/health/policy/long-term-care-looms-as-rising-medicaid-cost.html.

27. *Ibid.*

28. Schnurer, E. (August 15, 2014). Just how wrong is conventional wisdom about government fraud? *The Atlantic*. Retrieved from www.theatlantic.com/politics/archive/2013/08/just-how-wrong-is-conventional-wisdom-about-government-fraud/278690/.

29. Wessler, S. F. (June 14, 2014). Poll: Fewer Americans blame poverty on the poor, *NBC News*. Retrieved from http://www.nbcnews.com/feature/in-plain-sight/poll-fewer-americans-blame-poverty-poor-n136051.

30. Gilens, M. (2009). *Why Americans hate welfare: Race, media, and the politics of antipoverty policy*. Chicago: University of Chicago Press.

31. Stokes, B. (2013). Public attitudes toward the next social contract. Pew Research Center. Retrieved from http://www.pewglobal.org/files/pdf/Stokes_Bruce_NAF_Public_Attitudes_1_2013.pdf.

32. *Ibid.*

33. Allard, S. W. (2007). The changing face of welfare during the Bush Administration, National Poverty Center working paper series. Retrieved from http://www.npc.umich.edu/publications/u/working_paper07-18.pdf.

34. Lichter, D. T., & Jayakody, R. (2002).Welfare reform: How do we measure success? *Annual Review of Sociology*, 28, 117–141.

35. *Ibid.*

36. Ben-Shalom, Y., Moffit, R. A., & Sholz, J. K. (2011). An assessment of the effectiveness of anti-poverty programs in the United States. Retrieved from http://www.nber.org/papers/w17042.

37. *Ibid.*, p. 7.

38. Allard, S. W. (2007) The changing face of welfare during the Bush Administration, National Poverty Center working paper series. Retrieved from http://www.npc.umich.edu/publications/u/working_paper07-18.pdf.

39. *Ibid.*; Lowry, A. (February 4, 2014). Can marriage cure poverty? *New York Times Magazine*. Retrieved from http://www.nytimes.com/2014/02/09/magazine/can-marriage-cure-poverty.html.

40. MacGillis, A. (July 19, 2007). Obama says he, too, is a poverty fighter. *Washington Post*. Retrieved from http://www.washingtonpost.com/wp-dyn/content/article/2007/07/18/AR2007071802529.html.

41. Center on Budget and Policy Priorities (2015). Obama budget restores housing vouchers: Targets vouchers to reduce homelessness, help victims of domestic violence, keep families together. Retrieved from http://www.cbpp.org/research/housing/obama-budget-restores-housing-vouchers.

42. National Center for Homeless Education (2015). Federal data summary: School years 2011–2012 to 2013–2014, education for homeless children and youth. Retrieved from http://center.serve.org/nche/downloads/data-comp-1112-1314.pdf.

43. Center on Budget and Policy Priorities (2014). SNAP households experienced a benefits cut in November 2013. Retrieved from http://www.cbpp.org/food-assistance/snap-households-experienced-a-benefit-cut-in-november-2013.

44. Center on Budget and Policy Priorities (2012). How states have spent federal and state funds under the TANF Block Grant. Retrieved from http://www.cbpp.org/research/how-states-have-spent-federal-and-state-funds-under-the-tanf-block-grant.

45. Mencimer, S. (April 2, 2014). Paul Ryan has a plan for the poor: It's terrible. *Mother Jones*. Retrieved from http://www.motherjones.com/politics/2014/04/paul-ryan-budget-food-stamps-medicaid-block-grants.

46. Center on Budget and Policy Priorities (2012). How states have spent federal and state funds under the TANF Block Grant. Retrieved from http://www.cbpp.org/research/how-states-have-spent-federal-and-state-funds-under-the-tanf-block-grant.

47. Edelman, P. (2012) *So rich, so poor: Why it's so hard to end poverty in America*. New York: The New Press.

48. Center on Budget and Policy Priorities (2012). How states have spent federal and state funds under the TANF Block Grant. Retrieved from http://www.cbpp.org/research/how-states-have-spent-federal-and-state-funds-under-the-tanf-block-grant.

49. *Ibid.*

50. Center on Budget and Policy Priorities (2015). TANF continues to weaken as a safety net. Retrieved from http://www.cbpp.org/research/family-income-support/tanf-continues-to-weaken-as-a-safety-net.

51. Robles, F. (December 31, 2013). Florida law on drug testing for welfare struck down. *New York Times*. Retrieved from http://www.nytimes.com/2014/01/01/us/florida-law-on-drug-testing-for-welfare-is-struck-down.html; Ganeva, T. (October 17, 2015). Five reasons drug testing welfare recipients is profoundly stupid. *Salon*. Retrieved from http://www.salon.com/2015/10/17/5_reasons_drug_testing_welfare_recipients_is_profoundly_stupid_partner/.

52. Brodesser-Akner, C. (October 20, 2015). Tacking right, Christie now backs welfare drug-testing. *NJ.com*. Retrieved from http://www.nj.com/politics/index.ssf/2015/10/tacking_right_christie_now_backs_welfare_drug-test.html; Zezima, K. (June 23, 2014). Chris Christie has very complicated views on drugs. *Washington Post*. Retrieved from https://www.washingtonpost.com/news/post-politics/wp/2014/06/23/chris-christie-has-very-complicated-views-on-drugs/; Marley, P. (April 7, 2014). Scott Walker signs bills aimed at fighting Wisconsin heroin problems. *Milwaukee Wisconsin Journal Sentinel*. Retrieved from http://www.jsonline.com/news/statepolitics/scott-walker-to-sign-bills-aimed-at-fighting-wisconsin-heroin-problems-b99242123z1-254184721.html; Ganeva, T. (October 17, 2015). Five reasons drug testing welfare recipients is profoundly stupid. *Salon*. Retrieved from http://www.salon.com/2015/10/17/5_reasons_drug_testing_welfare_recipients_is_profoundly_stupid_partner/.

53. Edelman, P. (July 28, 2012). Poverty in America: Why can't we end it? *New York Times*. Retrieved from http://www.nytimes.com/2012/07/29/opinion/sunday/why-cant-we-end-poverty-in-america.html?pagewanted=all; CBPP (2015). TANF continues to weaken as a safety net. Retrieved from http://www.cbpp.org/research/family-income-support/tanf-continues-to-weaken-as-a-safety-net.

54. National Center for Children in Poverty (2015). Basic facts about low-income children: Children under 6 years, 2013. Retrieved from http://www.nccp.org/publications/pub_1097.html.

CHAPTER 4

1. National Research Council and Institute of Medicine; Shonkoff, J. P., & Phillips, D. A. (Eds.). (2000). *From neurons to neighborhoods: The science of early childhood development.* Washington, D.C.: National Academy Press.

2. Shonkoff, J. P. , & Bales, S. N. (2011). Science does not speak for itself: Translating child development research for the public and its policymakers. *Child Development*, 82(1), 17–32.

3. Shonkoff, J. P. (2010). Building a new biodevelopmental framework to guide the future of early childhood policy. *Child Development*, 81(1), 357–367.

4. Shonkoff, J. P., & Bales, S. N. (2011). Science does not speak for itself: Translating child development research for the public and its policymakers. *Child Development*, 82(1), 17–32.

5. Heckman, J. (2008). Schools, skills, and synapses. *Economic Inquiry*, 46(3), 289.

6. Sameroff, A. (2010). A unified theory of development: A dialectic integration of nature and nurture. *Child Development*, 81(1), 6–22; Shonkoff, J. P., Garner, A. S., Siegel, B. S., Dobbins, M. I., Earls, M. F., McGuinn, L., . . . & Wood, D. L. (2012). The lifelong effects of early childhood adversity and toxic stress. *Pediatrics*, 129(1), 232–246.

7. Rutter, M. (2006). *Genes and behavior: Nature–nurture interplay explained.* Oxford: Blackwell Publishers; Rutter, M., Moffitt, T. E., & Caspi, A. (2006). Gene-environment interplay and psychopathology: Multiple varieties but real effects. *Journal of Child Psychology and Psychiatry*, 47(34), 226–261.

8. Shonkoff, J. P., & Bales, S. N. (2011). Science does not speak for itself: Translating child development research for the public and its policymakers. *Child Development*, 82(1), 17–32.

9. *Ibid.*

10. *Ibid.*

11. *Ibid.*

12. McEwen, B. S. (2007). Physiology and neurobiology of stress and adaptation: central role of the brain. *Physiology Review*, 87(3), 873–904.

13. *Ibid.*

14. Shonkoff, J. P., Garner, A. S., Siegel, B. S., Dobbins, M. I., Earls, M. F., McGuinn, L., . . . & Wood, D. L. (2012). The lifelong effects of early childhood adversity and toxic stress. *Pediatrics*, 129(1), e232–e246.

15. *Ibid.*

16. *Ibid.*

17. *Ibid.*

18. Ibid.

19. Mulder, E. J. H., De Medina, P. R., Huizink, A. C., Van den Bergh, B. R. H., Buitelaar, J. K., & Visser, G. H. A. (2002). Prenatal maternal stress: effects on pregnancy and the (unborn) child. *Early Human Development*, 70(1), 3–14.

20. Shonkoff, J. P., Garner, A. S., Siegel, B. S., Dobbins, M. I., Earls, M. F., McGuinn, L., . . . & Wood, D. L. (2012). The lifelong effects of early childhood adversity and toxic stress. *Pediatrics*, 129(1), 232–246.

21. *Ibid.*; Propper, C. (2012). The early development of vagal tone: Effects of poverty and elevated contextual risk. In V. Malhomes & R. B. King (Eds.), *The Oxford handbook of poverty and child development*. New York: Oxford University Press, pp. 103–123.

22. Alkon, A., Wolff, B., & Boyce, W. T. (2012). Poverty, stress, and autonomic reactivity. In V. Maholmes and R. B. King (Eds.), *The Oxford handbook of poverty and child development*. New York: Oxford University Press, pp 221–239.

23. Shonkoff, J. P., Garner, A. S., Siegel, B. S., Dobbins, M. I., Earls, M. F., McGuinn, L., . . . & Wood, D. L. (2012). The lifelong effects of early childhood adversity and toxic stress. *Pediatrics*, 129(1), 232–246; Propper, C. (2012). The early development of vagal tone: Effects of poverty and elevated contextual risk. In V. Malhomes & R. B. King (Eds.), *The Oxford handbook of poverty and child development*. New York: Oxford University Press; pp. 103–123. Alkon, A., Wolff, B., & Boyce, W. T. (2012). Poverty, stress, and autonomic reactivity. In V. Maholmes & R. B. King (Eds.), *The Oxford handbook of poverty and child development*. New York: Oxford University Press, pp 221–239.

24. Felitti, V. J., Anda, R. F., Nordenberg, D., Williamson, D. F., Spitz, A. M., Edwards, V., . . . & Marks, J. S. (1998). Relationship of childhood abuse and household dysfunction to many of the leading causes of death in adults: The Adverse Childhood Experiences (ACE) Study. *American Journal of Preventive Medicine*, 14(4), 245–258.

25. *Ibid.*

26. *Ibid.*

27. Alkon, A., Wolff, B., & Boyce, W. T. (2012). Poverty, stress, and autonomic reactivity. In V. Maholmes & R. B. King (Eds.), *The Oxford handbook of poverty and child development*. New York: Oxford University Press, pp 221–239.

28. Felitti, V. J., Anda, R. F., Nordenberg, D., Williamson, D. F., Spitz, A. M., Edwards, V., . . . & Marks, J. S. (1998). Relationship of childhood abuse and household dysfunction to many of the leading causes of death in adults: The Adverse Childhood Experiences (ACE) Study. *American Journal of Preventive Medicine*, 14(4), 245–258.

29. Compas, B. E., Hinden, B. R., & Gerhardt, C. A. (1995). Adolescent development: Pathways and processes of risk and resilience. *Annual Review of Psychology*, 46(1), 265–293; Barrera, M., Prelow, H. M., Dumka, L. E., Gonzales, N. A., Knight, G. P., Michaels, M. L., . . . & Tein, J. (2002). Pathways from family economic conditions to adolescents' distress: Supportive parenting, stressors outside the family, and deviant peers. *Journal of Community Psychology*, 30(2), 135–152.

30. Drake, B., & Rank, M. R. (2009). The racial divide among American children in poverty: Reassessing the importance of neighborhood. *Children and Youth Services Review, 31*(12), 1264–1271.

31. Zeanah, C. H., & Scheeringa, M. (1996). Evaluation of posttraumatic symptomatology in infants and young children exposed to violence. *Zero to Three, 16*, 9–14.

32. *Ibid.*; Carter, A. S., Garrity-Rokous, E. F., Chazan-Cohen, R., Little, C., & Briggs-Gowan, M. J. (2001). Maternal depression and co-morbidity: Predicting early parenting, attachment security, and toddler social-emotional problems and competencies. *Journal of the American Academy of Child & Adolescent Psychiatry*, 40(1), 18–26; Westbrook, T. R., & Jones Harden, B. (2010). Pathways among exposure to violence, maternal depression, family structure, and child outcomes through parenting: A multigroup analysis. *American Journal of Orthopsychiatry*, 80(3), 386–400; Hans, S. L., Bernstein, V. J., & Henson, L. G. (1999). The role of psychopathology in the parenting of drug-dependent women. *Development and Psychopathology*, 11(4), 957–977; Whitaker, R. C., Orzol, S. M., & Kahn, R. S. (2006). Maternal mental health, substance use, and domestic violence in the year after delivery and subsequent behavior problems in children at age 3 years. *Archives of General Psychiatry*, 63(5), 551–560.

33. Carter, A. S., Garrity-Rokous, E. F., Chazan-Cohen, R., Little, C., & Briggs-Gowan, M. J. (2001). Maternal depression and co-morbidity: Predicting early parenting, attachment security, and toddler social-emotional problems and competencies. *Journal of the*

American Academy of Child & Adolescent Psychiatry, 40(1), 18–26; Westbrook, T. R., & Jones Harden, B. (2010). Pathways among exposure to violence, maternal depression, family structure, and child outcomes through parenting: A multigroup analysis. *American Journal of Orthopsychiatry*, 80(3), 386–400; Whitaker, R. C., Orzol, S. M., & Kahn, R. S. (2006). Maternal mental health, substance use, and domestic violence in the year after delivery and subsequent behavior problems in children at age 3 years. *Archives of General Psychiatry*, 63(5), 551–560.

34. Knitzer, J., Theberge, S., & Johnson, K. (2008). Reducing maternal depression and its impact on young children: Toward a responsive early childhood policy framework. Retrieved from http://academiccommons.columbia.edu/catalog/ac:126465; Morris, P. A. (2008). Welfare program implementation and parents' depression. *The Social Service Review*, 82(4), 579; Dodge, K. A. (1990). Developmental psychopathology in children of depressed mothers. *Developmental Psychology*, 26(1), 3.

35. Thompson, R., & Wiley, T. R. (2009). Predictors of re-referral to child protective services: A longitudinal follow-up of an urban cohort maltreated as infants. *Child Maltreatment*, 14(1), 89–99; Petterson, S. M., & Albers, A. B. (2001). Effects of poverty and maternal depression on early childhood development. *Child Development*, 72(1), 1794–1813.

36. Carter, A. S., Garrity-Rokous, E. F., Chazan-Cohen, R., Little, C., & Briggs-Gowan, M. J. (2001). Maternal depression and co-morbidity: Predicting early parenting, attachment security, and toddler social-emotional problems and competencies. *Journal of the American Academy of Child & Adolescent Psychiatry*, 40(1), 18–26.

37. Goodman, S. H., Rouse, M. H., Connell, A. M., Broth, M. R., Hall, C. M., & Heyward, D. (2011). Maternal depression and child psychopathology: a meta-analytic review. *Clinical Child and Family Psychology Review*, 14(1), 1–27.

38. Thompson, R., & Wiley, T. R. (2009). Predictors of re-referral to child protective services: A longitudinal follow-up of an urban cohort maltreated as infants. *Child Maltreatment*, 14(1), 89–99; Westbrook, T. R., & Jones Harden, B. (2010). Pathways among exposure to violence, maternal depression, family structure, and child outcomes through parenting: A multi-group analysis. *American Journal of Orthopsychiatry*, 80(3), 386–400; Conron, K. J., Beardslee, W., Koenen, K. C., Buka, S. L., & Gortmaker, S. L. (2009). A longitudinal study of maternal depression and child maltreatment in a national sample of families investigated by child protective services. *Archives of Pediatrics & Adolescent Medicine*, 163(10), 922–930.

39. Whitaker, R. C., Orzol, S. M., & Kahn, R. S. (2006). Maternal mental health, substance use, and domestic violence in the year after delivery and subsequent behavior problems in children at age 3 years. *Archives of General Psychiatry*, 63(5), 551–560; Huang, L. N., & Freed, R. (2006). The spiraling effects of maternal depression on mothers, children, families and communities (Issue Brief No. 2). Baltimore, MD: The Annie E. Casey Foundation.

40. Pollack, H. A., Danziger, S., Jayakody, R., & Seefeld, K. S. (2002). Drug testing welfare recipients—false positives, false negatives, unanticipated opportunities. *Women's Health Issues*, 12, 23–31; Nair, P., Schuler, M. E., Black, M. M., Kettinger, L., & Harrington, D. (2003). Cumulative environmental risk in substance abusing women: Early intervention, parenting stress, child abuse potential and child development. *Child Abuse & Neglect*, 27(9), 997–1017.

41. Hans, S. L., Bernstein, V. J., & Henson, L. G. (1999). The role of psychopathology in the parenting of drug-dependent women. *Development and Psychopathology*, 11(4), 957–977; Whitaker, R. C., Orzol, S. M., & Kahn, R. S. (2006). Maternal mental health, substance use,

and domestic violence in the year after delivery and subsequent behavior problems in children at age 3 years. *Archives of General Psychiatry, 63*(5), 551–560.

42. Hans, S. L., Bernstein, V. J., & Henson, L. G. (1999). The role of psychopathology in the parenting of drug-dependent women. *Development and Psychopathology, 11*(4), 957–977; Nair, P., Schuler, M. E., Black, M. M., Kettinger, L., & Harrington, D. (2003). Cumulative environmental risk in substance abusing women: early intervention, parenting stress, child abuse potential and child development. *Child Abuse & Neglect, 27*(9), 997–1017.

43. Whitaker, R. C., Orzol, S. M., & Kahn, R. S. (2006). Maternal mental health, substance use, and domestic violence in the year after delivery and subsequent behavior problems in children at age 3 years. *Archives of General Psychiatry, 63*(5), 551–560.

44. U.S. Government Accounting Office, 1998

45. Graham-Bermann, S. A., & Seng, J. (2005). Violence exposure and traumatic stress symptoms as additional predictors of health problems in high-risk children. *Journal of Pediatrics, 146*(3), 349–354; Westbrook, T. R., & Jones Harden, B. (2010). Pathways among exposure to violence, maternal depression, family structure, and child outcomes through parenting: A multigroup analysis. *American Journal of Orthopsychiatry, 80*(3), 386–400; Lieberman, A. F., & Van Horn, P. (1998). Attachment, trauma, and domestic violence. Implications for child custody. *Child and Adolescent Psychiatry Clinics of North America, 7*(2), 423; Zeanah, C. H., & Scheeringa, M. (1996). Evaluation of posttraumatic symptomatology in infants and young children exposed to violence. *Zero to Three, 16*, 9–14.

46. Westbrook, T. R., & Jones Harden, B. (2010). Pathways among exposure to violence, maternal depression, family structure, and child outcomes through parenting: A multigroup analysis. *American Journal of Orthopsychiatry, 80*(3), 386–400; Nair, P., Schuler, M. E., Black, M. M., Kettinger, L., & Harrington, D. (2003). Cumulative environmental risk in substance abusing women: early intervention, parenting stress, child abuse potential and child development. *Child Abuse & Neglect, 27*(9), 997–1017; Shonkoff, J. P., Garner, A. S., Siegel, B. S., Dobbins, M. I., Earls, M. F., McGuinn, L., ... & Wood, D. L. (2012). The lifelong effects of early childhood adversity and toxic stress. *Pediatrics, 129*(1), e232–e246; Belsky, J., & Jaffee, S. R. (2006). The multiple determinants of parenting. In D. Cicchetti & D. Cohen (Eds.), *Developmental psychopathology* (2nd ed.). Hoboken, NJ: Wiley, pp. 38–85.

47. Lynch, M., & Cicchetti, D. (2002). Links between community violence and the family system: Evidence from children's feelings of relatedness and perceptions of parent behavior. *Family Process, 41*(3), 519–532; McCurdy, K., Gorman, K. S., Kisler, T. S., & Metallinos-Kataras, E. (2012). Maternal mental health and child health and nutrition. In V. Maholmes & R. B. King (Eds.), *The Oxford handbook of poverty and child development*. New York: Oxford University Press.

48. Yeshuda, R., et al. (2015). Holocaust exposure induced intergenerational effects on FKBP5 methylation. *Biological Psychiatry,* DOI: http://dx.doi.org/10.1016/j.biopsych.2015.08.005

49. Shonkoff, J. P., Garner, A. S., Siegel, B. S., Dobbins, M. I., Earls, M. F., McGuinn, L., ... & Wood, D. L. (2012). The lifelong effects of early childhood adversity and toxic stress. *Pediatrics, 129*(1), 232–246.

50. Brooks-Gunn, J., & Duncan, G. J. (1997). The effects of poverty on children. *The Future of Children, 7*(2), 55–71.

51. Goldenberg, R. L., & Culhane, J. F. (2007). Low birth weight in the United States. *American Journal of Clinical Nutrition, 85*(2), 584S–590S.

52. Brooks-Gunn, J., & Duncan, G. J. (1997). The effects of poverty on children. *The Future of Children*, 7(2), 55–71; Goldenberg, R. L., & Culhane, J. F. (2007). Low birth weight in the United States. *American Journal of Clinical Nutrition*, 85(2), 584S–590S.

53. Hart, B., & Risley, T. (1995). *Meaningful differences in everyday parenting and intellectual development in young American children*. Baltimore, MD: Brookes.

54. Evans, G. W. (2004). The environment of childhood poverty. *American Psychologist*, 59(2), 77.

55. Heckman, J. J. (2006). Skill formation and the economics of investing in disadvantaged children. *Science*, 312(5782), 1900–1902.

56. Evans, G. W. (2004). The environment of childhood poverty. *American Psychologist*, 59(2), 77.

57. Phillips, D., Voran, M., Kisker, E., Howes, C., & Whitbook, M. (1994).Childcare for children in poverty: Opportunity or inequity? *Child Development*, 65, 472–492.

58. Aratani, Y. (2009). Homeless children and youth: Causes and consequences. Retrieved from http://www.nccp.org/publications/pdf/text_888.pdf.

59. Rafferty, Y., & Shinn, M. (1991). The impact of homelessness on children. *American Psychologist*, 46(11), 1170.

60. *Ibid.*

61. *Ibid.*

62. Children's Health Watch (n.d.).Overcrowding and frequent moves undermine children's health. Retrieved from http://www.childrenshealthwatch.org/upload/resource/crowdedmultimoves_brief_nov11.pdf.

63. Olivo, A. (March 28, 2010). Housing crisis drives families into overcrowded living conditions. *Chicago Tribune*. Retrieved from http://articles.chicagotribune.com/2010-03-28/classified/ct-met-overcrowded-housing-0328-20100327_1_foreclosures-housing-suburbs.

64. Breysse, P., Farr, N., Galke, W., Lanphear, B., Morley, R., & Bergofsky, L. (2004). The relationship between housing and health: children at risk. *Environmental Health Perspectives*, 112(15), 1583–1588.

65. Rauh, V. A., Landrigan, P. J., & Claudio, L. (2008). Housing and health. *Annals of the New York Academy of Sciences*, 1136(1), 276–288.

66. *Ibid.*

67. Evans, G. W. (2004). The environment of childhood poverty. *American Psychologist*, 59(2), 77.

68. Graziano, J. H., Loiacono, N. J., Moulton, N. J., et al. (1992). Controlled study of meso-2,3-dimercaptosuccinic acid (DMSA) for the management of childhood lead intoxication. *Journal of Pediatrics*, 120, 133–139.

69. Rauh, V. A., Landrigan, P. J., & Claudio, L. (2008). Housing and health. *Annals of the New York Academy of Sciences*, 1136(1), 276–288.

70. Krieger, J., & Higgins, D. L. (2002). Housing and health: Time again for public health action. *American Journal of Public Health*, 92(5), 758–768.

71. Rauh, V. A., Landrigan, P. J., & Claudio, L. (2008). Housing and health. *Annals of the New York Academy of Sciences*, 1136(1), 276–288.

72. Breysse, P., Farr, N., Galke, W., Lanphear, B., Morley, R., & Bergofsky, L. (2004). The relationship between housing and health: Children at risk. *Environmental Health Perspectives*, 112, 1583–1588; Williams, D. R., Sternthal, M., & Wright, R. J. (2009). Social determinants: Taking the social context of asthma seriously. *Pediatrics*, 123, S174–S184.

73. Morland, K., Wing, S., Diez-Roux, A., & Poole, C. (2002). Neighborhood characteristics associated with the location of food stores and food service places. *American Journal of Preventive Medicine, 22,* 23–29.

74. Beaulac, J., Kristjansson, E., & Cummins, S. (2009). A systematic review of food deserts, 1966–2007. *Preventing Chronic Disease, 6*(3), 1–10. http://researchonline.lshtm.ac.uk/491627/1/PCD63A105.pdf

75. Polhamus, B., Dalenius, K., Borland, E., Smith, B., & Grummer-Strawn, L. (2007). Pediatric nutrition surveillance report 2006. Atlanta, GA: Department of Health and Human Services, Centers for Disease Control and Prevention; Cusick, S. E., Mei, Z., & Cogswell, M. E. (2007). Continuing anemia prevention strategies are needed throughout early childhood in low-income preschool children. *Journal of Pediatrics, 150*(4), 422–428.

76. McCurdy, K., Gorman, K. S., Kisler, T. S., & Metallinos-Kataras, E. (2012). Maternal mental health and child health and nutrition. In V. Maholmes & R. B. King (Eds.), *The Oxford handbook of poverty and child development.* New York: Oxford University Press.

77. U.S. Centers for Disease Control (2013). Vital signs: Progress on child obesity. Retrieved from http://www.cdc.gov/vitalsigns/childhoodobesity/; Phipps, S. A., Burton, P. S., Osberg, L. S., & Lethbridge, L. N. (2006). Poverty and the extent of child obesity in Canada, Norway and the United States. *Obesity Reviews, 7*(1), 5–12.

78. Evans, G. W. (2004). The environment of childhood poverty. *American Psychologist, 59*(2), 77.

79. Evans, G. W., & Kantrowitz, E. (2002). Socioeconomic status and health: the potential role of environmental risk exposure. *Annual Review of Public Health, 23*(1), 303–331.

80. Schwartz, J. (2004). Air pollution and children's health. *Pediatrics, 113*(Suppl. 3), 1037–1043.

81. Metzger, R., Delgado, J. L., & Herrell, R. (1995). Environmental health and Hispanic children. *Environmental Health Perspectives, 103*(Suppl. 6), 25.

82. Sharkey, P. (2013). *Stuck in place: Urban neighborhoods and the end of progress toward racial equality.* Chicago: University of Chicago Press.

83. *Ibid.*

84. Garcia, E., & Weiss, E. (2014). Segregation and peers' characteristics in the 2010–2011 kindergarten class: 60 years after *Brown v. Board.* Retrieved from http://www.epi.org/publication/segregation-and-peers-characteristics/.

85. Finkelhor, D., & Ormrod, R. (2001). Homicides of children and youth. Retrieved from http://usdemo.missingkids.com/en_US/archive/documents/homicide_children.pdf.

86. Federman, M., Garner, T. I., Short, K., Cutter IV, W. B., Kiely, J., Levine, D., McGough D. & McMillen, M. (1996) What does it mean to be poor in America. *Monthly Labor Review, 119*(5), 3–17.

87. Bentley, M. E., Dee, D. L., & Jensen, J. L. (2003). Breastfeeding among low income, African-American women: power, beliefs and decision making. *Journal of Nutrition, 133*(1), 305S–309S.

88. Wright, R. J., Mitchell, H., Visness, C. M., Cohen, S., Stout, J., Evans, R., & Gold, D. R. (2004). Community violence and asthma morbidity: The Inner-City Asthma Study. *American Journal of Public Health, 94*(4), 625–632.

89. Kling, J. R., Liebman, J. B., & Katz, L. F. (2005). Bullets don't got no name: Consequences of fear in the ghetto. Retrieved from http://www.nber.org/mtopublic/boston/mto_boston_bullets.pdf; Lynch, M., & Cicchetti, D. (2002). Links between community violence and the family system: Evidence from children's feelings of relatedness and perceptions of parent behavior. *Family Process, 41*(3), 519–532.

90. Drake, B., & Rank, M. R. (2009). The racial divide among American children in poverty: Reassessing the importance of neighborhood. *Children and Youth Services Review*, 31(12), 1264–1271.

91. Sedlak, A. J., Mettenburg, J., Basena, M., Petta, I., McPherson, K., Greene, A., et al. (2010). *Fourth National Incidence Study of Child Abuse and Neglect (NIS-4): Report to Congress*. Washington, D.C.: U.S. Department of Health and Human Services; Administration for Children and Families; Office of Planning, Research, and Evaluation; and the Children's Bureau.

92. Lansford, J. E., Dodge, K. A., Pettit, G. S., Bates, J. E., Crozier, J., & Kaplow, J. (2002). A 12-year prospective study of the long-term effects of early child physical maltreatment on psychological, behavioral, and academic problems in adolescence. *Archives of Pediatrics &Adolescent Medicine*, 156(8), 824–830.

93. Jaffee, S., & Christian, C. W. (2014). The biological embedding of child abuse and neglect: Implications for policy and practice. *Social Policy Reports*, 28(1), 12.

94. Perry, B. D. (2002). Childhood experience and the expression of genetic potential: What childhood neglect tells us about nature and nurture. *Brain and Mind*, 3(1), 79–100.

95. Barrera, M., Prelow, H. M., Dumka, L. E., Gonzales, N. A., Knight, G. P., Michaels, M. L., . . . & Tein, J. (2002). Pathways from family economic conditions to adolescents' distress: Supportive parenting, stressors outside the family, and deviant peers. *Journal of Community Psychology*, 30(2), 135–152.

96. Werner, E. E. (1989). High-risk children in young adulthood: a longitudinal study from birth to 32 years. *American Journal of Orthopsychiatry*, 59(1), 72; Compas, B. E., Hinden, B. R., & Gerhardt, C. A. (1995). Adolescent development: Pathways and processes of risk and resilience. *Annual Review of Psychology*, 46(1), 265–293.

97. Davis, L. E. (2014), Have we gone too far with resiliency? *Social Work Research*, 38(1), 5–6.

CHAPTER 5

1. Burch, A. D. S., & Miller, C. M. (March 20, 2014). Innocents lost: Death by irresponsible parenting, bureaucratic inaction. *Miami Herald*. Retrieved from http://www.miamiherald.com/projects/2014/innocents-lost/stories/inglis/#storylink=cpy.

2. *Miami Herald* (n.d.). Innocents Lost database. Retrieved from http://www.miamiherald.com/projects/2014/innocents-lost/database/#134.

3. Stoelje, M. F. (December 28, 2013). Texas foster deaths hit grim record. *San Antonio Express News*. Retrieved from http://www.expressnews.com/news/local/article/Texas-foster-deaths-hit-grim-record-5098972.php#/0.

4. Wen, P. (May 25, 2014). The short, nomadic life of Jeremiah Oliver, failed by all. *Boston Globe*. Retrieved from http://www.bostonglobe.com/metro/2014/05/24/the-short-nomadic-life-jeremiah-oliver-failed-all/WTQcjXthTi3ruSwb7BuInO/story.html.

5. Levenson, N., & Wen, P. (April 29, 2014). Veteran manager Erin Deveney takes over as child welfare chief: Roche resigns under fire. *Boston Globe*. Retrieved from http://www.bostonglobe.com/metro/2014/04/29/one-day-after-top-state-leaders-call-for-dismissal-dcf-chief-olga-roche-patrick-administration-hold-press-conference/nB6hGFhKcs-jVAWkQW38i7L/story.html.

6. U.S. Department of Health & Human Services, Administration for Children and Families, Administration on Children, Youth and Families, Children's Bureau (2016). Child

maltreatment 2014. Available from http://www.acf.hhs.gov/programs/cb/research-data-technology/statistics-research/child-maltreatment.

7. Sedlak, A. J., & Broadhurst, D. D. (1996). Executive Summary of the Third National Incidence Study of Child Abuse and Neglect (NIS-3). Retrieved from https://www.ncjrs.gov/App/Publications/abstract.aspx?ID=166288.

8. Wald, M. (2014). Beyond child protection. In K. McCartney, H. Yoshikawa, & L. B Forcier (Eds.), *Improving the odds for America's children: Future directions in policy and practice.* Cambridge, MA: Harvard Education Press.

9. Plotnick, R. D., (1992). Income support for families with children. In P. J. Pecora, J. K. Whittaker, & A. N. Maluccio (Eds.), *The child welfare challenge: Policy, practice and research.* New York: Aldine De Gruyter; Goldman, J., Salus, M. K., Wolcott, D., & Kennedy, K. Y. (2003). *A coordinated response to child abuse and neglect: The foundation for practice.* Washington, D.C.: Office on Child Abuse and Neglect, Children's Bureau.

10. Cicchetti, D., & Lynch, M. (1993). Toward an ecological/transactional model of community violence and child maltreatment: Consequences for children's development. *Psychiatry,* 56(1), 96–118.

11. U.S. Department of Health & Human Services, Administration for Children and Families, Administration on Children, Youth and Families, Children's Bureau (2016). Child maltreatment 2014. Available from http://www.acf.hhs.gov/programs/cb/research-data-technology/statistics-research/child-maltreatment.

12. *Ibid.*

13. Stoltzfus, E. (August 25, 2005). *Race/ethnicity and child welfare.* Washington, D.C.: Congressional Research Service.

14. Harris, M., & Courtney, M. (2003). The interaction of race, ethnicity, and family structure with respect to timing of family reunification. *Children and Youth Services Review,* 25(5/6), 409–429.

15. Roberts, D. E. (2003). Child welfare and civil rights. *University of Illinois Law Review,* 171, Retrieved from http://scholarship.law.upenn.edu/cgi/viewcontent.cgi?article=1584&context=faculty_scholarship; Bartholet, E. (2009). Racial disproportionality movement in child welfare: False facts and dangerous directions. *Arizona Law Review,* 51, 871.

16. U.S. Department of Health and Human Services (2013). Recent demographic trends in foster care. Data brief 2013-1. Retrieved from http://www.acf.hhs.gov/sites/default/files/cb/data_brief_foster_care_trends1.pdf

17. Alexandre, M. (2010). *The new Jim Crow: Mass incarceration in the age of colorblindness.* New York: The New Press.

18. Full disclosure: I served as an expert witness for Children's Rights in this case.

19. Weekes, M. (February 22, 2014). Olga Roche needs bigger budget [letter to the editor]. *Boston Globe.* Retrieved from http://www.bostonglobe.com/opinion/letters/2014/02/22/roche-can-job-she-has-resources/XtlOawFsuLbFdXEgrZVK5J/story.html.

20. Horowitz, E. (June 2, 2014). Making children less vulnerable. *Boston Globe.*

21. Douglas, J. (May 21, 2012). Texas cuts efforts to prevent child abuse. *CBS DFW.* Retrieved from http://dfw.cbslocal.com/2012/05/21/texas-cuts-efforts-to-prevent-child-abuse/.

22. Klas, M. E. (March 11, 2014). Legislators propose improvements to "porous" child welfare system. *Miami Herald.*

23. Child Welfare League of America (2012). Sequestration and the impact on state child welfare budgets. Retrieved from http://www.cwla.org/advocacy/StateCharts.pdf.

24. Miller, C. M., & Burch, A. D. (March 16, 2014). Innocents Lost: Preserving families but losing children. *Miami Herald*.

25. *Ibid.*

26. Miller, C. M., & Burch, A. D. (March 16, 2014). Innocents Lost: The littlest victims of Florida's drug binge. *Miami Herald*.

27. Levenson, M. (May 29, 2014). Report on DCF creates furor: Agency not blamed for boy's death; Lawmakers rebuke group's findings. *Boston Globe*. Retrieved from https://www.highbeam.com/doc/1P2-36099310.html.

28. Levenson, M. (March 27, 2014). Audit turns up host of problems at DCF. *Boston Globe*.

29. Barth, R. P., Lloyd, E. C., Christ, S. L., Chapman, M. V., & Dickinson, N. S. (2008). Child welfare worker characteristics and job satisfaction: A national study. *Social Work*, 53(3), 199–209.

30. U.S. Department of Health and Human Services, The Children's Bureau (2016). Child maltreatment 2014. Retrieved from. http://www.acf.hhs.gov/sites/default/files/cb/cm2014.pdf#page=31

31. Zero to Three (2013). Changing the course for infants and toddlers: A survey of state child welfare policies and initiatives. http://www.zerotothree.org/policy/docs/changing-the-course-for-infants-and-toddlers.pdf

32. *Ibid.*

33. Zito, J. M., Safer, D. J., Gardner, J. F., Boles, M., & Lynch, F. (2000). Trends in the prescribing of psychotropic medications to preschoolers. *JAMA*, 283(8), 1025–1030.

34. Zito, J. M., Safer, D. J., Sai, D., Gardner, J. F., Thomas, D., Coombes, P., ... & Mendez-Lewis, M. (2008). Psychotropic medication patterns among youth in foster care. *Pediatrics*, 121(1), e157–e163.

35. Jaffee, S., & Christian, C. W. (2014). The biological embedding of child abuse and neglect: Implications for policy and practice. *Social Policy Reports*, 28(1), 12.

36. U.S. Centers for Disease Control and Prevention (2013). Tuskegee timeline. Retrieved from http://www.cdc.gov/tuskegee/timeline.htm.

37. U.S. Department of Health and Human Services (2015). The AFCARS Report: Preliminary FY 2014 estimates as of July, 2015, No. 20. Retrieved from https://www.acf.hhs.gov/sites/default/files/cb/afcarsreport22.pdf.

38. *Ibid.*

39. Chapin Hall, (2005). Foster care dynamics: 2000–2005. Retrieved from http://www.chapinhall.org/sites/default/files/old_reports/406.pdf.

40. U.S. Department for Health and Human Services (2012). Child welfare outcomes 2008–2011: Report to Congress. Retrieved from https://www.acf.hhs.gov/sites/default/files/cb/cwo08_11.pdf#page=7.

41. Newton, R. R., Litrownik, A. J., & Landsverk, J. A. (2000). Children and youth in foster care: Disentangling the relationship between problem behaviors and number of placements. *Child Abuse & Neglect*, 24, 1363–1374; Rubin, D. M., Alessandrini, E. A., Feudtner, C., Mandell, D. S., Localio, A. R., & Hadley, T. (2004). Placement stability and mental health costs for children in foster care. *Pediatrics*, 113, 1336–1341.

42. James, S. (2004). Why do foster care placements disrupt? An investigation of reasons for placement change in foster care. *Social Service Review*, 78(4), 601–627.

43. Dworsky, A., & Courtney, M. E. (2010). The risk of teenage pregnancy among transitioning foster youth: Implications for extending state care beyond age 18. *Child and Youth Services Review*, 32(10), 1351–1356.

44. National Campaign to Prevent Teen and Unplanned Pregnancy (2012). President Obama proposes focus on pregnancy prevention programs for youth in foster care. Retrieved from http://thenationalcampaign.org/blog/president-obama-proposes-focus-pregnancy-prevention-programs-youth-foster-care.

45. Estes, R. J., & Weiner, N. A. (2001). The commercial sexual exploitation of children in the US, Canada and Mexico. Retrieved from http://abolitionistmom.org/wp-content/uploads/2014/05/Complete_CSEC_oestes-weiner.pdf; Clawson, H. J., Dutch, N., Solomon, A., & Grace, L. G. (2009). Human trafficking into and within the United States: A review of the literature. Washington, D.C.: Office of the Assistant Secretary for Planning and Evaluation, US Department of Human and Health Services. Retrieved from http://aspe.hhs.gov/hsp/07/humantrafficking/LitRev/; Sewell, A. (November 27, 2012). Most of L.A. County youths held for prostitution come from foster care. *Los Angeles Times*. Retrieved from http://articles.latimes.com/2012/nov/27/local/la-me-1128-sex-trafficking-20121128.

46. U.S. Department of Health and Human Services (2015). The AFCARS Report: Preliminary FY 2014 estimates as of July, 2015, No. 22. Retrieved from. http://www.acf.hhs.gov/sites/default/files/cb/afcarsreport22.pdf

47. Berzin, S. C., Rhodes, A. M., & Curtis, M. A. (2011), Housing experiences of former foster youth: How do they fare in comparison to other youth? *Children and Youth Services Review*, 33, 2119–2126.

48. Dworsky, A., & Courtney, M. E. (2010). The risk of teenage pregnancy among transitioning foster youth: Implications for extending state care beyond age 18. *Child and Youth Services Review*, 32(10), 1351–1356.

49. National Campaign to Prevent Teen and Unplanned Pregnancy (2013). Why it matters: Teen childbearing and child welfare. Retrieved from http://thenationalcampaign.org/sites/default/files/resource-primary-download/childbearing-childwelfare.pdf.

CHAPTER 6

1. Heckman, J. J. (2008). The case for investing in disadvantaged young children. Retrieved from http://heckmanequation.org/content/resource/case-investing-disadvantaged-young-children.

2. The Committee has since changed its name to Prevent Child Abuse America.

3. Human children were not the first group for which a protective organization was formed in the United States; the Society for the Prevention of Cruelty to Animals was founded nearly ten years prior, and served as an inspiration for child protective programs.

4. Gomby, D. S., Culross, P. L., & Behrman, R. E. (1999). Home visiting: Recent program evaluations: Analysis and recommendations. *The Future of Children*, 4–26.

5. Daro, D. (2006). *Home visitation: Assessing progress, managing expectations*. Ounce of Prevention Fund and Chapin Hall Centre for Children; Sweet, M. A., & Appelbaum, M. I. (2004). Is home visiting an effective strategy? A meta-analytic review of home visiting programs for families with young children. *Child Development*, 75(5), 1435–1456.

6. Gomby, D. S. (2005). *Home visitation in 2005: Outcomes for children and parents*. Washington, D.C.: Committee on Economic Development.

7. Szalavitz, M. (March 2, 2009). Nurse home visits: A boost for low-income parents. *Time Magazine*.

8. Delaware Governor's Office (August 22, 2014). Governor's Weekly Message: Creating healthier communities through Nurse Family Partnership. Retrieved from http://news.

delaware.gov/2014/08/22/governors-weekly-message-creating-healthier-communities-through-nurse-family-partnership/.

9. Neuman, S. B. (2008). *Changing the odds: Seven essential principles of educational programs that break the cycle of poverty.* Westport, CT: Praeger.

10. Kristof, N., & WuDunn, S. (September 14, 2014). The way to beat poverty. *New York Times.* Retrieved from http://www.nytimes.com/2014/09/14/opinion/sunday/nicholas-kristof-the-way-to-beat-poverty.html?_r=0.

11. Neuman, S. B. (2008). *Changing the odds: Seven essential principles of educational programs that break the cycle of poverty.* Westport, CT: Praeger; Olds, D. L., Henderson Jr, C. R., Kitzman, H. J., Eckenrode, J. J., Cole, R. E., & Tatelbaum, R. C. (1999). Prenatal and infancy home visitation by nurses: Recent findings. *The Future of Children,* 9(1), 44–65.

12. The federal government, through its Home Visiting Evidence of Effectiveness (HomVEE) Project, contributes to the confusion regarding the impacts of NFP and other home-vising programs. For instance, the HomVEE website says that its conclusions are based on 21 studies of NFP. However, when one looks up those studies, they are mainly the original 3 studies (Elmira, Memphis, and Denver) plus various follow up assessments of the children and families participating in those three studies. See: U.S. Department of Health and Human Services, Administration for Youth and Families (n.d.) Nurse Family Partnership (NFP)®: Effects Shown in Research & Outcome Measure Details for Child Development and School Readiness Outcomes, at: http://homvee.acf.hhs.gov/Effects/1/Nurse-Family-Partnership--NFP--Effects-Shown-in-Research---Outcome-Measure-Details/14/Child-Development-and-School-Readiness/3/4

13. Coalition for Evidence-Based Policy (n.d.). Social programs that work: Nurse Family Partnership. Retrieved from http://evidencebasedprograms.org/1366-2/nurse-family-partnership.

14. The CEBP also found that at age two there were some differences between the nurse-visited children and those in the control groups. The nurse-visited children experienced about one-fifth fewer visits to health care providers for children's injuries or ingestions of harmful substances. However, the average rate of such encounters for all the children in the study during the two-year period was small. Those participating in NFP had an average rate of slightly below one half (0.43) of such a visit, and those in the control group had slightly above one half (0.56) visit per child. The nurse-visited children also had 78% fewer hospitalization for injuries or ingestions. The average number of days children were hospitalized for accidental injuries and ingestions during the first two years of the study was also small. Children in the control group were hospitalized an average of slightly less than one fifth (0.18) of a day and nurse-visited children spent an average of one twentieth 0(.04) of a day hospitalized over the two-year period. It's important to note that these findings are for the period during which the nurses were regularly visiting the NFP-enrolled families. These differences between NFP and control children disappeared in subsequent follow-up studies when the nurses were no longer visiting the families.

15. According to the CEBP, fewer NFP-participating children (1.7%) reported having used cigarettes, alcohol, or marijuana in the prior month than did their control-group peers (5.1%), and nurse-visited children showed symptoms of depression, anxiety, or similar mental health problems at a rate that was nearly 9 percentage points less. No differences in academic performance were found between the nurse-visited children and those in the control group. However, nurse-visited children in a subgroup of families Olds and his team identified as being at higher risk due to their mothers having "low psychological resources"

did show two modest educational impacts. At age twelve, these children scored an average of 6 percentile points higher on standardized reading and math achievement tests and had slightly higher grade-point averages (2.46 vs. 2.27) than control-group children from families at similar levels of risk.

16. Coalition for Evidence-Based Policy (n.d.). Social programs that work: Nurse Family Partnership. Retrieved from http://evidencebasedprograms.org/1366-2/nurse-family-partnership.

17. Unlike the Elmira study, in which the rate of substantiated child abuse and neglect reports was used to determine whether participation in NFP led to reductions in child maltreatment, Olds and his team did not measure child maltreatment in the Memphis study. Instead, they used health care encounters as a proxy for maltreatment occurrences and determined that nurse-visited children had somewhat lower rates of health care encounters for injuries and ingestions during their first two years of life and were hospitalized for such occurrences for fewer days than children in the control group. One would expect such a difference in the period in which the nurses were visiting, as they likely warned parents regarding hazards in the homes that could harm babies and toddlers and addressed concerns regarding minor injuries that would have otherwise resulted in contacting a pediatrician's office.

18. Olds, D. L., Kitzman, H. J., Cole, R. E., Hanks, C. A., Arcoleo, K. J., Anson, E. A., . . . & Stevenson, A. J. (2010). Enduring effects of prenatal and infancy home visiting by nurses on maternal life course and government spending: Follow-up of a randomized trial among children at age 12 years. *Archives of Pediatrics & Adolescent Medicine*, 164(5), 419–424.

19. "The above effects on use of government assistance resulted mainly from reductions during the first 9 years of the follow-up period; between years 10 and 12, the reductions were smaller and in most cases not statistically significant." Retrieved from http://evidencebasedprograms.org/1366-2/nurse-family-partnership.

20. An average of 1.08 subsequent births for the nurse-visited women versus 1.28 for the control group women during the children's first six years. Retrieved from http://evidencebasedprograms.org/1366-2/nurse-family-partnership.

21. Coalition for Evidence-Based Policy (n.d.). Social programs that work: Nurse Family Partnership. Retrieved from http://evidencebasedprograms.org/1366-2/nurse-family-partnership.

22. CEBP reports that in follow-up assessments when the children were four years old, there were no significant differences in the development of the nurse-visited children and their control-group peers. However, nurse-visited four-year-olds in the Denver families that Olds and his team had categorized as at higher levels of risk showed encouraging gains on assessments in the areas of language, behavior, and one aspect of mental development. Two years later, when the children were six years old, however, these gains had disappeared.

23. The CEBP website indicates that outcomes generally favored nurse-visited children in the higher risk category, with "a few reaching statistical significance"; however, it ruled that these findings were only "suggestive" due to a study limitation. Retrieved from http://evidencebasedprograms.org/1366-2/nurse-family-partnership.

24. The other significant difference was that slightly fewer of the NFP mothers reported experiencing domestic violence in the past six-month period, although the CEBP rated the validity of this finding as "in question." "Importantly, the effect on domestic violence may be valid, but could also have appeared by chance due to the study's measurement of a sizable number of maternal outcomes. Therefore, we believe this effect needs to be

confirmed in additional studies." Retrieved from http://evidencebasedprograms.org/1366-2/nurse-family-partnership.

25. The CEBP website does not list any outcomes for mothers in the Denver study after the age-four follow-up. Retrieved from http://evidencebasedprograms.org/1366-2/nurse-family-partnership.

26. Coalition for Evidence-Based Policy (n.d.). Social programs that work: Nurse Family Partnership. Retrieved from http://evidencebasedprograms.org/1366-2/nurse-family-partnership.

27. CEBP notes that differences in children's self-reported substance abuse "may be valid, but could also have appeared by chance due to the study's measurement of a sizable number of child outcomes at age 12. Therefore, we believe these effects need to be confirmed in additional studies." Retrieved from http://evidencebasedprograms.org/1366-2/nurse-family-partnership.

28. Hockenberry, S., &d Puzzanchera, C. (2015). Juvenile court statistics: 2013. Retrieved from http://www.ojjdp.gov/ojstatbb/njcda/pdf/jcs2013.pdf.

29. This difference was originally reported by Olds et al. to be thirty months for Memphis mothers at higher risk. CEBP's study of the data concluded that evidence for better outcomes for higher-risk mothers was only "suggestive." Retrieved from http://evidencebasedprograms.org/1366-2/nurse-family-partnership.

30. "The above effects on use of government assistance resulted mainly from reductions during the first 9 years of the follow-up period; between years 10 and 12, the reductions were smaller and in most cases not statistically significant." Retrieved from http://evidencebasedprograms.org/1366-2/nurse-family-partnership.

31. Cost of NFP in 2014 dollars, according to CEBP. Retrieved from http://evidencebasedprograms.org/1366-2/nurse-family-partnership.

32. Olds, D. L., Henderson Jr, C. R., Kitzman, H. J., Eckenrode, J. J., Cole, R. E., & Tatelbaum, R. C. (1999). Prenatal and infancy home visitation by nurses: Recent findings. *The Future of Children*, 9(1), 44–65.

33. Olds, D. L., Kitzman, H. J., Cole, R. E., Hanks, C. A., Arcoleo, K. J., Anson, E. A., ... & Stevenson, A. J. (2010). Enduring effects of prenatal and infancy home visiting by nurses on maternal life course and government spending: Follow-up of a randomized trial among children at age 12 years. *Archives of Pediatrics & Adolescent Medicine*, 164(5), 419–424.

34. Even for children in the Elmira study, the CEBP found no significant differences "in the percent engaged in economically productive activities at age 19 (e.g., work or school), or on lifetime use of welfare or other public assistance." Retrieved from http://evidencebasedprograms.org/1366-2/nurse-family-partnership.

35. MSNBC (September 24, 2014). One simple way to change poor kids' lives [segment of Krystal Clear show that discusses the "proven" benefits of NFP]; Goldberg, D. (December 1, 2014). State senator proposes $100 million for Nurse Family Partnership. *The Capitol*. Retrieved from http://www.capitalnewyork.com/article/albany/2014/12/8557498/state-senator-proposes-100-million-nurse-family-partnership.

36. Any adaptations or enhancements, such as having a social worker visit the most vulnerable families, or extending the duration of services for families in crisis, must be approved in advance by NFP headquarters.

37. Ingoldsby, E. M. (2010). Review of interventions to improve family engagement and retention in parent and child mental health programs. *Journal of Child and Family Studies*, 19(5),

629–645; Korfmacher, J., Green, B., Staerkel, F., Peterson, C., Cook, G., Roggman, L., . . . Schiffman, R. (2008). Parent involvement in early childhood home visiting. *Child & Youth Care Forum*, 37(4), 171–196; Nievar, M. A., Van Egeren, L. A., & Pollard, S. (2010). A meta-analysis of home visiting programs: Moderators of improvements in maternal behavior. *Infant Mental Health Journal*, 31(5), 499–520.

38. April 21, 2009, letter to President Obama. The authors are Deborah Daro, research fellow at the University of Chicago's Chapin Hall; Ken Dodge, Duke University professor of public policy; Heather Weiss, founder of the Harvard Family Research Project; and Edward Zigler, emeritus professor of psychology at Yale. See Haskins, R., Paxson, C., & Brooks-Gunn, J. (Fall 2009). Social science rising: A tale of evidence shaping public policy. The Future of Children Policy Brief. Retrieved from www.brookings.edu.

39. Bare, J. (2010). Philanthropy, evaluation, accountability, and social change. *Foundation Review*, 1(4), 90.

40. Schorr, L. B., & Yankelovitch, D. (February 18, 2000). In search of a gold standard for social programs. *Boston Globe*.

41. See Haskins, R., Paxson, C., & Brooks-Gunn, J. (Fall 2009). Social science rising: A tale of evidence shaping public policy. The Future of Children Policy Brief. Retrieved from www. brookings.edu.

42. Goldberg, D. (December 1, 2014). State senator proposes $100 million for Nurse Family Partnership. *The Capitol*. Retrieved from http://www.capitalnewyork.com/article/a.lbany/2014/12/8557498/state-senator-proposes-100-million-nurse-family-partnership

43. The larger cost savings amount comes from a published paper (Miller, T. [2015]. Projected outcomes of nurse-family partnership home visitation during 1996–2013, USA. *Prevention Science*, 16) featured on the NFP website that pools original data from Olds' three studies with that of a problematic Louisiana study and a study in the Netherlands (which has a far more extensive safety net than the United States), as well as a few other small studies. The paper acknowledges that cost savings to Medicaid are overstated due to Medicaid expansion for low-income families under the Affordable Care Act and other federal legislation, but states them nonetheless.

44. Haskins, R., Paxson, C., & Brooks-Gunn, J. (Fall 2009). Social science rising: A tale of evidence shaping public policy. The Future of Children Policy Brief. Retrieved from www. brookings.edu.

45. Like CHILD First and Early Head Start, discussed in Chapter 7; Nievar, M. A., Van Egeren, L. A., & Pollard, S. (2010). A meta-analysis of home visiting programs: Moderators of improvements in maternal behavior. *Infant Mental Health Journal*, 31(5), 499–520.

46. In the Elmira study, NFP failed to produce any lasting significant benefits to poor, single adolescents with only one child, although study results suggest it may have helped prevent low-birth-weight babies. Olds' team did not provide information as to whether the program specifically benefitted poor, single adolescents and their children in the papers they published regarding findings from the Memphis and Denver studies.

47. April 21, 2009 letter to President Obama. The authors are Deborah Daro, research fellow at the University of Chicago's Chapin Hall; Ken Dodge, Duke University professor of public policy; Heather Weiss, founder of the Harvard Family Research Project; and Edward Zigler, emeritus professor of psychology at Yale.

48. Barnett, W. S. (2010). Universal and targeted approaches to preschool education in the United States. *International Journal of Child Care and Education Policy*, 4(1), 1–12.

49. Magnuson, K., & Duncan, G. J. (October 2014). Can early childhood interventions decrease inequality of economic opportunity? Prepared for the Federal Reserve Bank of Boston Conference, Inequality of Economic Opportunity in the United States. Retrieved from http://www.bostonfed.org/inequality2014/papers/magnusun-duncan.pdf.

50. Barnett, W. S. (2010). Universal and targeted approaches to preschool education in the United States. *International Journal of Child Care and Education Policy*, 4(1), 1–12.

51. Magnuson, K., & Duncan, G. J. (October 2014). Can early childhood interventions decrease inequality of economic opportunity? Prepared for the Federal Reserve Bank of Boston Conference, Inequality of Economic Opportunity in the United States. Retrieved from http://www.bostonfed.org/inequality2014/papers/magnusun-duncan.pdf.

52. Minervino, J., & Pianta, R. (2013). Early learning: The new fact base and cost sustainability. The Bill and Melinda Gates Foundation. Retrieved from https://docs.gates-foundation.org/documents/Lessons%20from%20Research%20and%20the%20Classroom_September%202014.pdf.

53. Lipsey, M. W., Farran, D. C., & Hofer, K. G. (2015). A randomized control trial of the effects of a statewide voluntary prekindergarten program on children's skills and behaviors through third grade. (Research Report). Nashville, TN: Vanderbilt University.

54. *Ibid.*

55. U.S. Department of Health and Human Services (2011). History of Head Start. Retrieved from http://eclkc.ohs.acf.hhs.gov/hslc/hs/about/history.

56. As of 2015, only about one third of Head Start children were participating in full-day, year-round programs. Retrieved from http://eclkc.ohs.acf.hhs.gov/hslc/hs/news/blog/president-budget.html.

57. U.S. Department of Health and Human Services (2012). Third-grade follow-up to Head Start impact study. Retrieved from http://www.acf.hhs.gov/sites/default/files/opre/head_start_report.pdf.

58. Gibbs, C., Ludwig, J., & Miller, D.L. (2011). Does Head Start do any lasting good? NBER working paper #1752. Retrieved from www.nber.org/papers/w1752.

59. Kirp, D. L. (2007). *The sandbox investment: The preschool movement and kids-first politics.* Cambridge, MA: Harvard.

60. *Ibid.*

61. *Ibid.*; Schweinhart, L. J., Montie, J., Xiang, Z., Barnett, W. S., Belfield, C. R., & Nores, M. (2005). Lifetime effects: the High/Scope Perry Preschool study through age 40. Retrieved from http://www.highscope.org/Content.asp?ContentId=219.

62. *Ibid.*

63. Masse, L. N., & Barnett, W. S. (2002). A benefit-cost analysis of the Abecedarian early childhood intervention. Retrieved from http://files.eric.ed.gov/fulltext/ED479989.pdf.

64. *Ibid.*

65. Minervino, J., & Pianta, R. (2013). Early learning: The new fact base and cost sustainability. The Bill and Melinda Gates Foundation. Retrieved from https://docs.gates-foundation.org/documents/Lessons%20from%20Research%20and%20the%20Classroom_September%202014.pdf.

66. Kirp, D. L. (2007). *The sandbox investment: The preschool movement and kids-first politics.* Cambridge, MA: Harvard.

67. National Institute for Early Education Research. (2014).The state of preschool 2014. Retrieved from http://nieer.org/yearbook

CHAPTER 7

1. Shonkoff, J. (2010). Building a new biodevelopmental framework to guide the future of early childhood policy. *Child Development*, 81(1), 357–367.

2. *Ibid.*

3. Schorr, L., Farrow, F., & Sparrow, J. (2014). An evidence framework to improve results. Background Paper for the 2014 Harold Richman Public Policy Symposium: The Future of Evidence. Washington, D.C.: The Center for the Study of Social Policy.

4. Shonkoff, J. P., & Fisher, P. A. (2013). Rethinking evidence-based practice and two-generation programs to create the future of early childhood policy. *Development and Psychopathology*, 25(4), 1635–1653. doi:http://dx.doi.org/10.1017/S0954579413000813.

5. Lipsy, M. W., Farran, D. C., & Hofer, K. G. (2015). A randomized control trial of a state-wide voluntary prekindergarten program on children's skills and behaviors through third grade. Research Report. Nashville, TN: Peabody Institute, Vanderbilt University. Retrieved from http://peabody.vanderbilt.edu/research/pri/VPKthrough3rd_final_withcover.pdf.

6. Shonkoff, J. (2010). Building a new biodevelopmental framework to guide the future of early childhood policy. *Child Development*, 81(1), 357–367.

7. Knitzer, J., & Lefkowitz, J. (2006). *Pathways to early school success: Helping the most vulnerable infants, toddlers, and their families.* New York: National Center for Children in Poverty, Columbia University; Knitzer, J., Theberge, S., & Johnson, K. (2008). Reducing maternal depression and its impact on young children: Toward a responsive early childhood policy framework. Retrieved from http://academiccommons.columbia.edu/catalog/ac:126465; Full Frame Initiative (n.d.). The Full Frame Initiative: Changing systems, changing lives. Retrieved from http://fullframeinitiative.org/overview-of-the-full-frame-approach/; Schorr, L., Farrow, F., & Sparrow, J. (2014). An evidence framework to improve results. Background Paper for the 2014 Harold Richman Public Policy Symposium: The Future of Evidence. Washington, D.C.: The Center for the Study of Social Policy.

8. Zeanah, C. H., & Scheeringa, M. S. (1996). Evaluation of post traumatic symptoms in infants and young children exposed to violence. *Zero to Three*, 14(4), 9–14; Thompson, R. A., & Haskins, R. (2014). Early stress gets under the skin: Promising initiatives to help children facing chronic adversity. The Future of Children, Policy Brief, Princeton-Brookings. Retrieved from https://www.princeton.edu/futureofchildren/publications/docs/24_01_Policy_Brief.pdf.

9. Wagner, M., Spiker, D., Linn, M. I., & Hernandez, F. (2003). Dimensions of parental engagement in home visiting programs exploratory study. *Topics in Early Childhood Special Education*, 23(4), 171–187; Raikes, H., Green, B. L., Atwater, J., Kisker, E., Constantine, J., & Chazan-Cohen, R. (2006). Involvement in Early Head Start home visiting services: Demographic predictors and relations to child and parent outcomes. *Early Childhood Research Quarterly*, 21(1), 2–24; Korfmacher, J., Green, B., Staerkel, F., Peterson, C., Cook, G., Roggman, L., et al. (2008). Parent involvement in early childhood home visiting. *Child & Youth Care Forum*, 37(4), 171–196.

10. Hibel, L. C., Granger, D. A., Blair C., et al. (2011). Maternal sensitivity buffers the adrenocortical implications of intimate partner violence exposure during early childhood. *Development and Psychopathology*, 23, 689–701; Thomas, R., & Zimmer-Gembeck, M. J. (2011). Accumulating evidence for parent–child interaction therapy in the prevention of child maltreatment. *Child Development*, 82(1), 177–192; Webster-Stratton, C., Reid, M. J., & Hammond, M. (2001). Preventing conduct problems, promoting social competence: A parent

and teacher training partnership in Head Start. *Journal of Clinical Child Psychology, 30*(3), 283–302.

11. Schorr, L. B., & Schorr, D. (1988). *Within our reach: Breaking the cycle of disadvantage.* New York: Anchor Press/Doubleday.

12. Lowell, D. I., Paulicin, B., Carter, A. S., Godoy, L., & Briggs-Gowan, M. J. (2011). A randomized controlled trial of Child FIRST: A comprehensive home-based intervention translating research into early childhood practice. *Child Development, 82*(1), 193–208.

13. *Ibid.*

14. U.S. Department of Health and Human Services. (1994). *The statement of the Advisory Committee on Services for Families with Infants and Toddlers.* Washington, D.C.: Author.

15. Raikes, H., Love, J. M., Kisker, E. E., Chazan-Cohen, R., & Brooks-Gunn, J. (2004). What works: Improving the odds for infants and toddlers in low-income families. *Beacon of hope: The promise of Early Head Start for America's youngest children.* Washington, D.C.: Zero to Three, pp. 20–43.

16. US Department of Health and Human Services, Office of Head Start (2015). Early Head Start services snapshot: National 2013–2014. Retrieved from: https://eclkc.ohs.acf.hhs.gov/hslc/data/psr/2015/services-snapshot-ehs-2014-2015.pdf

17. Love, J. M., Kisker, E. E., Ross, C. M., Schochet, P. Z., Brooks-Gunn, J., Paulsell, D., . . . & Brady-Smith, C. (2002). Making a difference in the lives of infants and toddlers and their families: The impacts of Early Head Start. Volumes I–III: Final Technical Report/Appendixes/Local Contributions to Understanding the Programs and Their Impacts. Retrieved from http://www.researchgate.net/publication/234666754_Making_a_Difference_in_the_Lives_of_Infants_and_Toddlers_and_Their_Families_The_Impacts_of_Early_Head_Start._Volumes_I-III_Final_Technical_Report_and_Appendixes_and_Local_Contributions_to_Understanding_the_Programs_and_Their_Impacts.

18. When participating children were aged three, EHS was found to benefit families across a range of child, parent, and family self-sufficiency outcomes, although these impacts were modest in size. Impacts were strongest for African American children, families who enrolled in EHS during pregnancy, and families identified as being at medium levels of risk. Two years after the end of the program, when the children were aged five and heading to kindergarten, benefits from EHS continued in the areas of children's social and emotional outcomes, parenting, and parent well-being. Similar benefits emerged for families identified at being at the highest levels of risk, and impacts remained strong for African American children. Importantly, children whose participation in EHS was followed by two years of participation (at ages three and four) in Head Start, state-funded preschool, or center-based child care experienced the best overall impacts at age five, including those in academic skills. When the children in the study were in the fifth grade, follow-up assessments showed that only modest benefits related to social and emotional development remained for the entire group of children who had participated in EHS. African American children whose families had participated in EHS continued to benefit more than other EHS-participating children; they had fewer behavior and attention problems. Their parents were more involved with their child's school, showed greater support for their children's education, and reported less alcohol use. Hispanic mothers who participated in EHS had higher education attainment than their control-group peers. Disappointingly, however, benefits attributable to EHS disappeared for children and families in the highest-risk group; the EHS-participating children in this group actually scored *lower* on cognitive/academic assessments in grade five than their control-group peers. Researchers identified a few additional important findings. African American

and Hispanic children, but not whites, who had participated in EHS had better outcomes in the fifth grade than their control-group peers, but only when the EHS children had attended a preschool or formal early care and education program at ages three and four and were currently attending an elementary school in which a relatively low percentage of the study body was made up of low-income and poor students.

19. Kirp, D. L. (2007). The sandbox investment: The preschool movement and kids-first politics. Cambridge, MA: Harvard.

20. Minervino, J., & Pianta, R. (2013). Early learning: The new fact base and cost sustainability. Retrieved from https://docs.gatesfoundation.org/documents/Lessons%20from%20Research%20and%20the%20Classroom_September%202014.pdf.

21. *Ibid.*

22. McCann, C. (2014). Child care reauthorization: Twenty years in the making underway. Retrieved from http://www.edcentral.org/child-care-reauthorization-20-years-making-underway/.

23. Minervino, J., & Pianta, R. (2013). Early learning: The new fact base and cost sustainability. Retrieved from https://docs.gatesfoundation.org/documents/Lessons%20from%20Research%20and%20the%20Classroom_September%202014.pdf.

24. Shonkoff, J. (2010). Building a new biodevelopmental framework to guide the future of early childhood policy. *Child Development, 81*(1), 357–367.

25. Schorr, L., Farrow, F., & Sparrow, J. (2014). An evidence framework to improve results. Background Paper for the 2014 Harold Richman Public Policy Symposium: The Future of Evidence. Washington, D.C.: The Center for the Study of Social Policy.

26. Lowell, D. I., Paulicin, B., Carter, A. S., Godoy, L., & Briggs-Gowan, M. J. (2011). A randomized controlled trial of Child FIRST: A comprehensive home-based intervention translating research into early childhood practice. *Child Development, 82*(1), 193–208.

27. Schorr, L., Farrow, F., & Sparrow, J. (2014). An evidence framework to improve results. Background Paper for the 2014 Harold Richman Public Policy Symposium: The Future of Evidence. Washington, D.C.: The Center for the Study of Social Policy.

CHAPTER 8

1. Sharkey, P. (2013). *Stuck in place: Urban neighborhoods and the end of progress toward racial equality.* Chicago: University of Chicago Press.

2. Allen, S. F. (2003). Working parents with young children: cross-national comparisons of policies and programmes in three countries. *International Journal of Social Welfare, 12*(4), 261–273.

3. U.S. Bureau of Labor Statistics (2014). Characteristics of minimum wage workers, 2013. Retrieved from http://www.bls.gov/cps/minwage2013.pdf.

4. Center for Budget and Policy Priorities (2014). Working-family tax credits lift millions out of poverty. Retrieved from http://www.cbpp.org/blog/working-family-tax-credits-lift-millions-out-of-poverty.

5. Dahl, G., & Lochner, L. (2012). The impact of family income on child achievement: Evidence from the earned income tax credit. *American Economic Review.* Retrieved from http://www.aeaweb.org/articles.php?doi=10.1257/aer.102.5.192; Maxfield, M. (2013). The effects of the earned income tax credit on child achievement and long-term educational attainment. Retrieved from https://www.msu.edu/~maxfiel7/20131114%20Maxfield%20EITC%20Child%20Education.pdf.

6. Center on Budget and Policy Priorities (2016). Chart Book: The Earned Income Tax Credit and the Child Tax Credit. Retrieved from:http://www.cbpp.org/research/federal-tax/chart-book-the-earned-income-tax-credit-and-child-tax-credit

7. Lindsey, D. (2009). *Child poverty and inequality: Securing a better future for America's children.* New York: Oxford University Press.

8. Dubay, L., & Kenney, G. (2003). Expanding public health insurance to parents: Effects on children's coverage under Medicaid. *Health Services Research,* 38(5), 1283–1302; Fry-Bowers, E. K., Nicholas, W., & Halfon, N. (2014). Children's health care and the Patient Protection and Affordable Care Act: What's at stake? *JAMA Pediatrics,* 168(6), 505–506.

9. Center on Budget and Policy Priorities (2014). Chart book: The War on Poverty at 50, overview. Retrieved from http://www.cbpp.org/research/chart-book-the-war-on-poverty-at-50-overview; Hoynes, H. W., Schanzenbach, D. W., & Almond, D. (2012). Long-run impacts of childhood access to the safety net. National Bureau of Economic Research Working Paper No. 18535. Retrieved from http://www.nber.org/papers/w18535.

10. Child Welfare League of America. (n.d.) Recommended caseload standards. Retrieved from http://66.227.70.18/newsevents/news030304cwlacaseload.htm.

11. U.S. Department of Health and Human Services (2010). Caseload and workload management. Issue Brief. Retrieved from https://www.childwelfare.gov/pubPDFs/case_work_management.pdf.

12. U.S. Department of Health and Human Services (2015). The AFCARS Report: Preliminary FY 2014 estimates as of July 2015. Retrieved from http://www.acf.hhs.gov/sites/default/files/cb/afcarsreport22.pdf.

13. Fixen, A. (2011). Children in foster care: Societal and financial costs. Retrieved from http://www.afamilyforeverychild.org/Adoption/AFFECreportonchildreninfostercare.pdf.

14. Dozier, M., Lindhiem, O., Lewis, E., Bick, J., Bernard, K., & Peloso, E. (2009). Effects of a foster parent training program on young children's attachment behaviors: Preliminary evidence from a randomized clinical trial. *Child and Adolescent Social Work Journal,* 26(4), 321–332.

15. U.S. Department of Education (n.d.). IDEA 2004: Building the Legacy: Part C (birth to age 2). Retrieved from http://idea.ed.gov/part-c/search/new; U.S. Department of Health and Human Services, Child Welfare Information Gateway (n.d.) Child welfare and IDEA Part C. Retrieved from https://www.childwelfare.gov/topics/preventing/programs/earlychildhood/childwelfare/.

16. Zero to Three (2013). A developmental approach to child welfare services for infants, toddlers, and their families. Retrieved from http://main.zerotothree.org/site/DocServer/PDF__1_-Child_Welfare_Tool.pdf?docID=13381; Barth, R. P., Scarborough, A. A., Lloyd, E. C., Losby, J. L., Casanueva, C., & Mann, T. (2008). Developmental status and early intervention service needs of maltreated children. Final Report. U.S. Department of Health and Human Services. Retrieved from http://aspe.hhs.gov/sites/default/files/pdf/75351/report.pdf.

17. U.S. Department of Health and Human Services (n.d.). Child and family services review factsheet. Retrieved from http://www.acf.hhs.gov/sites/default/files/cb/cfsr_general_factsheet.pdf.

18. Minervino, J., & Pianta, R. (2013). Early learning: The new fact base and cost sustainability. Retrieved from https://docs.gatesfoundation.org/documents/Lessons%20from%20Research%20and%20the%20Classroom_September%202014.pdf.

19. BUILD Initiative (2015). Rising to the challenge: Building effective systems for young children and families: A BUILD E-Book. Retrieved from http://www.buildinitiative.org/Portals/0/Uploads/Documents/E-BookChapter1StateSystemsBuildingThroughGovernance.pdf.

20. American Psychological Association (2013). Poverty and high school dropout. Retrieved from http://www.apa.org/pi/ses/resources/indicator/2013/05/poverty-dropouts.aspx.

21. Aber, L., & Chaudry, A. (2010). Low-income children, their families and the Great Recession: What next in policy? Retrieved from http://eric.ed.gov/?id=ED510504.

22. Chertavian, G. (2012). *A year up: How a pioneering program teaches young adults real skills, for real jobs, with real success.* New York: Viking.

23. Kirp, D. L. (November 15, 2015). Giving it that new college try. *New York Times.*

24. The Children's Aid Society (n.d.). Carrera program components. Retrieved from http://www.childrensaidsociety.org/carrera-pregnancy-prevention/carrera-program-components.

25. Jim Casey Youth Opportunities Initiative (2013). Cost avoidance: The business case for investing in youth aging out of foster care. Issue Brief. Retrieved from http://www.jimcaseyyouth.org/sites/default/files/Cost%20Avoidance%20Issue%20Brief_EMBARGOED%20until%20May%206.pdf.

26. Courtney, M. E., Dworsky, A., Cusick, G. R., Havilcek, J., Perez, A., & Keller, T. (2007). *Midwest evaluation of the adult functioning of former foster youth: Outcomes at age 21.* Chicago: Chapin Hall Center for Children at the University of Chicago.

27. National Campaign to Prevent Teen and Unplanned Pregnancy (2014). Implementing an evidence-based pregnancy prevention program for youth in out-of-home care: Lessons learned from five implementing agencies. Retrieved from http://thenationalcampaign.org/sites/default/files/resource-primary-download/mpc_2.pdf.

28. Geller, A., Garfinkel, I., Cooper, C. E., & Mincy, R. B. (2009). Parental incarceration and child well-being: Implications for urban families. *Social Science Quarterly,* 90(5), 1186–1202.

29. Seymour, C. B. (1998). Children with parents in prison: Child welfare policy, program, and practice issues. *Child Welfare,* 77, 469–494.

30. Alexander, M. (2010). *The new Jim Crow: Mass incarceration in the age of colorblindness.* New York: The New Press.

31. Pew Research Center (2014). America's new drug policy landscape: Two-thirds favor treatment, not jail, for use of heroin, cocaine. Retrieved from http://www.people-press.org/2014/04/02/americas-new-drug-policy-landscape/; Pew Research Center (2014). Feds may be rethinking the drug war, but states have been leading the way. Retrieved from http://www.pewresearch.org/fact-tank/2014/04/02/feds-may-be-rethinking-the-drug-war-but-states-have-been-leading-the-way/.

32. Suárez-Orozco, C. (July 15, 2010). In the best interest of our children: Examining our immigration enforcement policy. Retrieved from http://www.apa.org/about/gr/issues/cyf/immigration-enforcement.aspx; Urban Institute (2010). Facing our future: Children in the aftermath of immigration enforcement. Retrieved from http://www.urban.org/research/publication/facing-our-future/view/full_report.

33. Toobin, J. (July 27, 2015). American limbo: While politicians block reform, what is happening to immigrant families? *The New Yorker.*

34. Schorr, L. (1988). *Within our reach: Breaking the cycle of disadvantage.* New York: Doubleday/Anchor.

35. MacGillis, A. (July 19, 2007). Obama says he, too, is a poverty fighter. *Washington Post*. Retrieved from http://www.washingtonpost.com/wp-dyn/content/article/2007/07/18/AR2007071802529.html.

36. This nearly 50% reduction is found using an absolute poverty line, similar to how poverty is measured in the United States. See pp. 1–2 in Waldfogel, J. (2010). *Britain's war on poverty*. New York: Russell Sage Foundation.

37. Waldfogel, J. (2010). *Britain's war on poverty*. New York: Russell Sage Foundation.

38. *Ibid.*

39. *Ibid.*

40. *Ibid.*

41. *Ibid.*

42. BBC News (June 25, 2015). UK has 2.3m children living in poverty, government says. Retrieved from http://www.bbc.com/news/uk-33266799; A. Garnham, personal communication, September 2, 2015.

43. A. Garnham, personal communication, September 2, 2015.

44. Gladwell, M. (2008). *Outliers: The story of success*. New York: Little, Brown, and Company.

Index